AF541737

POWER AND PURPOSE

POWER AND PURPOSE

Rediscovering Indian Foreign Policy in Amrit Kaal

Harsh V. Pant *and*
Anant Singh Mann

RUPA

Published by
Rupa Publications India Pvt. Ltd 2025
7/16, Ansari Road, Daryaganj
New Delhi 110002

Sales centres:
Bengaluru Chennai
Hyderabad Jaipur Kathmandu
Kolkata Mumbai Prayagraj

P-ISBN: 978-93-6156-559-5
E-ISBN: 978-93-6156-425-3

First impression 2025

10 9 8 7 6 5 4 3 2 1

Printed in India

To the students of Indian Foreign Policy

Contents

Prime Minister Jawaharlal Nehru addresses the nation at the Red Fort on 15 August 1947, marking India's first Independence Day.

Source: Wikimedia Commons

Rediscovering Indian Foreign Policy: An Introduction

The beginning of the third decade of the third millennium Anno Domini has seen India come to the forefront of the world's stage, with an ever-expanding remit of global responsibilities. Symbolic of this rise has been New Delhi's presidency of the Group of Twenty (G20), from December 2022 to November 2023, under the prophetic banner of 'वसुधैव कुटुम्बकम्',[1] which roughly translates to the idea that 'the entire world is one family'. Notwithstanding the general normative congruence between global and Indian values, exemplified by the prevailing rules-based global order, India has become exceedingly hard to ignore, not only on regional issues, but also on the international stage.

Since the turn of the century, India has outgrown the notion that its foreign policy quiver merely consists of ornaments of soft power, like Bollywood and yoga, and has, instead, proven the rising significance of its economic and military capabilities. Since the economic liberalization in the early 1990s, the Indian economy has expanded immensely. The World Bank estimates that its gross domestic product (GDP) has grown from less than half a trillion dollars in 2000 to over $3.5 trillion in 2023, overtaking the United Kingdom (UK) as the fifth largest global economy in 2021.[2]

Just as important as this rapid growth has been the great resilience India has shown in the relatively more contemporary context, with nations across the globe still recovering from the devastating impacts of the Covid-19 pandemic, facing severely compromised supply chains caused by the Russian invasion of

Ukraine and geopolitical instability across the Middle East[3] and other parts of the world. This has been further exacerbated by a weakening global economy, with uncontrolled inflation and stagnating productivity. Yet, at a time when the IMF has estimated a negative growth of -0.6 per cent for the UK in 2023, India is projected to continue to grow at over 6 per cent,[4] being the fastest growing economy of the top five global economies (See Graph 1).[5]

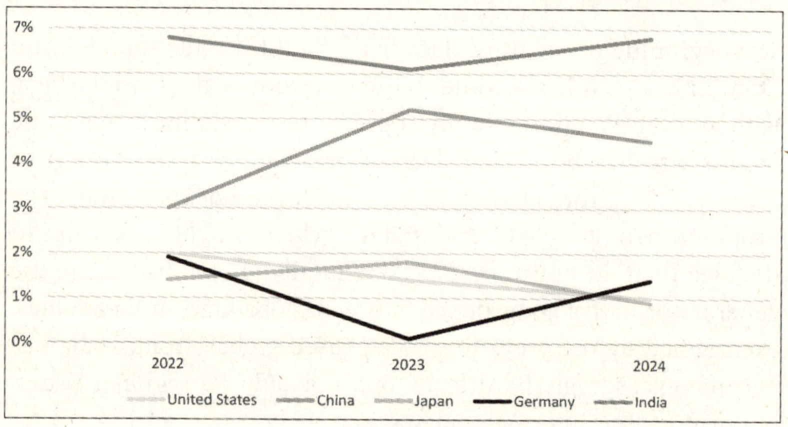

Graph 1: Growth projections for the five largest economies, 2022–24
Source: International Monetary Fund (IMF)[6]

Furthermore, India's extraordinary demographic dividend has only further strengthened the prospects of its continued and rapid economic rise. Estimations by the United Nations (UN) in 2023 indicated that, for the first time since 1950, China had lost its position as the world's most populous nation to India,[7] with its population surveyed to be around 1.425 billion, with an average age of twenty-seven. Understandably, analysts across the world remain bullish, to say the least, about New Delhi's rise and its consequently expanding global influence.

As a natural consequence of its growing GDP, India's military capabilities, and its ability to project its influence beyond its borders, have also notably increased. India's diplomatic engagement within its region has greatly matured, with policies like 'Look East' from the 1990s transitioning to 'Act East' in the 2010s.

Apart from diplomatic and economic progress, India has steadily built its military power. With its nuclear capabilities announced in the Pokhran-II tests of 1998, India's military position within its neighbourhood has gone from strength to strength. Its evolving capabilities and pivotal geostrategic position have, unsurprisingly, seen an expansion in its role, and its responsibilities in protecting the rules-based global order. More specifically, the rising significance of the Indo-Pacific region, with its growing security, connectivity, and economic issues, has presented challenges as well as opportunities for India.

India is strategically located at the centre of the Indo-Pacific, which is expected to become the gravitational centre for geopolitics and geo-economics in the twenty-first century. As a result, India has become a force to be reckoned with in its own neighbourhood, and a nation to be allied with in the wider Indo-Pacific region. Testament to the recognition of New Delhi's centrality in maintaining a 'Free and Open Indo-Pacific', is perhaps the progressively strengthening Quadrilateral Security Dialogue (Quad) between India, Australia, Japan and the United States. Partly due to aligning values and partly due to its worsening relationship with China, the coordination and collaboration between the 'West' and India have intensified, particularly over the past couple of decades.

The incumbent government, under Prime Minister Narendra Modi, is acutely aware of India's promise to both the citizens of its nation and the global community. The 2023 announcement of its vision for 2047, *Amrit Kaal*,[8] set a roadmap for India's transition into an advanced economy over the next twenty-five years, by when India would celebrate the centenary year of its Independence. The indisputable theme of India's rising prominence, in its role on the international stage and its promise to the aspirations of its citizenry, has naturally brought every single foreign policy decision it has taken under careful examination.

GROWING INTERNATIONALISM

Representative of this scrutiny has been the extensive Western critique of New Delhi's abstention from the UN General Assembly's resolution to condemn the Russian invasion of Ukraine. Juxtaposed with this has been the unprecedented expansion of the collaboration between India and the West, especially in key geopolitical regions like the Indo-Pacific. Naturally, an understanding of Indian foreign policy remains crucial in accurately explaining New Delhi's decision-making in both these competing spheres.

Since Independence in 1947, Indian foreign policy has traversed multifarious terrains, evolved continuously, and developed progressively in sophistication and efficiency. New Delhi's approach to its external affairs has transformed considerably, from the non-aligned isolationism of the past to the internationalism of the present. The keystone of this policy transition has been the adoption of 'issue-based alignments' in contemporary Indian foreign policy, which has allowed New Delhi the policy fluidity to stay relatively less vocal than the other Quad members in condemning Russia's invasion of Ukraine, while still strengthening its cooperation with the Quad members in a different geopolitical domain: the Indo-Pacific.

In reference to this significant shift, the foreign secretary Vijay Gokhale asserted in 2019: 'India has moved on from its non-aligned past. India is today an aligned state—but based on issues.' Emphasizing that it was time India became part of the rule-making process, Gokhale argued: 'In the rules-based order, India would have a stronger position in multilateral institutions.'[9] The foreign secretary was categorical that India's future would be largely shaped by the kind of role New Delhi managed to play in the G20 and the Indo-Pacific, clearly signalling the changing priorities of the Indian foreign policy establishment.

The reason why Gokhale's assertions did not raise many

eyebrows initially was that the Modi government, during its first term, managed to gradually, but decisively, shift the discourse on Indian foreign policy without many in the Indian strategic community recognizing it. Critics of the government continued to be sceptical about anything substantive changing, even as the government continued to re-evaluate the priorities of India's foreign policy, both in substance and style. Notably, in a lecture in 2015, Gokhale's predecessor S. Jaishankar had suggested that today's India 'aspire[s] to be a leading power, rather than just a balancing power', and as a consequence, it was willing 'to shoulder greater global responsibilities'. He, of course, was taking his cue from Prime Minister Modi himself, who, soon after taking office, had tasked his senior diplomats 'to help India position itself in a leading role, rather than just a balancing force, globally'.[10]

Later, in 2019, after being appointed as the Minister of External Affairs, Jaishankar gave an important lecture[11] which provides great insight into the Indian foreign policy of the Modi government in its second term, a prime ministerial term that would essentially form the foundation for New Delhi's foreign policy as it enters the next twenty-five years of its Amrit Kaal. Jaishankar declared that 'the real obstacle to the rise of India is not anymore the barriers of the world, but the dogmas of Delhi', stating his intention to provide 'an unsentimental audit of Indian foreign policy'. Jaishankar noted that India was at present standing at the 'cusp' of change with 'more confidence'. He argued that,

> ...a nation that has the aspiration to become a leading power someday cannot continue with unsettled borders, an unintegrated region and under-exploited opportunities. Above all, it cannot be dogmatic in approaching a visibly changing world order.

An important insight into contemporary Indian foreign policy is also provided by Jaishankar's elaborate treatise, *The India Way: Strategies for an Uncertain World* (2020).[12] In this, Jaishankar underlines the continuing importance of strategic autonomy in New Delhi's foreign policy. He articulates that New Delhi's foreign policy ultimately endeavours to advance its

> ...national interests by identifying and exploiting opportunities created by global contradictions [...] to extract as much [sic] gains from as many ties as possible [...] Leveraging the external environment to address bilateral imbalances.

Referring to the existing strategic imbalances with China, Jaishankar proposes that in the global context of 'multiple poles and greater choices',

> India must reach out in as many directions as possible [to] maximise its gains... In this world of all against all, India's goal should be to move closer to this strategic sweet spot.

Referring to the natural state of the world as one of 'multipolarity', and making the intentions of Indian foreign policy explicitly clear, Jaishankar states that 'there will be convergence with many but congruence with none' placing, in no uncertain terms, the continuing centrality of pragmatic 'issue-based alignments' or 'multi-alignments' and 'strategic autonomy' in the government's external calculus.[13] Naturally, this way of thinking remains rooted in the limitations and challenges being faced by contemporary India. While its economic growth has been nothing short of extraordinary, its economic development still has a long way to go.

Similar to any other developing economy, and especially with its inherited colonial structures, India continues to face significant domestic socioeconomic challenges. And while their evolution heretofore remains largely on a positive trajectory, India's external estimations have naturally been moulded by its efforts to negotiate its domestic necessities against the backdrop of a rapidly evolving global order. Rooted in this *pragmatic self-interest*, New Delhi has become increasingly adept at balancing competing interests.

This greater focus on pragmatism can be seen manifested right from the relationships it has created and delicately balanced in the Gulf region over the last decade, between Israel, Iran and the Gulf Cooperation Council (GCC), to its willingness to remain relatively neutral in Europe, amidst the Russian invasion of Ukraine, whilst still engaging with its European and Atlantic partners in other spheres like the Indo-Pacific. What is evident in this analysis is that history and legacy have continued to play a key part in New Delhi's foreign policy worldview, as it advances on its path to global leadership. Gauging the sequence of major milestones in its foreign policy over the last seventy-five years will help contextualize and better place its contemporary geostrategic decision-making.

WALK DOWN THE MEMORY LANE

With this evolution in New Delhi's foreign policy thinking, it is important to look back with the luxury of retrospection, and recognize the complex journey Indian foreign policy has undertaken, and discern the various milestones that have shaped its trajectory. For a nation that completed seventy-five years of its Independence in August 2022, this is also an attempt to take stock of the landmarks achieved, and the opportunities missed. This volume is a small endeavour in that direction. It presents seventy-five vignettes drawn from India's foreign policy journey over the last seven decades, to give the reader a short but hopefully holistic overview of the nation's journey within the global order, since its Independence in 1947. These annual vignettes have been selected based on their long-term impact on the Indian foreign policy journey. It is possible that some years will have more than one such landmark, and some years none, but the aim is to look at this journey through a chronological lens, by analysing landmark events from particular years.

Furthermore, to help structure this volume, the last seventy-five years are surveyed through a periodization of four parts: [1] State-building and the Nehruvian Outlook (1947–64); [2] Regional Consolidation and Antagonisms (1964–85); [3] Opening to the World (1985–2004); and [4] On the Path to Global Leadership (2004–present). Although the periodization of history comes with its own challenges, which includes the risk of oversimplification of history and the scarcity of clear-cut starting and ending points of historical periods, the above periodization has been consciously created to help capture, make intelligible, and draw out the major themes in the trajectory of Indian foreign policy.

The first period has been classified as 'State-building and the Nehruvian Outlook', as, at this time, India had just succeeded in its long-fought struggle for independence. The theme of this period was very much based on its colonial experience, and its consequent focus on maintaining its sovereign agency by rebuilding its economy in an international environment that was anything but conducive to it. Although the end of the Second World War, and the fact that it had recently gained independence, made it a time of great optimism for the nation, it was severely dampened by the bifurcation of the world into two global camps: the Soviet Union and the United States.

Amidst these goliaths, the challenge of retaining its agency was addressed by New Delhi through the conduit of its non-aligned ideology, and the championing of the Global South and the other recently decolonized nations, both of which helped conceive the Non-Aligned Movement. Jawaharlal Nehru's idealism and internationalism saw India vociferously participate in the diplomatic challenges of the day, right from supporting the ideals of global peace and nuclear disarmament to the Suez crisis and the situations in Korea and Vietnam. Bearing the legacy of its own freedom struggle, New Delhi saw it as a duty to lead the global community, and other recently decolonized nations, to a more equitable world. Unfortunately, India's confidence in its position as the leader of the Third World was greatly damaged by its fallout, and consequent war, with China in the early 1960s. This jolt of the early 1960s helped catalyze the early transition of New Delhi's strategic thinking, from the righteousness of its idealism to the stark realities of an increasingly Hobbesian international system.

Regional consolidations and antagonisms came to define the post-Nehru era, till the mid-1980s. The pragmatism of this phase saw New Delhi unshackle itself from the constraints of non-alignment, and initiate limited cooperation with the superpowers, amidst external vulnerabilities, domestic turmoil and economic tribulations. This period of recovery also witnessed New Delhi's enhanced focus on regional consolidation, with the creation of Bangladesh and a greater Indian assertion in its neighbourhood. On the international stage, the initiation and socialization of China into the international community in 1971 by the US was countered by India's distinctly strengthening relationship with the Soviet Union, and the landmark signing of the Treaty of Peace, Friendship, and Cooperation between New Delhi and Moscow the same year.

The pragmatism of this phase allowed New Delhi the policy manoeuvrability of taking major steps to open its economy in the latter part of the 1980s, eventually allowing for a major transition of economic policies in the early 1990s. The liberalization of the economy massively helped consolidate it, and catalyze an enduring phase of growth in India's GDP, which has not since abated, except for short periods of global volatility. The fall of the Soviet Union in the early 1990s also gave India the strategic space to reconsider its global position, laying the foundations for its endeavour to maintain its strategic autonomy, a luxury that was not afforded to it in the previous era of the Cold War.

This new thinking was evident through the creation of India's 'Look East' policy, its changing diplomatic position towards the Gulf region, particularly Israel, and its strengthening ties with the United States. New Delhi's desire for protecting its strategic autonomy led to it finally crossing the nuclear Rubicon, with the declaration of the success of the Pokhran-II nuclear tests in 1998. Later, in 1999, New Delhi successfully defended its territorial integrity in Kargil against the Pakistani army's military opportunism. India had, by the turn of the century, largely achieved its vision of protecting its sovereign agency and maintaining its geopolitical autonomy, with an increasing global interest in its burgeoning GDP and economic potential.

These strong foundations of economic growth and strategic autonomy laid the groundwork for the fourth and concurrent period of India's path to global leadership. This phase has seen a stark change in India's approach to the international system and worldview, with its expanding global participation and internationalism. Symbolic of this phase is perhaps New Delhi's role in the much-overlooked relief efforts during the Indian Ocean Tsunami of 2004. India's credentials as key regional protector of the global commons was confirmed with the creation of the Tsunami Core Group, along with the United States, Australia and Japan, aligning on values and directly providing relief to nations across the littoral regions of the Indian Ocean. The core group crucially laid the foundations upon which the Quadrilateral Security Dialogue was formed in 2007, and which has only gone from strength to strength since 2017.

Crucially, this period also began with the US-India nuclear deal, seeing an expanding cooperation between India and the West. The creation of the BRICS forum and the continuing maintenance of a strong relationship with Russia provide great insight into the skilful balance New Delhi had created in its external relations. The financial crisis of 2008 only confirmed the multipolar reality of the international system further, with the West increasingly being overshadowed by the rise of Asian economies. In this environment of economic rebalancing and increasing regionalism, New Delhi chose to expand its international engagement. The global realization of India's position, and its willingness to engage in the rules-based global order, has led not only to it shouldering greater responsibility, but also to growing global expectations for India to play its part on the international stage.

Examples like the creation of an 'Act East' policy, or New Delhi's massive outreach during the pandemic years, with the supply of vaccines and personal protective equipment, are indicative of this changing terrain. India took the reins of the G20 in 2022–23, at a time when the international system faced vulnerabilities and challenges of considerable gravity. For the rules-based global order, New Delhi represents a bastion of hope in an increasingly unstable global environment. Being the largest liberal democracy in the world, New Delhi has continued to defy the odds in its rise to global prominence, at a time when the structures of the global order are undergoing major transitions. Whether it is the rise of right-wing movements across the globe, the unveiling of a revisionist China, or the weakening global economy, New Delhi's path to global leadership will continue to be moulded by the rapidly transitioning international system.

Essentially, this volume endeavours to create a tableau vivant of Indian foreign policy through the lens of the seventy-five specifically chosen events since Independence. The centrality of this legacy remains an important pillar in understanding the foundations of India's foreign policy. This is not to insinuate that foreign policy remains fixed in the sands of time, but is, instead, to highlight the extent of influence these events have had in both shaping and justifying the contemporary positioning in India's foreign policy. The chronological analysis of seventy-five events allows for not only a comprehensive coverage of the seventy-five-year-long pre-Amrit Kaal period, highlighting the significance of certain events, but also a depth of analysis, engaging with events across diplomatic, military, economic and cultural dimensions which have underpinned Indian foreign policy. Apart from providing an account of key foreign policy events over the past seventy-five years, this volume also fulfils two other purposes.

First, it aims to provide the reader with an insight into an empirical understanding of what has created contemporary Indian foreign policy, by sticking to Leopold von Ranke's assertion of the value of understanding history for what it is. This is done by structuring each note in a similar method, each containing an introduction to the event, a qualitative survey of competing perspectives and views, and a description of its importance in shaping Indian foreign policy. The analysis relies on a combination of primary and secondary sources, including government press releases, documented speeches, secondary literature and grey literature, among others.

Second, this volume aims to provide a window into contemporary foreign policy for future analysts and historians, to broadly understand how Indian foreign policy was perceived seventy-five years post its Independence, as it enters the next phase of its Amrit Kaal. This will be possible by analysing the biases behind the curation of events this book has collated through its presentism, as many events may lose their significance in the years to come, while others grow in relevance. These variances will essentially represent the delta between contemporary Indian foreign policy and its subsequent formulations at infinite points of time in the future.

THE FOUR WAVES

Prime Minister Jawaharlal Nehru meets with Chinese Premier Zhou Enlai and Madam Sun Yat-sen in 1954 in Peking.

Source: Wikimedia Commons

Wave 1

1947–64: State-building and the Nehruvian Outlook

In the aftermath of Independence, Indian foreign policy was shaped by the vision of its first Prime Minister Jawaharlal Nehru, who sought to establish India as a non-aligned, independent and responsible member of the global community. This period laid the foundations for India's principled approach to international affairs, seeking autonomy in decision-making while promoting global peace and cooperation. The challenges of this period would test the feasibility of its idealism in a turbulent world, setting the stage for a more pragmatic approach in the subsequent phase.

1947

1. INDEPENDENCE AND PARTITION

The formative cornerstone of Indian foreign policy has remained the cataclysmic bifurcation of the Indian subcontinent. Although the events of 1947 saw India gain independence, it also established the groundwork for one of its most persistent security challenges, in carving out Pakistan, essentially its theoretical antithesis. The colonization and systematic exploitation of the previous two centuries had left the Indian economy on its knees, with abject poverty, insufficient food security, and a largely agrarian economy, which had yet to benefit from the wave of industrialization. Along with this, even the key indicators of the modern Westphalian state were remarkably weak, with the inheritance of an India whose *population* faced a calamitous humanitarian and refugee crisis, with an undefined *territory*, a newly formed *government*, and a *sovereignty* open to being questioned. Against this backdrop, state-building became, naturally, the top priority for its government. Along with economic restructuring, political consolidation remained a fundament in its nascent years, exemplified by the protection of Kashmir, the consequent war with Pakistan, and the integration of Hyderabad and Junagadh. Tensions between India and Pakistan continued to simmer till the Liaquat-Nehru Pact, which marked the first bilateral agreement for crisis diffusion between the two nations.

This geopolitical complexity that arose from the Partition was only entangled further by the integration of the princely states, which reserved the agency of choice in their decision to join the newly formed nations. Although Vallabhbhai Patel of the Indian National Congress was widely successful in his efforts to convince the Princes to accede to the Indian Union, several states, like Junagadh, Hyderabad and Kashmir, proved to be problematic. While the first two states were integrated through a mixture of Machiavellian persuasion and police action, Kashmir's willingness to delay its decision led to the first war between India and Pakistan in 1947. The decision was deferred till the eleventh hour, and was only catalyzed after a Pakistani invasion threatened to capture its capital, Srinagar. Subsequent to Kashmir's accession, India deployed its forces and engaged with Pakistani forces, leading to the first Indo-Pak War. The war continued till the Karachi Agreement in 1949, by which time India had successfully protected the capital and pushed back the invaders, taking control of two-thirds of Kashmir, including the Kashmir Valley, the Jammu province and Ladakh. The conflict over Kashmir, as well as managing a progressively hostile relationship with Pakistan, became an all-pervasive influence on the bilateral relationship, and has continued to remain a key feature in New Delhi's foreign policy.

Coupled with the lack of clear boundaries was also one of the century's most devastating refugee crises, in which, estimates indicate, around a million people were killed and tens of millions were displaced. Religious minorities on both sides were widely persecuted in the course of sectarian violence, riots and mass killings that were caused by the paranoia created by the abrupt, impulsive, and grossly mismanaged departure of the British colonial regime from the subcontinent. The humanitarian disaster continued, with tensions on both sides, and finally concluded with the signing of the Liaquat-Nehru Pact in 1950. The Liaquat-Nehru Pact was pivotal in bringing stability to the subcontinent, which had theretofore been ravaged by violence. Crucially, the Pact provided for the protection of minorities on both sides by various mechanisms, including the setting up of Minority Commissions in both nations, to enforce its implementation.[1] The Pact effectively pacified tensions and allowed each government to, instead, initiate efforts to address the urgent necessities of growth and development, something which the Indian subcontinent had been starved of, as it was subjected to the structures of colonial exploitation, which had only recently been dismantled.

India's first Prime Minister Jawaharlal Nehru led a government which was profoundly aware of the desperation of its circumstances, and the deep necessity to modernize its economy and protect the dignity of its external sovereignty. The first government also had the unenviable task of drawing up from scratch its plan of engagement with the rest of the world, whilst bearing the burdens of the Partition and managing an adversarial relationship with Pakistan, a relationship which has continued to cast its shadow on Indian external policy. The Partition of India, and its postcolonial legacy, have remained foundational events in shaping the foreign policy of the nation, and defining its identity, values, and the direction in which its understanding of its own role on the global stage has evolved.

1950

2. THE KOREAN CRISIS

The Korean crisis, beginning with North Korea's invasion of South Korea in June 1950, proved to be one of the most devastating humanitarian crises in the post-war period, with conservative estimates indicating more than a million civilian deaths, caused by military forces from both sides.[2] The Korean crisis also represented one of the first instances of the catastrophe that awaited nations that became collateral damage caught in the struggle for global domination between the United States (US) and the Soviet Union (USSR). This period, which later came to be known as the era of the Cold War, continued to define the state of international relations for more than four decades, ending in the early 1990s.

The complex contemporary history of Korea began to unfold in 1945, with the nation getting divided into two parts, the north under the control of the USSR, and the south administered by the United States. The two governments that grew out of foreign domination on the two parts of Korea subscribed to the political and economic structures of the Cold War blocs that sustained them. Hostilities between the two governments continued, with the eventual invasion of the South by the North in 1950. Other developments in the Cold War, which preceded this invasion, included the worsening of hostilities between the two blocs, the Berlin airlifts of 1948–49, the formation of the North Atlantic Treaty Organization (NATO) in 1949, and the Soviets conducting a successful nuclear test in 1949.

The Korean crisis was also the moment when Indian foreign policy engaged in one of its first significant international efforts to support a peaceful resolution of conflict. Despite it being beyond the boundaries of the Indian security calculus, India actively took part in the peace-building efforts. Being an outwardly neutral nation at the time, India did not provide field combatants, but instead supplied a medical unit, which assisted around 200,000 wounded people and carried out 2,300 field surgeries in the duration of the crisis.[3] It also provided a second contingent, called Custodian Force India, which assisted in the repatriation of the prisoners of war (POWs).

On the diplomatic stage, India played a crucial role in negotiating a peaceful settlement. Apart from its active participation in the United Nations to find a durable and lasting solution to the larger crisis, India also helped negotiate on the fate of more than 2,00,000 POWs between the two Cold War blocs. While the UN endorsed voluntary repatriation, the Communist Bloc demanded forced repatriation. Two commissions were constituted by the United Nations General Assembly, one tasked to supervise the ceasefire, and the other tasked with the repatriation of the POWs. India, with its neutral position, was made the chairman of the latter, which helped facilitate the protection and relocation of POWs who refused to be repatriated.

The Korean War was a defining moment for Indian foreign policy, in which it recognized that its own peace and security were fundamentally linked to wider regional and global security challenges. India's willingness to rise to the occasion and engage internationally barely three years post-Independence, has remained representative of its awareness of its duty towards the global community. More broadly, the impacts of the crisis, and its clear positivist linkages with the evolution of the Cold War, resonated deeply in Indian foreign policy. The polarization of the globe into two nuclear-powered blocs had brought the prospect of a catastrophic war perilously close to reality during this crisis. Unlike the Second World War, both sides now had cataclysmic capabilities, borne by nuclear weapons. Notwithstanding the nuclear option, the Korean crisis had also been representative of the devastation that was possible for nations caught in the crossfire, from widely available conventional weapons systems.

The urgency of not falling into this web of warring blocs became profound in New Delhi's strategic vision. Although the ideas of self-sufficiency, sovereignty in external decision-making, and an anti-imperial stand had been incorporated by India since its struggle for independence, the Korean crisis further catalyzed and highlighted the fundamental significance of maintaining a policy of non-alignment in a dangerously polarized international system. Furthermore, in contrast to strategic alignments, New Delhi strengthened its appeal to the Third World to remain removed from the politics of the Cold War, and, instead, stand together, united in solidarity with one another, to support decolonization and collaborate on development. Beyond being a petri dish for Nehru's policy of neutrality, which, at the time, predated the idea of non-alignment, the crisis showcased that India was diplomatically capable of punching far beyond its weight, just three years after its Independence, and despite the inheritance of fragile economic structures and military capabilities. Against this backdrop, New Delhi's foreign policy achievement in functioning as an unbiased agent of peace in a complex international crisis earned it extensive global credibility.

3. THE INDIA-NEPAL TREATY OF PEACE AND FRIENDSHIP

The Indo-Nepalese Treaty of Peace and Friendship, signed in 1950, was one of the first few efforts by India to consolidate its regional relationships and boundaries, the others being treaties signed with Bhutan in 1949 and Sikkim in 1950. Containing ten Articles and a letter of exchange, the Indo-Nepalese treaty established a framework for a 'special relationship' recognizing their historical association, congruence of values, economic and cultural linkages, and security requirements, in an effort to perpetuate peace in the region. The preamble of the treaty stated that both nations recognized 'the ancient ties which have happily existed…desiring still further to strengthen and develop these ties and perpetuate peace'. The first article of the treaty further substantiated that both the nations 'agree mutually to acknowledge and respect the complete sovereignty, territorial integrity and independence of each other'.[4] Notably, Articles 6 and 7 of the treaty laid the groundwork for open borders and the granting of special privileges to each other's citizens, which has continued to define the friendly bilateral relationship between the two nations.

Whilst India's treaty with Nepal was similar to the treaties it had with Bhutan and Sikkim, to the extent that they represented landmarks of cooperation and collaboration, the Nepalese treaty remained the most neutral. Unlike the Bhutanese treaty, which yielded its foreign policy to the control of India, or the Sikkimese one which made it a protectorate of India, the Nepalese treaty only dealt with strategic matters. It affirmed, firstly, as Article 2 stated, that the two nations would 'inform each other of any serious friction or misunderstanding with any neighbouring State likely to cause any breach in the friendly relations'. Secondly, Article 5 stipulated that Nepal would 'be free to import, from or through the territory of India, arms, ammunition or warlike material and equipment necessary for the security of Nepal'. New Delhi viewed these clauses to be absolute, in terms of being assured of both the neutrality of Nepal in the ongoing geopolitical posturing between the two Cold War blocs, and the security of a strong buffer on its northern boundaries.

From Nepal's perspective, the treaty was crucial in saving its independence from the expansionist policies being practised by China in its neighbouring region, Tibet. This was a significant cause of concern, as Nepal shared a border of nearly 1,400 kilometres with China. Furthermore, being a landlocked Himalayan nation, enclosed by China and India on either side, Kathmandu relied heavily on its neighbours for critical requirements, which included trade, commerce and energy supplies. Being unwilling to enter into negotiations with Beijing, which was concurrently planning its own territorial expansion, Kathmandu sought refuge in the promise of New Delhi, with its vocal support for anti-imperialism, strategic neutrality, and history of cultural interconnectedness. The bargain was clear for Kathmandu: while India would gain a friendly and neutral ally to its north, Kathmandu would gain a pivotal relationship, securing its sovereignty against Beijing's expansionism.

From India's perspective, an important driver of this treaty, as well as other treaties it made with its neighbours on its Himalayan frontier, was New Delhi's endeavour to protect the neutrality of its neighbourhood from the divisiveness of the Cold War. Furthermore, the newly independent India was acutely aware of its own security vulnerabilities across its northern borders, with Pakistan on either side, the rise of China's adventurism in Tibet, and the prospect of an expanding communist influence in Nepal. India was also understandably concerned with Communist China's claim that Tibet was China's palm, and Nepal, Bhutan, Sikkim, Ladakh and Arunachal Pradesh were its five fingers. India's treaties with Bhutan and Nepal, within the first few years of its Independence, effectively addressed these issues by granting formal recognition to the relationship, and strengthening India's strategic positioning and security on its northern frontier.

Although there have been attempts to amend it, the Indo-Nepal treaty of 1950 has been foundational in constructing Indian foreign policy with its northern neighbour, and continues to be used as a framework for engagement. Beyond strategic imperatives, the treaty also laid the foundations for regional economic cooperation and people-to-people relations, eventually underpinning India's Neighbourhood First policy. The treaty essentially manifested India's perception of its role as a security guarantor in its neighbourhood, with Article 5 allowing for the free access and import of 'warlike material and equipment necessary for the security of Nepal', from or through India. Along with its role of a security guarantor, the relationship between the two has naturally been lopsided, with New Delhi bringing significantly more to the table than Kathmandu.

1954

4. THE DETONATION AT BIKINI ATOLL

On 1 March 1954, the United States detonated their largest-ever thermonuclear device, known as Castle Bravo. The detonation was part of a broader programme for testing high-yield nuclear devices. It was called Operation Castle, which had completed its first successful test, called Ivy Mike, in 1952. The device was detonated at Bikini Atoll, part of the Marshall Islands, which had been the location for nuclear weapons research since 1946. The Marshall Islands are two chains of twenty-nine low-lying coral atolls, situated north of the equator, between Australia and Hawaii. The Islands were captured by the US in 1944 from Japan, which had ruled it since 1914. Notwithstanding Operation Castle's achievement in advancing the design of thermonuclear weapons, the serious misjudgement of its yield led to the worst incident of nuclear contamination in US history. A yield of five to six megatons was expected from the nuclear device, but the test delivered a yield of 15 megatons, estimated to be a thousand times more powerful than the US nuclear weapons used in Hiroshima and Nagasaki in 1945.

Although Castle Bravo was not the largest nuclear weapon to ever be tested, it represented a worrying and rapid advancement from the US's initial success in developing a hydrogen bomb in 1952. The critical fallout of the explosion occurred in the Rongelap, Rongerik, Alinginea and Utirik atolls in the Marshall Islands, impacting the inhabitants of the islands for years after the testing. The explosion sent irradiated dust through the atolls.

Traces of radioactive material were discovered as far as Japan, Australia, India, Europe and the United States, with the nuclear fallout spreading over about 7,000 square miles.

The successful detonation of the 15-megaton bomb by the United States was a significant milestone, in both the development of nuclear capabilities and the developing arms race between the two Cold War blocs. Along with enhancing the American power projection, the detonation catalyzed discussions around nuclear non-proliferation and related environmental and humanitarian ramifications. This event also significantly helped shape India's growing non-aligned stance, making evident the dangers of an uncontrolled arms race between the two blocs in an increasingly polarized geopolitical scenario. It had become certain that the use of nuclear weapons would have wide-scale ramifications, far beyond the realms of the Soviet Union and the United States, especially against the backdrop of the recently concluded Korean crisis. It had also become apparent that even the mere testing of nuclear weapons, with their expanded yield, posed a significant threat to the environment through its contamination of the Earth's atmosphere. The remnants of the explosion and the debris that gradually fell back over large portions of the globe, the radioactive fallout, was increasingly seen as the greatest danger in nuclear war.

This detonation, dubbed Castle Bravo, saw India take the lead on non-proliferation efforts, with Nehru's proposal to the United Nations requesting nuclear-armed states for 'some sort of what may be called "Standstill Agreement", in respect at least, of these actual explosions, even if arrangements about the discontinuance of production and stockpiling must await more substantial agreements among those principally concerned'. This proposal, and the posturing of Indian foreign policy, were specifically significant, as they not only reinforced its advocacy for restraint, but also strengthened the image of India as the face of what would later be described as the Non-Aligned Movement.

Castle Bravo was representative of the arms race in its full stride, with the United Nations estimating an annual average of fifty-five nuclear tests conducted between 1955 and 1989. Furthermore, it reported that in 1962 a total of 178 nuclear tests were conducted, with the preceding year seeing the world's largest nuclear weapon ever, called the Tsar Bomb, being detonated by the Soviet Union at the Novaya Zemlya site, near the Arctic Circle. The non-proliferation advocacy had quite clearly permeated into both the blocs, with a Limited Test Ban Treaty being signed in 1963 between the United States, United Kingdom and the Soviet Union. It banned all nuclear tests in the atmosphere, in space, or underwater. However, weapon expansion programmes continued, as the treaty did not include underground explosions.

Nehru's proposal remains one of the first to push for a global halt to nuclear weapons testing, as a step towards ending the nuclear arms race and preventing nuclear proliferation. This activism also characterized Indian foreign policy for years to come, as one which chiefly valued the ideal of peaceful coexistence and international peace and security as a fundamental goal, which it saw to be increasingly at risk due to polarization and the divisive nature of the Cold War. Although India's nuclear policy has naturally evolved with the passage of time, Nehru's proposal for a 'standstill' agreement remains representative of New Delhi's continuing and strong advocacy for international nuclear disarmament. Closer to home, Nehru made significant progress in developing India's relationship with its northern neighbour.

5. PRIME MINISTER NEHRU'S VISIT TO CHINA

The Indian prime minister's return visit to China in 1954 has been described as one of Nehru's most important external visits, and was also one of the first visits to China by the representative of a non-communist nation. It is estimated that a million people lined up to greet the Indian PM in Beijing. Nehru was well aware of the significance of the meeting in creating a constructive bilateral relationship, and also recounted that Chairman Mao Zedong similarly believed that 'both countries were struggling for peace. They had had more or less common experiences in recent history and both countries needed peace to reconstruct their economies as both were industrially backward'.[5] Nehru had prolonged meetings with several other key figures, including Premier Zhou Enlai, other principal ministers, the Dalai Lama, and the Panchen Lama, among others.

Just four years prior to this, in 1950, India was the first nation from a non-socialist bloc to recognize the People's Republic of China. Crucially, this visit was also preceded by the mutual agreement on the Panchsheel ('five principles') between the two governments in June 1954, which propagated the values of equality and cooperation, while agreeing on non-aggression, respect for each other's sovereignty, non-interference, and peaceful coexistence. Notably, the Panchsheel agreement was first mentioned in April 1954 in what was officially known as the 'Agreement on Trade and Intercourse Between Tibet Region of China and India', which, significantly, accepted China's suzerainty over Tibet.

In retrospect, however, some analysts argue that the Sino-Indian diplomatic developments in 1954 laid the foundations for New Delhi's misinformed and misaligned conciliatory approach to its northern neighbour. They further suggest that New Delhi's adamant belief in a future of peaceful Sino-Indian bilateral relations, and its resolute support for the same, had allowed it to make the unamendable faux pas of accepting China's suzerainty over Tibet. Others propose that this policy concession was made in return for China's acceptance, through the Panchsheel agreement, of the existing border demarcated by the McMahon Line drawn in 1914 jointly by the United Kingdom and Tibet. Nehru, during his visit to Beijing, did bring up the border question with Zhou, including the fact that Chinese maps had included Indian territory in them. However, no agreements were made apart from a verbal confirmation and a commitment by Zhou that those maps were insignificant, as they were reproductions of old maps, and that the People's government had not had the time to revise them.[6]

Nehru's efforts had created a bilateral relationship which allowed for the existence of conditions in which the boundary dispute could finally be discussed, with Zhou acknowledging and, on several occasions, even offering Nehru a package deal to resolve the issue of the disputed areas. Unfortunately, a compromise on the border question was simply not acceptable, Nehru stated, as it not only meant that India would have to 'accept the border claimed by China', but also put the rest of its borders up for discussion and renegotiation.[7]

An important aspect of Nehru's decision-making, throughout the chronological sequence of the Sino-Indian developments in 1954, was an emphasis on not only cultivating a peaceful Sino-Indian relationship but also ensuring the continuance of a Third World solidarity and neutrality, which had been championed and cultivated by him. The integration of Beijing into the international community, to ensure that it functioned within the accepted rules and norms institutionalized within the global order, was seen as pivotal in reining in any Chinese expansionism or adventurism in their shared neighbourhood. New Delhi was the first non-socialist nation to recognize China in 1950; it supported the People's Republic's membership of the United Nations,[8] and, according to some accounts, even passed over an offer by the United States to a permanent seat at the UN Security Council in the 1950s in favour of China.[9]

Nehru's policy of appeasement towards Beijing has often been seen as emblematic of his values-driven foreign policy, and its ineffectiveness in dealing with the issue at hand. It has consequently been noted for its inherent idealism, striving for an international environment, a world which simply did not exist, and a relationship which was characteristically one-sided, with little or, at best, measured reciprocation from Beijing.

Notwithstanding this wider foreign policy critique, the importance of the 1954 visit cannot be overstated; China represented, to India, a crucial stakeholder in the region, and to a large extent determined whether the regional dynamics would be congruent to the global power blocs, or resistant to this bifurcation. The visit ensured, to a large extent, that at least for the near future the latter could be expected, with Chairman Mao stating that 'India is a promising nation, a great nation.... Every piece of good news from India makes us happy. When India gets better, the world benefits.'[10] Nehru's visit in 1954 had been successful for all intents and purposes, as far as the bilateral relationship was concerned, as it had reached a crescendo, which would not be achieved thereafter. The visit also marked a major milestone for Nehru's internationalism, and strengthened the ideas of an Asian solidarity and non-alignment within the region. This visit marked perhaps the highest point of optimism in Sino-Indian relations, which has not been relived since.

1955

6. INDIA AT THE BANDUNG CONFERENCE

The Asian-African Conference of 1955, also known as the Bandung Conference, was held in Indonesia, co-sponsored by India, Indonesia, Sri Lanka, Myanmar and Pakistan, and was attended by twenty-nine nations from across Asia, the Middle East and Africa. The attending nations built on the principles of Panchsheel, promoted African and Asian economic and cultural cooperation, and championed the idea of a global decolonization. At the end of the conference, a communiqué was signed which included several tangible objectives, like the promotion of economic cooperation and cultural exchange, the protection of human rights, abstinence from Cold War alignments, and the protection of the principle of self-determination and peaceful coexistence, and called for the end of racial discrimination wherever it occurred globally. As the decolonization process was still in progress, the participating nations took it upon themselves to speak for nations that had yet to become independent.

This final resolution eventually led to the creation and the strengthening of the Non-Aligned Movement, which aimed to take a stand against the global bifurcation caused by the Cold War. The conference, to a great extent, embodied Indian foreign policy in the 1950s. Nehru, along with the Indonesian President Sukarno, was a key figure in its organization and what has often been described as his 'Bandung moment'. Apart from representing African-Asian solidarity, the conference set the stage for a wide South-South solidarity, recognizing the importance of economic development and political consolidation to counter neo-colonial forces and the underdevelopment that had been bequeathed to them by their colonial pasts.

Throughout the conference, Prime Minister Nehru had gone to considerable lengths to integrate the Chinese Communist government into the international system, and more specifically, the grouping of the Third World nations. The Ministry of Foreign Affairs of the People's Republic of China highlighted the precariousness of its position during its participation in the conference, as 'hostile forces at home [in China] and abroad did not want to see Chinese Communists making their voice heard on the world stage or New China raising its international profile'.[11] Multiple accounts describe Nehru, leveraging India's position as a key player of Asian regionalism, chaperoning and introducing China's Premier Zhou to the various sponsoring and participating nations at the conference. Without New Delhi's sponsorship, Beijing would have had to invest significant diplomatic capital and make considerable concessions to establish those relationships, especially with the relative newness of its regime, and the international contestation against the sovereign representation of China, with the continuing UN-recognized legitimacy of Chiang

Kai-Shek's Republic of China. Interestingly, others point out that India's patronage of China within the forum represented both the highest point of the bilateral relationship between the two nations, and ironically also the beginning of its decline, with the growing Chinese perception of being patronized and subordinated as a junior partner by India, in its role as a leader of the Third World.[12]

More broadly, the Bandung Conference was the precursor to the Belgrade Summit's establishment of the Non-Aligned Movement, which largely adopted the principles agreed upon at Bandung. In its establishment of a Third World solidarity, the conference also provided recently decolonized nations with a viable alternative to protecting their sovereignty, without completely aligning to one of the two Cold War blocs. The platform provided by the conference had proved vastly successful in allowing New Delhi to project its vision for global peace and neutrality for the Third nations, which had little to gain and plenty to lose from the ongoing US-Soviet Great Game. New Delhi's foreign policy had effectively realized its vision, and constructed the foundation of Third World cooperation through the unanimous agreement over norms and conventions that were institutionalized in the subsequent Belgrade Summit.

For Indian foreign policy at the time, the conference was a crucial conduit to showcase to the world a Third World solidarity, shield the greater region from the outside forces of the Cold War, and critically embed the 'Five Principles of Coexistence', recently formalized in agreement with China, in the larger region and community of the Global South. This event was a major moment in the history of Indian foreign policy, and perhaps the closest it has ever come to realizing the idealism of the Nehruvian outlook. In an increasingly perilous geopolitical condition, Bandung was the first time these recently decolonized nations had finally found a suitable platform to project their ideas, collaborate, take a stand, and punch far beyond their diplomatic weight in economic and material terms.

7. PRIME MINISTER NEHRU'S VISIT TO MOSCOW

Following Nehru's initial visit to the Soviet Union in 1927, this was his first visit in his capacity as India's prime minister. India was also well on its way through successfully implementing its First Five-Year Plan (1951–56), making considerable strides towards establishing its socialist ideals. In fact, its Second Five-Year plan emphasized the need for establishing a 'Socialist Pattern of Society', making its ideological alignment increasingly congruent with the Soviet Union. Furthermore, having already visited both the United States and China in his capacity as India's prime minister, in the preceding years, Nehru's visit to the Soviet Union was long overdue.

In June 1955, Nehru spent about half a month touring Moscow and Leningrad, as well as visiting many Soviet republics, from Ukraine to Turkmenistan. Reciprocating this gesture of goodwill, Nikolai Bulganin and Nikita Khrushchev visited India later the same year. Nehru's visit was particularly important to both the evolution of Indian foreign policy and the geopolitical landscape at the time. Nehru's visit in 1955 was of particular political, economic and cultural importance, as it established the foundation upon which any further collaboration and partnership would be built between the two governments. During their trip to India, Bulganin and Khrushchev crucially came out in support of India's positions on both Kashmir and Goa.

Notably, Nehru's visit also followed Pakistan's growing alignment with the Western Bloc, with it joining both the Central Treaty Organization (CENTO) and the Southeast Asia Treaty Organization (SEATO). This visit also strengthened India's credentials with respect to its non-aligned stance, as it expressed India's willingness to engage with both the blocs in a constructive manner to perpetuate global peace. Nehru's efforts to socialize China into the international order, rein in any potential military adventurism, and bridge the divide between the two blocs, was manifested during these trips, with his outward support for China to be given a seat in the United Nations Security Council.

Towards the end of the trip, an Indo-Soviet joint statement was issued on 21 June 1955, titled the 'Nehru-Bulganin Joint Statement', which described the converging values and interests of both the nations. It laid down a broad agreement between the two governments on several international issues, and discussed the cooperation and collaboration over several spheres, including the economic, cultural and technical ones. The USSR supported India's calls for international disarmament, and more broadly, it supported India's role on the global stage as an advocate for the ideals of neutrality and global peace. The Soviet support for India's self-perceived role for itself on the global stage was deeply impactful for Nehru.

During the return visit, Nehru, in an internal note, accounted for the delta between the USSR and the West's responses towards India's internationalism and diplomatic activism in projecting its beliefs and values to the rest of the world.[13] He recorded that the Soviet willingness to understand and express confidence in New Delhi's foreign policy activity was evidenced by their support for its inclusion in international conferences on Indochina and Korea. In contrast to this, the West had responded to India's rising international prestige with 'anger and resentment', and persistently had an 'over-bearing attitude', rooted in past colonial relationships.

In this note, Nehru did refer to his concern for the Soviet leadership's unequivocal public support for India, along with their denunciation of the West. In the period after 1955, Soviet economic support continued to increase, particularly for heavy industrial projects in the public sector. While New Delhi continued to practise its policy of non-alignment, its ideological convergence with the Soviet Union continued to represent, for the West, a significant change in its policy. The irony of this view consists in the fact that this was indeed Nehru's first visit to the USSR, having visited the US nearly six years before this, in 1949, just a couple of years after India's Independence. Perhaps the foundation of this Indo-Western policy divergence lay in the policy dissonance of the West, with its export of liberal policy on the one hand, juxtaposed with its legacy of colonialism, and support for imperialist ideals on the other. It is important to note that in 1955, India had only just decolonized the territories of Pondicherry, and Dadra and Nagar Haveli, and it had yet to successfully liberate and decolonize Goa, and Daman and Diu. The ratification of Pondicherry's merger into India took six years to pass by the French, and the rest were colonies of Portugal, which made significant international efforts to retain them.

While India did not strategically align with the Soviet Union with the successive trips of 1955, a collaboration between the two nations flourished, and steadily expanded over the next three decades. Nehru's sojourn in the Soviet Union was received extremely well within Russia, and left a lasting and positive impression on Mikhail Gorbachev, a student at the time, who wrote, in his memoirs, of his attendance of Nehru's visit to his university, with great fondness and respect. The monumental significance of this visit was testament to the diplomatic seeds it had sown, from which Russo-Indian relations would proliferate, expand and deepen over the coming decades, eventually to form a core part of Indian foreign policy and its geopolitical considerations.

1956

8. THE SUEZ CRISIS

The diplomatic and military crisis that took place over the Suez was perhaps one of the greatest concerns for both regional and wider global political stability in 1956. The crisis was chronologically preceded, and precipitated, by the Egyptian President Gamal Abdel Nasser's nationalization of the French and British-owned Suez Canal Company, which was, in turn, a retaliation to the West's withdrawal from financing the Aswan Dam project. The funding for the project had been withdrawn under various pretexts, and was seen by Nasser as a Western attempt to influence its policy. Just three months after the Suez Canal's nationalization, Egypt was invaded, under various pretexts, by Israel, the United Kingdom and France, in a war that began on 19 October 1956 and lasted nine days. The 'tripartite aggression' and invasion was called off by combined pressure from the Soviet Union and the United States. Apart from there being evident signs of Western imperialism in these events, India was particularly concerned as it was one of the major users of the canal—any blockages would have detrimental effects both economically and politically, with its Second Five-Year Plan just beginning in 1956. India heavily relied on navigating through the Suez for supplies of trade and energy.

Nehru was conscious of the magnitude of the crisis, and is said to have noted the importance of not just bringing about a peaceful settlement, but he also wanted to ensure that the canal would be available to be used as before. India had, since its Independence, developed a special relationship with Egypt, through which it had aimed to expand its support for secular nationalism in West Asia, and establish friendly relations within the region. Nehru had described the relationship as a 'spirit of brotherliness', and Nasser had come to rely on Nehru's advice on a variety of issues of international security. Nehru had consistently discouraged Nasser from joining either of the superpowers, and suggested that he maintain the non-alignment stance of his nation. The foreign policy convergence between India and Egypt developed to the extent that, along with Josip Broz Tito of Yugoslavia, Nehru and Nasser became symbols of unity for the Non-Aligned Movement across Asia, Africa and Europe.

The crisis threatened to create a dangerous precedent if the non-aligned nations did not unite in opposition, even if it was only diplomatic, against the onslaught on the sovereignty of the nations of the Global South. Reacting to the invasion,

India actively lobbied the United States to intervene and bring an end to the hostilities. In a letter to the US Secretary of State, Nehru described the magnitude of the event and its impact on international relations, claiming that 'the whole future of the relations between Europe and Asia' hung in the balance.[14] The Suez crisis was undeniably a dangerous development for the world at the time, with contemporaneous developments like the national uprising in Hungary and the Algerian War of Independence. The prospect of the escalation and spread of the conflict to the rest of the region was a matter of great concern within Indian strategic circles.

India played a pivotal role in bringing together the African and Asian nations in supporting the America-sponsored 'Uniting for Peace' resolution in the United Nations. Consequently, the UN established the UN Emergency Force (UNEF) as a peacekeeping force, in which India for the first time provided armed troops, which were placed in the Sinai Peninsula. Notably, the UNEF was commanded, between December 1959 and January 1964, by an Indian, Lieutenant-General P. S. Gyani. Nehru's uncompromising stand for the protection of Egypt's territorial sovereignty and dignity made significant advances for India's popularity within the region, also representing the height of India's pro-Arab policy. India had made a concerted effort to reconcile the geopolitical interests of the Western nations with a rising torrent of Arab nationalism. New Delhi's relentless, but responsible, support for a relatively weak Arab state, in the face of coordinated Western coercion, represents the core of Indian foreign policy at the time, which was characterized by its internationalism and foreign policy activism.

Indian foreign policy had managed to walk the diplomatic tightrope of supporting decolonization whilst still mediating between the two sides, and substantially contributing to the resolution of the crisis. Characteristic of India's non-aligned policy, it allowed it to remain relatively neutral throughout the crisis, while still engaging vigorously, through the UN, to ultimately arrive at a solution to the crisis. India's actions throughout this crisis consolidated its global reputation, enhanced its political capital, and reinforced its commitments towards the principles of multilateralism, non-alignment, anti-imperialism and global peace.

9. THE APSARA NUCLEAR RESEARCH REACTOR

The achievement of criticality by the Apsara nuclear reactor in 1956 was an extraordinary accomplishment on India's part. Apart from the Soviet Union, and ahead of China and Japan, India became the first Asian nation to accomplish a feat of this kind, all within less than a decade of its Independence. The reactor was developed with assistance from the United Kingdom, which supplied the enriched uranium fuel, and was a significant advancement for Indian research capabilities. It helped transition its scientific research from being purely theoretical to having a platform for its application.

The Atomic Energy Establishment, Trombay (AEET), established in 1954, later renamed the Bhabha Atomic Research Centre (BARC) in 1966, developed the reactor and described it as a pool-type thermal reactor of 1 MW power. The reactor was developed in record time at the Trombay campus of BARC, with the decision to build the reactor made in March 1955 and the achievement of criticality within just a year and a half, in August 1956.[15] The Indian nuclear programme had developed significantly within the first decade of India's Independence, right from its first efforts after the Government of India passed the Atomic Energy Act in August 1948, with Homi Jehangir Bhabha as its Chairman, to achieving criticality in record time. Notably, even before the Partition, Bhabha had orchestrated the establishment of the Institute of Fundamental Research in 1945, with assistance from Sir Dorabji Tata Trust. Bhabha had written to the Trust, asserting that 'when nuclear energy has been successfully applied for power production in say a couple of decades from now, India will not have to look abroad for its experts but will find them ready at hand'.[16]

Bhabha, essentially the founder of the Indian atomic energy programme, noted that the Apsara reactor was a critical stepping stone for India to begin mastering nuclear reactor technology. The reactor provided a pivotal platform for the production of radioisotopes, neutron activation analysis, neutron-induced fission studies, forensic research, beam tube research, shielding experiments, neutron radiography, neutron detector testing, seed radiation, and radio-biology research, among others. The reactor was ultimately shut down in 2010, and replaced by the 2 MW Apsara-U, which achieved criticality in 2018. In 2023, the *Times of India* reported that the Apsara reactor would be converted into a museum to commemorate the extraordinary leap that took place in Indian scientific research in 1956, serving as the 'cradle for the development of nuclear technology in India'.[17]

The creation of the reactor also represented a major foreign policy milestone, as it saw India embed itself deeper into the global nuclear debate. At the conference on the Statute of the International Atomic Energy Agency (IAEA) in 1956, Bhabha articulated in response to the prospect of controlling plutonium processing, that it remains the 'inalienable right of states to produce and hold fissionable material required for peaceful power programmes'. India continued to play a crucial role in the negotiation to create the IAEA since 1954, eventually becoming a permanent part of its board of governors, when it was later established in 1957.

Along with India's success with Apsara, in 1956 India also entered into an agreement, known as the Colombo Plan, with Canada and built the 40 MW CIRUS (Canadian-Indian Reactor, United States) reactor, which went critical in 1960, producing weapons-grade uranium. Plutonium for Pokhran-I, India's first 'peaceful' nuclear test, was also obtained from the CIRUS reactor. The 1950s and 1960s marked the first phase of India's nuclear policy, in which it pursued, as Nehru described, a 'peaceful nuclear programme' to further science and energy requirements, and not to develop nuclear weapons. This policy, however, began to evolve with China's increasing hostility, the war in 1962, and its development of nuclear weapons in 1964. Notably, just before Independence, in 1946, Nehru stated that he hoped 'Indian scientists will use the atomic force for constructive purposes. But if India is threatened, she will inevitably try to defend herself by all means at her disposal.'[18]

At the time, India's unwillingness to weaponize this capability only further bolstered its position on the world stage as a non-aligned nation which fundamentally championed global peace and stability. Apart from laying the foundations for greater scientific partnership, and collaboration with other like-minded nations, the success of Apsara also provided India with a platform to engage and cooperate with the wider international community on nuclear diplomacy, adding to its foreign policy an important nuclear dimension. The criticality achieved by the Apsara reactor in 1956 remains a monumental milestone for India, moulding its foreign policy, enhancing its status on the global stage, and accelerating its scientific and nuclear research.

1958

10. PRIME MINISTER NEHRU'S VISIT TO BHUTAN

Prime Minister Nehru's unplanned visit to Bhutan in 1958 became a major landmark in Indo-Bhutanese relations, marking the first-ever visit to the country by an Indian prime minister. The route he had taken, despite being the most frequented and convenient one, had no systems of mechanized transport beyond the Sikkim border. In defiance of medical caution and government reluctance, Nehru, at the age of sixty-nine, along with the Indian diplomatic mission, made this 105-kilometre journey on foot, using yaks to negotiate the steep terrains. Indian helicopters available to the Air Force at the time could not cross the outer ranges of the Himalayas.

The special relationship between India and Bhutan had already been established just after India's Independence. In 1948, the Bhutanese King Jigme Dorji Wangchuck, the third Druk Gyalpo of Bhutan, visited India, and soon afterwards, the Indo-Bhutanese 'Treaty of Perpetual Friendship and Peace' was signed in Darjeeling in 1949. India recognized Bhutan's sovereignty in this treaty, reverted the Dooars,[19] and increased their annual subsidy to ₹5 lakh. In return, Bhutan declared, as stated in Article 2, that it would continue to 'be guided by the advice of the Government of India in regard to its external relations'. Interestingly, a similar language was used by Bhutan in the Treaty of Punakha, which it had signed with the British in 1910. Along with this, the treaty provided for free trade and commerce, an assurance that India would not interfere with internal Bhutanese matters, and 'equal justice' to the citizens of each of the two countries.

For India, this treaty was an important landmark, as it provided it the assurance that Bhutan would be able to develop and function as a strong buffer state against the increasingly belligerent China. This evolution in relations was hastened by an increasingly aggressive China, which had claimed stretches of both Indian and Bhutanese territories as its own. Furthermore, India's behaviour towards its smaller and weaker neighbour was an important manifestation of its foreign policy, and gave credibility to its ideals of peace and mutual prosperity.

Nehru, recognizing the importance of this symbolism, stated in his 1959 trip to Bhutan that 'some may think that that since India is a great and powerful country and Bhutan a small one, the former might wish to exercise pressure on

Bhutan. It is, therefore, essential that I make it clear to you that our only wish is that you should remain an independent country'. Nehru further reiterated India's support for Bhutan to continue to 'remain an independent country, choosing your own way of life and taking the path of progress according to your own will'. Nehru articulated that both the nations should live with 'mutual goodwill as members of the same Himalayan family and that freedom for both should be safeguarded so that none from outside could do harm to us'.[20] This visit was particularly remarkable not only from a strategic angle, but also, it crucially catalyzed the opening up of the Bhutanese kingdom to the world outside, through the conduit of India.

Notwithstanding India's benefit of gaining a strategic ally, Nehru's trip had also been pivotal in protecting the Himalayan kingdom's unique identity and self-imposed detachment from the rest of the world. For Bhutan, its policy of isolation from international politics had to be reinforced with support from India, with significant developments in its neighbourhood which included the invasion of Tibet by the People's Liberation Army in 1950, the annexation of Bhutanese enclaves in Tibet, and an increasing presence of Chinese troops near the Bhutanese border, against the backdrop of Chinese territorial claims.

This treaty had effectively addressed all these concerns, and had gone several steps further in securing a crucial ally in India, which has since continued to support the development and the protection of the Himalayan kingdom's sovereignty. India was pivotal in assisting Bhutan to become a member of the Colombo Plan in 1963, the Universal Postal Union in 1968, and finally, the United Nations in 1971. Each of these memberships, culminating with the UN one, was crucial in protecting the independence of Bhutan, expanding its recognition as a sovereign nation, and gradually integrating it into the international system, at its own desired pace. Breaking out of its isolationism, Bhutan leveraged this visit to secure its sovereignty through increasing security, economic and strategic support from India, while expanding its international presence. The significance of this trip has been far-reaching for Indo-Bhutanese relations, with its foundation being firmly fixed in Nehru's assertions, and the declaration of India's support for the unquestioned sovereignty and independence of Bhutan.

1959

11. THE DALAI LAMA SEEKS POLITICAL ASYLUM

After an unsuccessful Tibetan uprising in March 1959, which had aimed for the complete withdrawal of China from the region, the Dalai Lama, along with an entourage of eighty people, reached the Assam Rifles outpost of Chutangmu, near Tawang, on 31 March 1959, to request asylum in India. A few days later, in April, the Dalai Lama met Prime Minister Nehru in Mussoorie, and was officially granted political asylum in India. Following their leader, trudging through the snow and treacherous terrains, via Tawang, the Brahmaputra Valley and various other routes, were also tens of thousands of Tibetans seeking shelter and safety from repression in the hands of the People's Liberation Army. Although the Indian government welcomed most of the asylum seekers, the refugee inflow also set in motion an administrative, security and humanitarian crisis.

The People's Liberation Army had, by the latter part of March 1959, ruthlessly supressed any remaining resistance in Tibet, and by 28 March, the Chinese Premier Zhou Enlai had formally announced the dissolution of the Kashag, the Tibetan local government, handing over political control to the 'Preparatory Committee of the Tibetan Autonomous Region'. Zhou had called for the people of Tibet to unite and create a 'democratic and socialist' new Tibet.

While India's gesture in providing asylum to the Tibetan leader fell in line with its humanitarian principles, it massively strained its relations with China. Along with this asylum, the subsequent creation of a Tibetan government-in-exile in Dharamshala in April 1959 saw Nehru crossing the Rubicon in the context of Sino-Indian relations. The event damaged India's relations with China beyond rapprochement, as Nehru's decision had contradicted the Chinese President Zhou Enlai's warning not to grant the Tibetan leader refuge in India. This was seen by the Chinese government as both a direct interference in China's internal affairs and a breach of the bilaterally agreed-upon principles of the Panchsheel understanding. By the autumn of 1959, two clashes had occurred on the Sino-Indian border.

The reasons as to why India gave the Dalai Lama political asylum in 1959 remain debated. For China, the issue of Tibet, and its own worsening relations with India, also led to it receiving diplomatic censure from the Soviet Union, with the latter supporting India's position. In a heated conversation between the Soviet leader Nikita Khrushchev and Mao, Khrushchev stated that 'the events in Tibet are the fault of the Communist Party of China, not Nehru's fault'.[21] Later, in 1960, due to rising Sino-Soviet bilateral disputes, China and the Soviet Union broke off diplomatic relations. China had continued to view India's position on Tibet as an attempt to 'grab Tibet' and turn it into a buffer zone. Contravening Beijing's perception, New Delhi had, through the 1950s, gradually come to recognize Beijing's suzerainty over the region of Tibet, and reduced its interactions and weakened its ties with Tibet, in an effort to strengthen its relations with Beijing.

New Delhi's act of grand accommodation was seen to be pivotal in providing a basis for a broad programme of cooperation between the two nations and the rest of the developing world against the two nuclear-powered Cold War blocs. Nehru had continued to believe that the collection of policies that had been designed to appease China, and demonstrate India's willingness to engage constructively, could win over China, and create a powerful sense of unity in the Global South. Through the 1950s, these policies included India's acceptance of China's suzerainty over Tibet, its position on issues in Korea, its support for the PRC's admission into the UN, and the passing over of the offer for a place in the UNSC in favour of China, among many others.

However, Nehru's policy towards China and Tibet likely changed, seeing that its repeated overtures to Beijing through the decade remained unreciprocated, instead witnessing a rise in Chinese belligerence. The importance of their shared cultural roots and religiosity should not be underestimated. Nehru was innately sensitive to the 'sentimental' and 'cultural' interests in Tibet, which had widespread support across India. India had, once before, also provided refuge to the fourteenth Dalai Lama's predecessor, the thirteenth Dalai Lama, in Darjeeling in 1918. The thirteenth Dalai Lama had also refused to surrender to Chinese suzerainty over Tibet, and only returned after a few years, when the Chinese had been successfully rejected and the Dalai Lama's supremacy re-established.

The granting of political asylum has represented a watershed in Indian foreign policy, as, in retrospect, it further accentuated the mutual distrust between China and India that had been brewing since the Chinese invasion and annexation of Tibet in the early 1950s, and it also symbolized the point at which Sino-Indian hostilities began escalating. The schism between China's Chairman Mao and Nehru widened, with Mao subsequently labelling Nehru 'a reactionary' and 'an expansionist'. More broadly, this event has continued to cast its shadow over contemporary Sino-Indian relations, with the provision of asylum continuing to remain a key area of disagreement between both the Indian and the Chinese governments.

1960

12. THE SIGNING OF THE INDUS WATER TREATY WITH PAKISTAN

The signing of the Indus Water Treaty between India and Pakistan on 19 September 1960 put to rest one of the major post-Partition disputes between the two governments. India and Pakistan had attempted to settle this issue with several bilateral initiatives since 1948, with the World Bank joining the discussions as a mediator in 1952, and tabling its proposal in 1954, which was accepted by India. After several further amendments, this proposal was eventually accepted by Pakistan and consequently signed in 1960. The Treaty provided for a division of the water of the Indus River System that originated in Tibet, with India being allocated the control of the three eastern rivers, Beas, Ravi and Sutlej, while Pakistan was granted control of the three western rivers, the Indus, Chenab and Jhelum.

The Treaty had normative as well as functional values, as it crucially laid down administrative and institutional mechanisms for the management of the basin. It mandated biannual meetings between the two nations, the arrangement of technical visits to construction sites, and encouraged the exchange of details about the water flow and the quantum used. This helped set up a structured procedure for the exchange of information and the management of disputes that could potentially arise in the future. In retrospect, the Treaty has proved to be one of the world's most effective interstate water-sharing efforts, with most of the bilateral water disputes between the two nations continuing to be resolved diplomatically.

The distribution of the water of the Indus Basin was not dealt with by the erstwhile colonial government, which had hastily retreated from the subcontinent. Cyril Radcliffe, who was responsible for the demarcation of the borders, is said to have had acknowledged the importance of the Indus Basin for both India and the newly created Pakistan, but did not make any specific recommendation, and had simply hoped that the new governments would find a solution.[22] This solution, although not long-lasting, was reached with the chief engineers of both East Punjab (India) and West Punjab (Pakistan) signing a Standstill Agreement on 20 December 1947. This agreement had held that until the end of the rabi crop on 31 March 1948, the status quo of the water allocation of the Indus Basin irrigation system would be maintained. Unfortunately, the cooperation transformed into conflict, as Pakistan did not take any initiative to negotiate or extend the agreement, and on 1 April 1948 the agreement expired, and India halted the supply of water to several canals in Pakistani territory.[23]

Salman M.A. Salman and Kishor Uprety note the gravity of the situation for Pakistan, as it faced the prospect of not being able to irrigate 5.5 per cent of its cropland in the crucial kharif sowing season. Following through this via an Inter-Dominion Conference, a new agreement was signed on 4 May 1948, under which both East and West Punjab recognized the need to resolve the issue in the spirit of friendship and goodwill. East Punjab assured that it would not stop water supplies suddenly, without providing time for West Punjab to develop other sources, and the agreement provided for the gradual decrease of water being supplied to Pakistan, and for it to develop alternative sources. While the Inter-Dominion Agreement collapsed with disagreements over its interpretation, it provided a modus vivendi which kept this complex situation from unravelling further, till the signing of the Indus Water Treaty in 1960.

The agreement was formally denounced by Pakistan in 1950 with it proposing third-party intervention, which was strongly opposed by India—the latter had instead urged that the Inter-Dominion Agreement be made permanent. Later, in 1952, both the nations agreed to have the issue mediated through the conduit of the World Bank, which had committed not to adjudicate on the conflict. The inclusion of the World Bank was significant, as it pivoted from approaching the issue purely along its political aspects, but also focused on its functional aspects. This marked the beginning of several proposals and counterproposals from either side, which finally culminated in the signing of the Treaty in 1960.

Apart from setting a major normative precedent for sharing international waters between riparian nations, the Treaty also symbolized the possibility for Indo-Pakistani cooperation, and safeguarded against the weaponization of water within the subcontinent. Notwithstanding the criticism, and the various efforts to modify the Treaty in the last six decades, it has continued to be the bedrock of Indo-Pakistani relations. The relevance of the Treaty has continued unabated, as it has withstood several wars and frequent periods of heightened tensions. Indian foreign policy has continued to negotiate new and changing challenges with Pakistan around the Indus River System, through the constructs of this Treaty. It will continue to be fundamental for any further negotiation to evolve the water-sharing agreement, especially against the backdrop of climate change and the potential exacerbation of water shortage forecasted for the subcontinent.

13. PREMIER ZHOU ENLAI OF CHINA IN INDIA

Under pressure from the Soviet Union to resolve the territorial disputes with India, and facing greater threats like the United States and Japan to its east, the Chinese Premier Zhou Enlai made an extraordinary overture by flying to Delhi in April 1960. Against the backdrop of border skirmishes, and despite problems with Mao, this trip was made by Zhou in an attempt to salvage the situation and settle the border disagreement peacefully. Roughly put, Zhou had come with a package deal in which the border would be delimited; if India accepted China's control over Aksai Chin, China would recognize the McMahon Line, accepting India's control over Arunachal Pradesh. However, Nehru declined this territory swap, as he believed that 'our borders are not negotiable'.

It is important to note that China's outreach was underscored by several factors, which included the unravelling of its relationship with the Soviet Union, the heightening border tensions with India, and the prospect of hostilities with the United States and Japan. The Soviet Union had not only taken a neutral position on the Sino-Indian border question, but it had also withdrawn its experts and its economic contracts with China by early 1960. The border issue with India was also proving to be explosive, with major skirmishes already taking place in the latter half of 1959. Adding to this situation, China was indeed being surrounded from all sides, with ever-expanding hostilities and trust deficits with the Western Cold War bloc.

A lot of these sentiments can be seen to be manifested in Beijing's note to New Delhi in May 1959, in which it declared that 'the enemy of the Chinese people lies in the east—the US imperialists have many military based in Taiwan, in South Korea, Japan and in the Philippines which are all directed against China', further stating that 'China's main attention and policy to struggle are directed to the east, to the west Pacific region, to the vicious and aggressive US imperialism, and not to India....our principal enemy is US imperialism'. These policy drivers had also seen China make significant border agreements with Nepal and Burma in the 1960s.

However, unfortunately for Zhao's endeavour, the proposed fundament of the negotiations could not be accepted by India. In a series of exchanges between the two prime ministers in the build-up to the 1960 visit, Nehru, in a letter dated 5 February 1960, articulated that 'in the latest note from the Government of the People's Republic of China, emphasis has been laid on our entire boundary never having been delimited. That is a statement which appears to us to be wholly incorrect, and we cannot accept it. On that basis there can be no negotiations.' Nehru further stated that 'although any negotiations on the basis you have suggested are not possible, still—I think it might be helpful for us to meet'.[24]

Zhou's visit did not bear any significant fruit, with him stating, 'after seven days of talks, although, unlike what we expected, no agreement has been reached for the settlement of the boundary question'. Zhou further noted that the only developments regarding the border issue were:

> ...the two sides have unanimously agreed that the officers of the two sides should meet and examine, check and study the factual material relevant to the boundary question and submit report to the Governments of the two countries. Both sides have also agreed that while the officials of the two countries are holding meetings, all efforts should be made to avoid friction and clashes in the border areas. These agreements have been set forth in the Joint Communique of the two Prime Ministers. We hold that these agreements have a bearing on the maintenance of tranquillity on the border and on the continued search for avenues to a reasonable settlement of the boundary question.[25]

This trip and Zhou's offer have been frequently described as 'the point of no return' in the trajectory of the Sino-Indian border dispute, which eventually culminated in war two years later, in 1962. Nehru's decision to reject Zhou's proposal has been subject to extensive analysis, ranging from being oversimplified as short-sighted and influenced by the anti-China lobby, to instead a consideration of the reality in which this decision was made. It all happened against the backdrop of a strong anti-China public sentiment, in which a 'barter' would not be accepted; constitutional hurdles which would require a two-thirds approval by the parliament to cede Indian territory; and an understanding that this may not be a 'final settlement', with China only becoming more emboldened to expand its territorial claims within the region.

Notwithstanding the various deliberations about why the proposal fell through, it indeed marked a momentous occasion, and an opportunity for both sides to de-escalate the border situation. This event was also an important landmark, as it provided a glimpse into the decaying reality of the Asian solidarity that Indian foreign policy, at the time, had sought to realize through its overtures to China. Perhaps for Nehru, the greatest disillusionment took place when China, through deceit and force, as Neville Maxwell notes in *The Times* in 1960, 'simply annexed it [Aksai Chin] and killed Indian soldiers on its soil'.

14. THE INITIATION OF SOVIET MILITARY SUPPORT

Apart from Russia's Nikita Khrushchev's visit to India in early 1960, Indian President Rajendra Prasad's return visit and the agreements signed on expanding economic, cultural and scientific cooperation in 1960 also, crucially, marked the beginning of India's expanding military collaboration with the Soviet Union. This represented the first shift away from New Delhi's dogmatic abstinence from any form of military cooperation, towards the rise of more pragmatic considerations. A now declassified report from the Chinese Foreign Ministry in 1963 stated that the 'Soviet Union began military aid to India in 1960 in the wake of the incident at Kongka Pass', referring to one of the first significant Sino-Indian border skirmishes, in which nine Indian police personnel were killed in action. The report further noted that the extent of the Indo-Soviet military cooperation eventually spanned 'road building machinery to military aircrafts', further protesting that 'the Soviet Union has refused to give us [China] complete equipment for making MiG-21 aircraft [sic], but has sold it to India' in 1962.[26] A declassified CIA report from 1973 has estimated that this military support had begun in November 1960. This remains a crucial event in the evolution of Indian foreign policy, as the 1960s saw an exponential increase in Soviet military support, as is explained by both the aforementioned reports.

While this Indo-Soviet military exchange began as early as 1955, with two Il-14 transport aircraft being sent to India, this cooperation flourished from 1960 onwards, the same year in which the sale of twenty-four Il-14 transport aircraft to India was finalized. The extent of this military exchange was significant, with another CIA report from 1972 estimating that in just over a decade, from 1960, up to the time when the report was written, the Soviet Union had delivered equipment worth more than $1.1 billion to India. It further suggested that the average amount was over $130 million after 1965, and included MiG-21 fighters, MI-8 helicopters, SA-2 surface-to-air missiles, tanks, and OSA-class guided missile patrol boats within the same period.

For the Soviet Union, which was dealing with a spiralling relationship with China and its growing bilateral antagonism, India represented a key pillar of friendship and stability within Asia. From the perspective of Moscow, it was critical that India had the right external support and capabilities to protect this stability against the backdrop of increasing regional instability. For New Delhi, its strengthening relationship with the Soviet Union and their military support were crucial with the diplomatic fallout it had faced with China, with the previous heated rhetoric over the provision of political asylum to the Dalai Lama, Beijing's growing expansionist tendencies, boundary disagreements, and the subsequent skirmishes in 1959. Furthermore, the expanding flow of arms to Pakistan from the US, in exchange for base facilities, had also threatened to create an imbalance in the regional equilibrium, especially with Pakistan's procurement of some F-104 Starfighters from the US in 1961–62.

Furthermore, scholars like P. Chari contend that the non-availability of Western arms pushed India further towards the Soviet Union to meet this dire necessity. At several different points, New Delhi had reached out through Y.B. Chavan, the

Minister of Defence from 1962 to 1966, to both the United States and the United Kingdom for military assistance, which was not provided.[27] Following the Sino-Indian War in 1962, the First Five-Year Defence Plan was formulated in 1964, which laid out several objectives to modernize and enhance India's capabilities. It aimed to bring India's armed forces and equipment up to date, and to help it achieve self-reliance in the shortest possible time.[28] The Soviet Union had effectively filled this vacuum by supplying India with military assistance, and setting up local assembling facilities. The MiG-21 remains symbolic of this defence framework, with a gradual increase in indigenous components in its construction over time, reaching 60 per cent in 1972.

The importance of this event is far-reaching for Indian foreign and security policy, as a new element had been introduced that brought it significant leverage. Although, in essence, India continued to position itself as a non-aligned nation, its relationship with the Soviets continued to expand thereafter, right up till the end of the Cold War. This relationship only strengthened in leaps and bounds, creating one of the greatest legacies of the Cold War for India. Russia has continued to be considered India's 'all-weather friend'. Notably, even up to 2022, India's military structure has continued to be heavily dependent on Russian military imports. Indian foreign policy has had to evolve while navigating this relationship, carefully observing its dependencies and security necessities.

1961

15. THE ANNEXATION OF GOA

Code-named Operation Vijay, the annexation of Goa, and Daman and Diu, in mid-December 1961 finally freed India from the shackles of Portuguese imperialism, after more than 450 years of colonial rule. The military manoeuvre lasted just short of two days, and involved the mobilization of the Indian air, sea and land forces. The liberation of Goa was demanded by the Indian government as non-negotiable, right from the nation's Independence in 1947. Despite pressure from the United States and the West to refrain from intervening, Nehru took the decision to annexe the Portuguese colony by deploying the military. Portugal, a founding member of NATO, along with the Western nations of US, UK and France proposed a resolution at the UN Security Council for a ceasefire and the withdrawal of Indian forces. Crucially, this was vetoed by the Soviet Union.

The prelude to Goa's liberation was characterized by Portugal's growing obstinacy about retaining its colonial possessions, reinforced by the authoritarian dictatorship of the corporatist Estado Novo under António de Oliveira Salazar. Portugal had continued to deny the repeated calls for decolonization that had begun as early as 1928, with the establishment of the Goa Congress Committee by Tristão de Bragança Cunha. By the early 1950s, Portugal had refused to entertain any Indian requests to open negotiations, as it claimed that this issue was non-negotiable. By 1953, India had withdrawn its diplomatic missions from Lisbon, and within a year or so, India had also levied economic sanctions on Portugal. Later, in 1955, Portuguese authorities fired upon a procession of more than 5,000 unarmed satyagrahis,[29] who had gathered to mark the seventh anniversary of India's Independence from British colonial rule.[30] Following this, India shut its consul office in Goa. As years of diplomatic effort and India's policy of settling the issue peacefully had been consistently disregarded by the Portuguese, Nehru took the decision to intervene with the help of the military.

Consequently, through the Constitution (Twelfth Amendment) Act, 1962, India proceeded to integrate these territories, as it had done with the Portuguese-controlled Dadra and Nagar Haveli in 1954 through the Constitution (Tenth Amendment) Act, 1961. Goa remained under army administration till June 1962, after which a power transition took place in which a civilian government was installed, and Goa, Daman and Diu were officially declared union territories. The annexation was a major symbol for India's perceived role as the leader of the Non-Aligned Movement and a champion of global decolonization, with many African nations encouraging Nehru to 'show the way'. A government-controlled radio in Ghana announced that the people of Ghana 'hail the liberation of Goa and long for the day when our downtrodden brethren in Angola and other Portuguese territories in Africa are also liberated'.[31]

Interestingly, preceding the military intervention, in October 1961, during a seminar in Delhi organized by the Indian Council for Africa, delegates from across existing Portuguese colonies spoke of their discontent and the ruthless suppression they were subjected to. African delegates also showed their dissatisfaction with India's slow policy of working towards a peaceful resolution for Goa, and were waiting impatiently for India to lead the campaign for freedom from Portuguese colonial suppression. J. Ferreira Viana of Angola was recorded to have said that the insistence of India on following peaceful methods was adversely impacting national revolution movements in other Portuguese colonies; another Angolan delegate apparently said that the Portuguese empire would cease to exist if Goa was to become free.

Fascinatingly, D.P. Singhal in his work in 1962 conjectured that the liberation of Goa could perhaps build the momentum for antifascist forces in Portugal to overthrow the Salazar regime.[32] Indications thereof had already begun showing, with an attempted coup in Beja in southern Portugal a fortnight after Goa's liberation. Following the loss of its colonial territories in India, this pro-colonial regime engaged in the Portuguese Colonial War to suppress nationalist movements in its colonies in Angola, Guinea-Bissau and Mozambique—this started in 1961 and only ended with the Carnation Revolution military coup and the overthrowing of the Estado Novo in 1974.

By the early 1960s, international support for colonial regimes had also begun to change, with a marked transition in policy evident even in the most conservative quarters of British politics, underscored by the British Prime Minister Harold Macmillan's famous 'winds of change' speech in South Africa, in which he acknowledged that 'the wind of change is blowing through this continent. Whether we like it or not, this growth of national consciousness is a political fact'. The outcomes of the events in Goa would eventually gather momentum to end colonial rule in Portuguese Angola, Portuguese Mozambique and Portuguese Guinea.

More importantly, this event fell in line with the Indian government's bid to consolidate its own territorial integrity. The eviction of the Portuguese colonial state also represented the removal of the last vestige of the legacy of imperialism that had plagued the subcontinent for several centuries. Notwithstanding the Western censure, India's actions brought it widespread acclaim across non-Western, developing, recently independent, and still colonized nations, strengthening both its regional influence and international stature.

1962

16. THE FIRST SINO-INDIAN WAR

The war between India and China took place in both the eastern and western sectors of the Sino-Indian border and lasted just over a month, between October and November 1962, culminating in a decisive Chinese victory. The war was preceded by an increasing frequency of Sino-Indian border skirmishes since 1959, expanding mutual political suspicions and leading to a fundamentally differing interpretation of the shared border. China's unilateral declaration of a ceasefire on 20 November 1962, and its simultaneous withdrawal to its pre-war position (known as the Line of Actual Control), effectively ended the war.

India's relationship with China had continued to deteriorate through the latter half of the 1950s, with strong evidence that India's persistent policy of appeasement had failed to bear any significant fruit. Beijing had, instead, continued to become more belligerent. The early 1960s had also seen China become increasingly cornered and threatened, encircled by hostile actors, with perilously disintegrating ties with the Soviet Union along its northern border, increasing hostilities with Japan and the US to its east, and growing border disputes with India to its south. After extensive pressure by the Soviet Union, Beijing had attempted to resolve the border dispute, with Mao Zedong committing to Khrushchev, in a conversation on 2 October 1959, that 'the border issue with India will be decided through negotiations'. Off the back of this, Zhou Enlai had made his visit to India in 1960, which unfortunately did not generate any significant success.[33]

Later, in 1961, China had begun carrying out patrols along the McMahon Line, and entered Indian-administered territory. In response to this, India launched its infamous 'forward policy', under which it aimed to counteract China's incursions into its territory by setting up outposts behind Chinese troops, in an effort to cut off their supply lines and force them to return to China. John Garver notes that this policy saw initial success, as Chinese forces withdrew when confronted by advancing Indian outposts. Following this, Mao convened a Central Military Commission in which, after several deliberations, a decision was made to stop withdrawing when confronted by new Indian outposts, and instead to counter-encircle them under a policy of 'armed coexistence'.

While the policy of armed coexistence had eroded the basic assumption of the forward policy, instead of re-examining it and adjusting it appropriately, New Delhi sought to make it more aggressive, and not simply to occupy vacant territory, but also to push back Chinese posts which were already occupied. Matters came to a head when both nations planned manoeuvres and counter-manoeuvres to claim Thagla Ridge. With reports by the People's Liberation Army that India might attack its positions on Thagla Ridge, Mao declared war, stating,

> ...we fought a war with old Chiang [Kai-shek]. We fought a war with Japan, and with America. With none of these did we fear. And in each case we won. Now the Indians want to fight a war with us. Naturally we don't have fear... Since Nehru sticks his head out and insists on us fighting him, for us not to fight with him would not be friendly enough. Courtesy emphasizes reciprocity.[34]

The narrative around the war has been considerably wide-ranging, from China's portrayal as an aggressor to India's vast political miscalculations of both its relationship with China and its own military preparedness. The Brooks-Bhagat report, a retrospective assessment sanctioned by the Indian Army, sheds light on these strategic misjudgements on the part of Krishna Menon and Nehru, as well as India's military unpreparedness. Notwithstanding the extensive analysis performed so far on the various aspects of the event, there exists a unanimous consensus regarding the epistemic upheaval it caused in the framework of Indian foreign policy.

China's unilateral disengagement ended perhaps the single most diplomatically humiliating episode in the annals of contemporary Indian history, moulding Indian foreign policy to an extraordinary extent. The precipitous military defeat, at the hands of a nation which was perceived as something of an ally just a decade earlier, jolted New Delhi out of the Nehruvian phantasmagoria of peace and friendship with Beijing rooted in Third-Worldism. With the Nehruvian outlook's natural inclination towards idealism, India's foreign policy theretofore had been commanded by its focus on key principles like non-alignment, internationalism, pro-Third-Worldism, and peaceful coexistence. These foundations led to the formation of a foreign policy that was characterized by its positive-sum international calculations, and an intransigent conviction about the incorruptible solidarity of the Global South. The Sino-Indian War helped catalyze India's transition from its Nehruvian inertia, and gradually move its foreign policy along more pragmatic lines, recognizing the fundamental realities of *realpolitik* within the international system. Its antagonistic relationship with China has continued to remain a key hurdle for Indian global aspirations, and a critical factor to navigate for Indian foreign policy.

1963

17. THE CEDING OF SHAKSGAM VALLEY

The souring of Sino-Indian relations after the war in 1962, and the perception of India as a strategic concern for both Pakistan and China, led to the natural convergence of interests among its northern neighbours, with the signing of three significant agreements which included a trade agreement, a civil aviation agreement and a boundary agreement. The Sino-Pakistan Boundary Agreement signed in Peking on 2 March 1963 between Chen Yi and Zulfikar Ali Bhutto, the Chinese and Pakistani foreign ministers respectively, delineated a common border between the two nations. The agreement also represented one of the first indications of this geopolitical shift, laying the nascent foundations of the relationship and controversially ceding 5,180 square kilometres of Indian territory, the Trans-Karakoram Tract, also known as the Shaksgam Valley, by Pakistan to China. This Valley is part of the Hunza-Gilgit region, which was a portion of Kashmir occupied by Pakistan and a point of dispute between India and Pakistan. The agreement was made up of seven articles, of which the sixth stated that the agreement was subject to renegotiation once the Kashmir dispute was resolved between India and Pakistan.

The agreement was described as illegal by New Delhi, as it pointed out that Islamabad and Beijing did not, in fact, share a common boundary and that the region covered by the agreement was a part of the Indian territory of Kashmir, as had been formally acceded by the ruler of the erstwhile princely state in 1947. Although the Sino-Pakistan relationship was still thawing from Pakistan's close associations with the Western Bloc, being part of both SEATO and CENTO, the signing of this agreement by the Pakistani and Chinese foreign ministers set the stage for an expanding scope for cooperation and collaboration. The region's geography is of particular importance, with it bordering the Xinjiang province of China to its north, the Siachen Glacier region to its east, and the northern regions of Pakistan-occupied Kashmir (PoK) to its west and south. Effectively establishing a link between Pakistan and China, the surrendering of the Shaksgam Valley formed a critical component of connectivity and infrastructure between the two countries, with the eventual construction of the Karakoram highway.

Some have interpreted the event as a major concession by Islamabad, which would not have been made without President Ayub Khan's willingness to befriend the People's Republic of China. Others have explained this agreement as an expression of Beijing's vindictiveness towards New Delhi.[35] The Sino-Pakistani border negotiations had already started in 1961, and the agreement to negotiate the border was announced in May 1962.[36]

The cession of this strategically important and disputed territory by Pakistan significantly complicated India's security challenges, not only by questioning India's territorial integrity but also by expanding its concerns about external hostility across a majority of its land borders. The Sino-Pakistan Agreement saw India's willingness to remain non-aligned become even more challenging to maintain, adding a layer of complexity to regional balancing and creating the prospects for two-front hostility, and increasingly pushing India into the Soviet sphere. The ceding of

Shaksgam Valley has remained an important landmark, catalyzing India's expanding affiliation with the Soviet Union till the end of the Cold War, and shaping Indian foreign policy significantly with the complications that it added to India's border and security milieu.

The agreement was a watershed for Sino-Pakistani relations, after which the two countries collaborated across a wide range of activities, with China not only providing it with key military capabilities, like missile and nuclear technology, but also becoming the largest economic investor in Pakistan. This relationship has continued to strengthen in the following century, with Pakistan being absorbed into China's Belt and Road Initiative.

President Ronald Reagan and Prime Minister Indira Gandhi outside the Oval Office in 1982.

Source: White House Photographic Collection

Wave 2

1964–85: Regional Consolidation and Antagonisms

Following Nehru's idealism, in this phase Indian foreign policy shifted towards a more realist approach, driven by a focus on regional security and strategic autonomy. This period reflects a significant evolution of India's foreign policy, where idealism was tempered by the need to navigate complex regional realities.

1964

18. INDIA AND SRI LANKA FOR THE INDIAN OCEAN ZONE OF PEACE

Following the Bandung Conference in 1955, the Non-Aligned Movement (NAM) had hit full stride, with its first summit taking place in September 1961 in Belgrade, Yugoslavia. The summit drew on the principles agreed upon at the Bandung Conference, which included objectives like the promotion of economic cooperation and cultural exchange, the protection of human rights, abstinence from Cold War alignments, and the principles of self-determination and peaceful coexistence, and called for the end of racial discrimination wherever it occurred globally.

The significance of the Belgrade meet in institutionalizing Third-Worldism is evident in its frequent description as the

'Third World's Yalta', much like how, in 1945, the Yalta Conference brought together Prime Minister Winston Churchill of the United Kingdom, President Franklin D. Roosevelt of the United States, and General Secretary Joseph Stalin of the Soviet Union to discuss what post-Second World War peace would look like. The Belgrade Summit was seen as its parallel in the Third World, bringing together President Joseph Broz Tito of Yugoslavia, President Gamal Abdel Nasser of Egypt, and Prime Minister Jawaharlal Nehru of India to discuss the place and role of the Third World in the post-Second World War period.

Subsequent to Belgrade, the second NAM Summit was held in Cairo, Egypt, in October 1964. Crucially, the Cairo meet took place against the backdrop of a severely damaged Third World unity, with Sino-Indian relations plummeting following the catastrophic war in 1962, the Algerian-Moroccan war of 1963, the Indonesian-Malayan skirmishes over Borneo that began in 1962–63, and the cataclysmic Congo crisis. The Cairo Summit revealed a damaged Third World unity, with deepened divisions and the absence of clarity and consensus on the direction it was going to take, with two factions developing around the issue of the expansion of NAM membership. On one side, there was Yugoslavia which supported the idea of a universal approach to membership, which would be open to all regardless of geography. On the other side, there was Indonesia, supported by China, which supported a narrower Afro-Asian regionalism when it came to expansion.

Although the universalist concept eventually succeeded, the Cairo meet also symbolized India's transition away from Nehruvian idealism, allowing it to take its first steps towards a more pragmatic worldview. During the summit, in a significant step, Prime Minister Sirimavo Bandaranaike of Sri Lanka called for the denuclearization and the removal of military bases from the Indian Ocean Region (IOR), and proposed that the IOR be turned into a Zone of Peace. Being a neighbouring littoral nation,

India forthwith supported the initiative, and went on to become one of its greatest exponents till the end of the 1970s. Apart from being one of the early antecedents of the 'free and open Indo-Pacific' concept, the Zone of Peace initiative became a key conduit of Indian foreign policy during what were perhaps two of its most turbulent decades: the 1960s and the 1970s, in the course of which it fought two wars with Pakistan and one with China.

India's advocacy of the Zone of Peace initiative has been analysed extensively, with most interpretations highlighting its genesis in Nehruvian foreign policy idealism, which essentially aimed at dismantling extra-regional interference and politics as well as imperialistic military bases, and thwarting any neo-colonial interests. Although this does capture the essence of the initiative, others, like Yogesh Joshi, point at the rise of an innate power politics and *realpolitik* pragmatism in India's approach to the initiative. Joshi proposes that far from curtailing external presences in the IOR, India started encouraging it, on the basis of its changing strategic security calculations in a continuing attempt to balance China and Pakistan within the region.

The legacy of the Zone of Peace concept has continued to remain an important aspect of Indian foreign policy. It has evolved from its initial function of simply balancing the great powers during the Cold War to becoming a mainstay of contemporary Indian foreign policy, as an arena for its diplomatic projection. While the Zone of Peace concept may not be synonymous with the free and open Indo-Pacific concept, it has remained an integral and enduring objective, one that has continued to align with New Delhi's broader foreign policy goals within the Indo-Pacific. These include fostering economic growth, ensuring regional stability and security, protecting the freedom of navigation, supporting humanitarian initiatives and counterterrorism activities, among others.

1965

19. THE SECOND INDO-PAK WAR OF 1965

The War of 1965 between Pakistan and India began with the infiltration of around 7,000 Pakistani insurgents into Kashmir on 5 August, and ended with the United Nations Security Council (UNSC) resolution for a ceasefire, which was to take effect on 22 September 1965. Although some accounts of the war describe the outcome as 'inconclusive', as both sides claimed a victory, objectively India had successfully countered Pakistan's machinations to achieve a military victory through its Operation Gibraltar, and the subsequent Operation Grand Slam. The former aimed to covertly infiltrate Kashmir, and the latter aimed to capture the strategic town of Akhnoor in Jammu. Furthermore, not only had India successfully thrown off Pakistan's military adventurism, but it had also secured the greater spoils of war, occupying 1,920 square kilometres of Pakistani territory, compared to the 540 square kilometres of Indian territory captured by Pakistan.

Other evidence-based assessments, including a report by the American Central Intelligence Agency on 1 October 1965, concluded that 'in finite military terms India won the September war with Pakistan. India seized the most territory and suffered less relative loss in manpower and materiel. Moreover, when the ceasefire occurred, India was in a much better position to continue the fighting.'[1] Notwithstanding the UNSC resolution, ceasefire violations continued to be committed by both the sides, threatening a larger region with further escalations and instability within the Indian subcontinent. The Soviet Union played a significant role in bringing both sides to the table, and hosted peace negotiations between the two nations in Tashkent, Uzbekistan. At this meet, the Tashkent agreement was signed on 10 January 1966, between Prime Minster Lal Bahadur Shastri of India and President Mohammad Ayub Khan of Pakistan. Both countries agreed to withdraw their positions to pre-August lines by 25 February 1966.

The Tashkent agreement was arguably path-breaking in terms of the relationship between the two nations, as it not only brought the hostilities to an end, but also resulted in both the nations reaffirming their obligation to the UN Charter and not to resort to force, and instead to settle their disputes through peaceful means, further agreeing that along with a cessation of the conflict both sides would withdraw their positions to the status quo that existed before 5 August 1965, by 23 February 1966. Although the agreement has been denounced by certain factions on both sides as unsatisfactory, it remains a remarkable Soviet feat, and an important historical precedent for mutual understanding between the two nations.

For India, the War of 1965 was equally significant in its symbolism, as it secured a restoration of trust in the ability of the Indian armed forces to protect its territorial integrity, after the catastrophe of the War of 1962. The enhanced level of preparedness of India's frontline forces in 1965 can be gauged through a report commissioned by India's Ministry of Defence in 1992. It stated, through a retrospective analysis, that only 14 per cent of its frontline ammunition had been used, and it had twice the number of Pakistani tanks at the time the ceasefire was declared. Ironically, the same report relates that while India's frontline was well equipped, its military intelligence was found wanting. General J.N. Chaudhuri, on being questioned whether India would win if the war was prolonged, informed the prime minister that most of India's frontline ammunition had been expended, and that there was also considerable loss of tanks.

More broadly, the war impacted Indian foreign policy. However, the impact was not in terms of degree but in terms of type. It catalyzed New Delhi to shake off the veneer of 'non-alignment', the remnants of its Nehruvian legacy, which had been exposed by the divisive nature of the war, and move towards a stronger alignment with the Soviet Union. This was driven, in part, by the United States and the United Kingdom's refusal to supply India with weaponry, and their inability to rein in their ally Pakistan, which was part of both the Western alliances, SEATO and CENTO. Disappointingly for India, apart from China, Turkey, Iran and Saudi Arabia, Indonesia, which was one of the founding members of the NAM, had broken its neutrality, and openly supported Pakistan.

New Delhi had, through the progression of the 1960s, become increasingly dependent on Soviet imports for armaments, and developed what has been described as a 'special relationship' with Moscow. This watershed event allowed for an even greater spillover in Russo-India collaboration, and set a key fundament in Indian foreign policy for the remainder of the Cold War. More practically, the war is also attributed to have led to the creation of the Research and Analysis Wing (RAW) to bolster India's external intelligence-gathering abilities. It also led to several military enhancements in the command and control of its armed forces.

1966

20. DEVALUATION AND ADJUSTMENTS

India faced one of its first major economic crises in 1966, with dangerously high fiscal deficits, unnervingly low foreign exchange reserves, and consistently uncompetitive exports. Exacerbating these weak fundamentals of the economy was an eclectic mix of internal and external factors that drove the domestic economy into a state of crisis. These included the destructive economic legacy of the wars of 1962 and 1965, a drought and the consequent threat to India's food security in the spring of 1966, and an overvaluation of the Indian rupee (₹). Added to this mix was also the overbearing pressure exerted by the International Monetary Fund (IMF), the World Bank, the Aid India Consortium, and the United States administration, to enact structural economic reforms to secure foreign capital investment and aid. Throughout the 1960s, the deficit in India's balance of payments was extensively bridged by foreign aid. Consequently, with few alternatives, on 6 June 1966, the Indian rupee was devalued by 57.5 per cent, increasing from ₹4.76, to ₹7.50 per US dollar. Along with this, other policy measures included the imposition of several countervailing export duties, the removal of some export subsidies, and a reduction in import duties.

This was the second time in history that the Indian rupee was devalued, the only other instance being the incident of 1949 in which a decision to devalue the British pound spilled over into India and the rupee was devalued, as it was pegged to the British pound. Subsequent to 1966, the next significant foreign exchange crisis and devaluation took place in 1991, when India more extensively liberalized its economy. More broadly, the devaluation of a nation's currency is a significant reset in its financial system, as its impacts necessarily reverberate into the sinews of its economy. It is essentially the deliberate downward adjustment of the official exchange rate which reduces a currency's value. By contrast, a revaluation is an upward change in a currency's value. A devaluation makes a nation's currency cheaper relative to other foreign currencies, making its exports relatively less expensive and foreign products more expensive. While its effects, i.e. reducing imports and increasing exports, may help ease a nation's balance of payments deficit, the IMF suggests that the impact of this sudden change can also drive inflation. As imports become more expensive, nations are seldom able to immediately substitute them with domestic production. This can, in turn, affect economic growth as the government is generally forced to increase interest rates to rein in inflation.

In the context of India, it appears that although the drawbacks existed, most have argued that it remained an unavoidable reality. Beyond the endogenous and exogenous catalysts mentioned above, New Delhi's economic policy, in the form of its Second Five-Year Plan (1956–61) using deficit financing to promote heavy industrialization, had simply proved ineffective, instead creating a foreign exchange crisis. The subsequent Third Five-Year Plan (1961–66), unfortunately, also bore the legacy of low foreign exchange reserves, proving ineffective in changing the economy's trajectory, also beset with fundamental structural challenges, like wars and a drought. The nation's foreign exchange deficit grew a staggering nine-fold between 1955 and 1966. These unavoidable economic circumstances forced New Delhi to accept the terms demanded by the IMF and the West, and implement major structural changes to its economy, as foreign aid had remained a key instrument for easing its balance of payments deficit. The move was widely unpopular for Prime Minister Indira Gandhi's government at the time, with a considerably strong opposition in parliament, accusing the government of selling itself to the World Bank and the United States. It must be noted that less than two decades before this incident, the ideals of economic self-reliance had been embedded in India's independence movement, its subsequent Independence, and its governance thereafter. This was, understandably, unpalatable for the nation's identity, as it feared losing control of its own economic policy.

Eventually, when the promised aid package failed to materialize, disenchantment, the seeds of which had already been sown in New Delhi's relationship with Washington, only continued to grow progressively. A natural distrust also grew in India for international organizations like the World Bank. While New Delhi's politics had already transitioned from its legacy of idealism, the devaluation also marked for its economy the end of an age of idealism and optimism, and the start of one characterized by a growing sense of disenchantment with the international economic system. The devaluation had ramifications abroad as well; Qatar, Oman and the UAE, countries which used the Gulf rupee issued by the Reserve Bank of India, were forced to withdraw their circulation and create their own currencies. While some may be right in arguing that the devaluation was required, it was indeed mistimed, and perhaps too little and too late. Although the economy benefitted, the incident remained a core memory for New Delhi's expanding trust deficit with the West, embedding it even further in the Soviet camp.

21. 'FOOD FOR PEACE'

Since 1954, the United States had, under its 'food for peace' programme enabled by its Public Law (PL) 480 legislation, provided nations in need with shipments of grain. India had benefitted immensely from this programme, importing significant quantities of grain throughout the remainder of the 1950s, till the end of the 1960s, against the payment of the Indian rupee equivalent of its cost in US dollars. Over this period, several agreements were made between the two governments regarding the terms of the shipments of grain. The arrangement had remained an important bridge between inadequate domestic agricultural production, which had consistently been outpaced by domestic consumption, while not adversely affecting its foreign exchange reserves.

This arrangement, however, was called into question in 1966, with President Lyndon B. Johnson politicizing it in an attempt to control New Delhi's position on the Vietnam War. In retaliation for its limited success, and Prime Minister Indira Gandhi's signing of a joint Gandhi-Kosygin communiqué in July 1966 in Moscow, which condemned imperialists for deteriorating world affairs, the Johnson administration began to limit the shipments being sent to India under PL 480. The deliberate delay of shipments, and consequently the overstretched supply chains, reduced India to what has been described as a ship-to-mouth existence. The sense of humiliation caused by the Johnson administration's Machiavellian decisions in 1966 left a lasting impression on New Delhi's foreign policy calculus. Sharada Prasad, the press adviser to the prime minister, reminisces about Indira Gandhi clenching her fingers tightly while on the phone with President Johnson, stating after the call, 'I don't want us ever to have to beg for food again.'[2] Coupled with the domestically unpopular decision to devalue India's currency in June 1966, based on what would eventually be a false promise of American aid and foreign investment, New Delhi faced a rude awakening in its tryst with the liberal experiment.

The PL 480 agreement had unarguably been an important instrument in New Delhi's economic policy. Although the idea of this agreement was to build the nation's buffer stock of grain and bolster its food security, a large proportion of it was consumed. Bridging the deficit between its domestic food consumption and production, while still not depleting its foreign exchange reserves, this agreement had also enabled the Second Five-Year Plan (1956–61) to focus on its aim of rapid industrialization. Notwithstanding the feasibility of such an arrangement, the fact remained that such a compromise could create a fundamental dependency, which would be sustained until domestic production was increased to match consumption.

David Sorenson proposes three models for the American approach to the PL 480 arrangement. First, from an American perspective, on the surface the PL 480 initiative enabled it to fulfil its humanitarian ambition, consisting of its moral commitment to feed the world's hungry. Through an economic lens, this arrangement also assisted in disposing of surplus American produce. It further stimulated American shipping interests and created a base of development capital, designed to establish markets for its other agricultural produce in the receiving nations. Through a national security lens, however, it becomes evident that such a relationship of dependency could eventually be weaponized to facilitate its policies of communist containment, while also rewarding nations with which it maintained strategic ties. This has been aptly described by Kristin Ahlberg as 'Machiavelli with a heart!'

It appears from India's experience with the PL 480 that each of these models held true. The first two prevailed for the majority of the arrangement, with the national security model catching India unawares in 1966. The humiliation caused by the conduct of American *realpolitik* in 1966 marked an important milestone for India, proving to it, through clear, positivist evidence, that the exercise of sovereignty in its external affairs depended to a great extent on its domestic self-sufficiency. The economic disequilibrium in its agricultural consumption and production had proved to be a glaring vulnerability when it came to preserving a sovereign foreign policy. As a reaction to this experience, New Delhi declared 'plan holidays' between its Third and Fourth Five-Year Plans, between 1966 and 1969, actively prioritizing the strengthening of its agricultural sector and facing the consequences of its decision of currency devaluation. The period which followed saw an agricultural transformation, referred to as the Green Revolution, which drastically enhanced its capacity for domestic food production.

With a combination of policy change and conducive weather conditions, the *New York Times* reported that between 1970 and 1971, India produced 107.8 million tons of food grain, about 3 million tons more than what was forecasted, permitting India to shake off the shackles of PL 480 for the period of the war with Pakistan fought for the liberation of Bangladesh. The experience of PL 480, one of the most publicly visible vestiges of its post-Independence dependencies, remained a key motivator for New Delhi to focus on expanding India's internal capacity, and simultaneously widened its trust deficit with the United States.

1967

22. INDIA AND CHINA BORDER CLASH AT NATHU LA AND CHO LA

In September 1967, clashes between the Indian Army and China's People's Liberation Army (PLA) broke out across two high-altitude passes: Nathu La and Cho La, along the China-Sikkim border. This represented one of the most significant escalations between India and China after the War of 1962, matching in scale and significance the clashes in Tulung La in 1975 and the Doklam standoff in 2017. Casualties amounted to hundreds on both sides, with China's *The People's Daily* (14 September) warning the Indian troops of 'another taste of China's iron fist', referring to the War of 1962.

According to Indian reports, the dispute started with China's forward posts digging bunkers in Sikkimese territory and Indian troops laying barbed wire fences to demarcate the disputed boundaries. According to Indian reports, on 11 September, following another dispute over boundaries, Chinese troops returned to their bunkers and commenced machine gun and mortar fire against Indian troops. Despite the fierce fighting, which continued till 14 September, the Indian troops held their posts and yielded no ground. Notably, the Nathu La incident redeemed faith in the level of India's military preparedness and capabilities along its northern border. Following this, on 1 October, clashes and firing went on for the entire day at Cho La, where the PLA saw little success, with Indian troops not only holding their positions but also driving the PLA three kilometres back, with effective mortar and field artillery support.

With scant evidence of any achievement, China made a significant effort to capture the narrative, and control the optics of the encounter. Its media was on the front foot, spewing propaganda about India being the aggressor and the PLA launching a 'resolute and powerful counterattack'. Beijing media continued to allude to the injustices and the interference in its affairs carried out by an 'anti-China' lobby of the 'US imperialists', 'Soviet Revisionists', and 'Indian reactionaries'. Notably, a CIA report at the time reported a Soviet build-up on the Chinese border, sending in tanks, which would eventually erupt in the form of the Sino-Soviet border conflict in 1969.

While the reasons why this clash did not translate into war remain debated, analysts like Taylor Fravel point at a reduction in the Chinese claim over the territory as one of the core reasons for it to initiate the hostilities. China's border positions were not as assertive as they had been in 1962, as India had since then undertaken a large-scale military transformation, which included doubling the size of its army, equipping its frontline troops better, and enhancing its military preparedness. Adding to this, the period was also one of uncertainty for the PLA, as it was going through the most unstable period of China's Cultural Revolution.

The clashes of 1967 were a watershed moment as the event essentially reset the relationship between India and China, which had theretofore been coloured with the defeat in 1962. The border thereafter saw a prolonged period of peace, with the Tulung La clashes in 1975 being the last reported instance of a shot being fired along the Sino-Indian border till the Sino-Indian skirmishes in 2020. The Sikkim sector of the shared border has remained relatively peaceful. Although Sikkim was recognized as an Indian protectorate in 1950, through a referendum in 1975 it joined the Indian Union. Later, in 2003, China finally recognized the Sikkim frontier. The Sino-Indian diplomatic reset had worked, with clear, positivist evidence, unlike during the 1965 War with Pakistan, where China made consistent threats on its northern border. During the 1971 War with Pakistan and the Liberation of Bangladesh, China did not intervene despite America encouraging China to distract India during its advance. Notwithstanding the relationship reset, China continued to support insurgencies in India's Northeast.

The 1967 border clash served as an important symbol for New Delhi. Having given China a 'bloody nose', it broke the myth of its invincibility. For the rest of the globe, India redeemed some credibility on the international stage. India's strategic success in the incident was further bolstered by the fact that its government remained undeterred by this act of neighbourly aggression and retained confidence in its own military capabilities. In her first statement on the second incident at Cho La, Prime Minister Indira Gandhi simply said that she 'hoped that it would only prove to be a local affair like the previous exchange at Nathu La'.[3] The status quo that was established after this event became one of the key bulwarks of the Sino-India relationship. Even though both the nations remained cautious with one another, it set a lasting precedent against further military adventurism by Beijing, with the intimidating prospect of the kind of response it should expect to receive from its neighbour to its south.

1968

23. INDIA OPTS OUT OF THE TREATY ON NON-PROLIFERATION OF NUCLEAR WEAPONS

New Delhi's approach to nuclear weapons has remained consistent at its core, continuing with its call for universal disarmament. India's decision to opt out of signing the Treaty on the Non-Proliferation of Nuclear Weapons (NPT) in 1968 is often seen as a contradiction when juxtaposed with its efforts to the contrary, being one of the first nations to call for an end to nuclear testing in 1954, as Nehru proposed a 'standstill agreement' at the United Nations. India remains one of the four nations, along with Pakistan, Israel and South Sudan, not to have signed the NPT. The NPT represents the only binding multilateral commitment to prevent the spread of nuclear weapons and technology, to further the goal of complete nuclear disarmament and promote cooperation among nations in the peaceful use of nuclear energy. Focusing on these objectives, the treaty was made up of ten articles, and was negotiated between 1965 and 1968 by a body called the Eighteen Nation Disarmament Committee (ENDC), set up by the UN in 1961.

The negotiations of 1965 were dominated by the Soviet Union and the United States, which appeared to set up constraints for non-nuclear-weapon states (NNWS), while merely paying lip service to the road to disarmament for nuclear-weapon states (NWS). In this regard, India made considerable contributions to the process of the negotiations, working with other NNWS to unanimously pass the General Assembly Resolution 2028 (XX) on 19 November 1965, which called for the ENDC to give 'urgent consideration' to its five principles.[4] Unfortunately, these demands were ignored and no such guarantees were provided by the superpowers when the final treaty emerged in 1968.

In January 1964, the United States and the Soviet Union came together in Geneva for a meeting which has been described as the 'nuclear Yalta', and among other topics, they crucially agreed that a NNWS would be defined as any state which has not manufactured and exploded a nuclear device before 1 January 1967. As India had yet to develop and test a weapon, it was categorized as a NNWS. Finally, when the treaty was presented for signatures, it contained the 'grand bargain' enshrined in Articles II and IV which required countries to give up any present or future plans to develop nuclear weapons, in return for access to nuclear energy for peaceful use. Notwithstanding the relinquishment of the right to develop nuclear weapons by NNWS, the treaty did little to ensure disarmament among the NWS. Furthermore, the NPT, by referring to nuclear weapons without defining them, and including any other nuclear explosive device, had factored in the relinquishment of all systems intended for peaceful nuclear explosion (PNE). Theretofore, nuclear contracts consisting of a restrictive clause only prohibited their use for military purposes, instead of prohibiting all explosions.

Essentially, the NPT had been curated to contain the 'horizontal' proliferation of nuclear weapons, and did little to check the 'vertical' proliferation of nuclear weapons. The former is the acquisition of nuclear capability by NNWS, through the testing and attainment of nuclear weapons, and the latter is effecting a proliferation of nuclear weapons by NWS, through the testing, production and stockpiling of nuclear weapons. The NPT had essentially been designed to function as an instrument that stratified the international system into 'nuclear haves' and 'nuclear have-nots'. This was an important consideration for India's nuclear policy, which was forced to become more nuanced as a response to the nuclear tests conducted by China since 1964.

Unfortunately for New Delhi, the NPT had proved insufficient in ensuring a general disarmament, a foreign policy objective which India had long been in favour of. The treaty, instead, threatened to reduce New Delhi's policy manoeuvrability and endanger its sovereignty at a time when its military was still reviving from the debacle of 1962. It was completely unacceptable, from a national security point of view, that the NPT would constrain India as a NNWS and prevent it from availing the option of using nuclear technology for peaceful or military purposes, while China, as a NWS, had free rein to continue the proliferation of nuclear weapons. The circumstances in the 1960s helped considerably to change India's nuclear policy, seeing PM Indira Gandhi authorize the development of nuclear capabilities in 1972, and eventually seeing it conduct its first peaceful nuclear explosion in 1974. While India's refusal to join the NPT as a NNWS was a significant milestone in the trajectory of its nuclear policy, its approach to the issue of nuclear disarmament has continued to be consistent. India's Foreign Minister Jaswant Singh stated in 2000:

> India's policies have been consistent with the key provisions of the NPT that apply to nuclear weapon states. These provisions are contained in Articles I, III and VI.... India has been a responsible member of the international nuclear

non-proliferation regime and will continue to take initiatives and work with like-minded countries to bring about stable, genuine and lasting non-proliferation, thus leading to a nuclear-weapon-free-world.

1970

24. THE CALL FOR A 'SOUTH-SOUTH' COOPERATION

The bifurcation that had taken place during the preceding conference of the Non-Aligned Movement in Cairo in 1965, between supporters of the regionalist concept and those of the universalist concept, had somewhat subsided, with the universalist concept prevailing. The regionalist concept, backed by China and Indonesia, supported a narrower Afro-Asian regionalism in the expansion of the group, while the universalist one, backed by Yugoslavia, supported a more universal approach to membership, which would be open to nations from all geographical regions. Partly, the regionalist approach collapsed as the Afro-Asian Conference, which was to be held in Algeria, was called off due to the 1965 coup d'état there. The Lusaka Summit was pivotal in the institutionalization of the NAM. It called for regular summits every three years, and established a standing committee of sixteen NAM member-nations who would coordinate the preparation for summits. Furthermore, the Lusaka Summit built the groundwork for the adoption by the United Nations General Assembly, in December 1971, of a resolution declaring the Indian Ocean 'for all time as a zone of peace'.

These steps were particularly important as the NAM had faced several challenges since its first meet in 1961, which included the expansion of its membership and the contemporaneous détente between the US and the Soviet Union. Beyond its contribution to the institutionalization of the movement, the Lusaka Summit also helped bolster the decolonization movement, which had already gained significant momentum with the earlier UN Declaration on Decolonization. Most importantly, the Lusaka Summit's declaration on 'Non-Alignment and Economic Progress' took cognizance of the threat to international peace, security and the sovereignty of newly independent countries, from the progressively widening gap between rich and poor nations.

To this end, the declaration called for the 'international machinery to bring about rapid transformation of the world economic system particularly in the fields of trade, finance and technology so that economic domination yields to economic cooperation and economic strength is used for the benefit of the world community'. It further asserted the important role of the United Nations 'in safeguarding the independence and sovereignty of the non-aligned nations'. Crucially, it also called for self-reliance through direct action in its Declaration on Non-alignment and Economic Progress. This proposed the idea that expanding economic cooperation among developing nations would bolster the concept of self-reliance in an asymmetric international economic system.

Notwithstanding the variety of subjects discussed during the meet, the Lusaka Summit was the first time that the economic proposals of the NAM nations were articulated and formalized. Building on this momentum, the succeeding summit held in Algiers in 1973 seeded the concept of the New International Economic Order (NIEO). Referring to the existing state of unfavourable economic structures, Prime Minister Indira Gandhi warned that 'powerful vested interests, domestic and foreign, are combining to erect new structures of neo-colonialism'. Building on this, she called for a unique 'South-South Cooperation', stating that there existed 'greater complementarity amongst our [developing] economies than between economies of the developed countries'. Referring to trade and cooperation among the countries of the Global South, the prime minister stated that this had thus far been 'left virtually unexplored', and through such cooperation, the Global South could 'diversify [their] trade, safeguard it against the caprices of international commerce, and reduce [their] dependence on middlemen and brokers'. It further called for cooperation in the 'fields of development—generation of power, development of agriculture, improvement of roadways, railways and telecommunications, the expansion of higher education and training in science and technology'.[5]

The Lusaka Summit has continued to represent New Delhi's commitment to the development of the Global South on its own terms, and without the strings of structural dependencies created by the international economic system. Apart from being a victory with regard to the success of the universalist approach of the NAM, Lusaka had provided a platform for India to bring into focus for the Third World the neo-colonial structures and the vestiges of imperialism that still remained. The idea of South-South Cooperation has, since the summit, remained a cornerstone of Indian foreign policy and its approach to the rest of the developing world. New Delhi's efforts in Lusaka had contributed towards creating a re-energized NAM, with a clear focus on correcting global economic injustices, effectively saving the group from becoming redundant, as had been feared, with the emergence of factions at the Cairo Summit in 1964. The continuation of the NAM was integral to New Delhi, both as a central element in its own foreign policy and as a confirmation of its position at the helm of the Third World.

1971

25. THE TREATY OF PEACE, FRIENDSHIP, AND COOPERATION

The signing of the Russo-Indian Treaty of Peace, Friendship, and Cooperation on 9 August 1971 saw India enter what was perhaps its most consequential arrangement in the Cold War era. Consisting of twelve Articles, the treaty was signed by India's Foreign Minister Swaran Singh and Soviet Foreign Minister A.A. Gromyko, and set the highest standards of cooperation and symbolized an alignment of interests in the context of international and regional security challenges. Although Article IV of the treaty,[6] and Foreign Minister Singh in his address to the Lok Sabha,[7] maintained India's subscription to its non-aligned principles, the treaty did symbolize a marked transition in New Delhi's foreign policy approach, expanding its collaboration with the Soviet Union. To the extent that the non-aligned policy had evolved, the Indian foreign minister recognized this shift in his address and stated that 'the world is presenting a rapidly changing and dynamic picture. There is a change in the configuration of various world forces. Our policy of non-alignment is a dynamic policy which can be adapted to these changing situations.'

Srinath Raghavan articulates that while the treaty was drafted relatively swiftly after its initiation in 1969, accommodating India's non-aligned policy and removing any mentions of a military alliance, New Delhi's hesitations, fearing a fallout with both the United States and China, forestalled further progress. Far from a strategic Indo-Soviet consensus, the subsequent signing of the treaty represented more of a convergence of strategic imperative for both the parties.

From a Soviet perspective, a major catalyst for entering this arrangement was based in the growing Sino-Soviet ideological battle and was accentuated by the border clashes between China and the Soviet Union over the Ussuri River island, in March 1969. The clashes escalated to the extent that nuclear rhetoric and threats were being hurled by both sides, and it led to the Chinese leadership fleeing Beijing, and it remains the first and only time that China placed its nuclear forces on a full alert status.[8] A declassified CIA memorandum sent to Henry Kissinger from Helmut Sonnenfeldt on 18 August, nine days after the treaty was signed, refers to the Ussuri River clashes as a catalyst for the Soviet Union expanding its diplomatic alliances, to ensure there is no 'loss of face' in its deteriorating relationship and prospects of confrontation with China.

India, on the other hand, had resisted giving in to this treaty, including during the beginning of the East Pakistan humanitarian crisis in 1971. The turning point for New Delhi is seen by many to be the US Secretary of State Henry Kissinger's covert trip to China via Pakistan. The decision to cross the Rubicon was based on a reported conversation between Kissinger and the Indian ambassador to the US, L.K. Jha, in which Kissinger communicated that the US would not get involved if China intervened in a war between India and Pakistan.[9] Within a month of Kissinger's trip, the treaty was signed on 9 August. Quite clearly, for Moscow the strategic imperative embodied by the Ussuri incident, and for New Delhi, Kissinger's trip, were the underpinning dual forces that drove the treaty to its realization.

Notwithstanding the strategic significance of this treaty, and its effect on New Delhi's policy of non-alignment, it successfully maintained the core tenets of its strategic autonomy. Discerningly, a memorandum to President Nixon, just hours after its signing, stated that 'while the Treaty represents no substantial change in Indo-Soviet relations, it reinforces the increasing closeness of view…[reflecting] a Soviet recognition of the preeminence [sic] of its interests… and India's recognition of the geopolitical necessity… [implying no] change in India's desire for close relations with the United States'. While the treaty had ushered in a period of closer cooperation, it, by no means, represented a break in its non-aligned principle, being actually an evolved version of it. It was met with censure from the Western media and widespread domestic criticism. Notably, Atal Bihari Vajpayee of the Bharatiya Jana Sangh described Moscow's 'deliberate avoiding of the term Bangladesh' in the treaty as 'a Soviet stab in India's back'.[10] The Jana Sangh also criticized the treaty as having 'mortgaged the country' to the

Soviets, further noting that it was 'aimed at China's encirclement', which was 'born of Sinophobia and the [Indian] Government's Russophile policy'.[11]

The treaty, however, served as a pivotal instrument during India's subsequent war with Pakistan and the Liberation of Bangladesh, ensuring that no external influence intervened in the matter. The treaty symbolized the rise of New Delhi's pragmatism, and its *realpolitik* approach to its foreign policy, prioritizing strategic necessities over the dogma of its inherited foreign policy principles. The traditional understanding of non-alignment had visibly evolved, from the near absolute abstinence from foreign engagement on a strategic level to protecting the nation's *strategic autonomy* through pragmatic arrangements. New Delhi had, instead, truly maintained its non-alignment, to the extent of protecting independence of judgement and excluding itself from military pacts and alliances. The treaty has remained a key milestone for how India practises its foreign policy and also a cornerstone for Indian diplomacy and its international engagement throughout the Cold War. While the treaty lasted only twenty years, it was subsequently extended for another twenty, and then replaced by another treaty of friendship between India and Russia, characterizing the relationship with a 'special and privileged strategic partner'.

26. THE LIBERATION OF BANGLADESH

The third Indo-Pakistani War lasted just under two weeks, between 3 and 16 December 1971, and resulted in a decisive Indian victory and the Liberation of Bangladesh. Fought on India's eastern and western frontiers, the war was a culmination of escalating tensions over an internal Pakistani crisis in its erstwhile eastern province. The Pakistani General Election of 1970, which was also the first general election since its independence in 1947, had bifurcated the state, with the resounding victory of the Awami League under Sheikh Mujibur Rahman in the east. It won 167 out of a total of

313 seats in the National Assembly. The Pakistan People's Party, under Zulfikar Ali Bhutto, representing Pakistan's west, came in second, with eighty-seven of the remaining seats. Resenting the prospects of an eastern-ruled federal government, including the possibility of forming a constitution based on Rahman's liberalism and the Six-Point Movement, which supported greater autonomy for East Pakistan, President Yahya Khan continued to delay the inauguration of the National Assembly. As a reaction to this injustice, widespread strikes and protests broke out in East Pakistan, which continued to escalate, culminating in an unscrupulous crackdown on them by the Pakistani military.

After outlawing the Awami League, the infamous Operation Searchlight was executed by the Pakistani military in March 1971, which aimed to eliminate all Bengali opposition and suppress its population, eventually precipitating the Bangladesh Genocide of 1971. A Pakistani journalist broke the story to the Western media, through *The Sunday Times* (UK), reporting that he had 'witnessed the brutality of "kill and burn missions" as the army units, after clearing out the rebels, pursued the pogrom in the towns and villages', and further recounted seeing 'whole villages devastated by "punitive action"'.[12] Estimates of the genocide indicate that around 3 million people were slaughtered, 30 million were internally displaced, and around 10 million refugees fled to India.[13] The refugee crisis in the subcontinent essentially became the conduit through which the civil war in Pakistan spilled over into India. To address this situation, marked by economic challenges created by the inflow of refugees, Prime Minister Indira Gandhi finally made a decision, in April 1971, to support the Bangladeshi forces of resistance to the genocide, the Mukti Bahini, with training, equipment and logistical support.

Noting India's overt assistance to the Mukti Bahini, the progressively growing indefensibility of East Pakistan, and the prospect of a direct conflict with India as an unavoidable and imminent development, Pakistan chose to conduct pre-emptive air raids on 3 December against multiple Indian airbases along its western border. The air raids, code-named Operation Chengiz Khan, marked the official beginning of the war. Unfortunately for Pakistan, its Six Day War-esque emulation of Israel's swift victory fell significantly below their expectations, as the tides of the war rapidly turned in India's favour. By 16 December, the Pakistani Eastern Command signed its instrument of surrender yielding around 90,000 Pakistani troops as prisoners of war, consequently becoming one of the largest military surrenders in the world since the end of the Second World War.

India's 'finest victory' in the 1971 War has been one of the defining moments for its foreign policy in the late twentieth century. The military triumph had elevated its status as the undisputed pre-eminent power in the subcontinent. Diplomatically, the government had laid the groundwork for the eventuality of war exceptionally well, with the prime minister conducting several tours to Moscow, London, Washington and Paris in mid-1971 to seek support and spread awareness about the ongoing humanitarian crisis in its eastern border. Barring the US, these visits resulted in the UK, the USSR and France sending letters to President Yahya Khan requesting a political settlement and the release of Sheikh Mujibur Rahman. Crucially, prior to these visits, India had also signed the Treaty of Friendship with the Soviet Union which proved pivotal in ensuring that there would be no external interference in the event of a conflict with Pakistan. Throughout the war, in the UN Security Council and the subsequent General Assembly's 'Uniting for Peace' debate, Soviet support counteracted significant pressure from the US. The latter had created and deployed its Task Force 74, from its Seventh Fleet, into the Bay of Bengal on 15 December to intimidate India at the height of war. In response, the Soviet Union diverted several naval vessels from the Persian Gulf to the Indian Ocean on 18 December.[14]

The broader impacts of the 1971 War on Indian foreign policy cannot be overstated. The intransigent support received by Pakistan from the US—whether during the genocide in Bangladesh or during the Indo-Pakistani War—further drove India towards the Soviet Union. The military humiliation led Islamabad to spiral into an arms race with New Delhi, with both nations reconsidering their nuclear options as a natural sub-optimal outcome, rooted in the dilemma of anticipating each other's strategic decisions.[15] The 1971 War is more than just a pillar in the colonnade of Indian foreign policy, as it has continued to represent the triumph of its strategic manoeuvring while not compromising on its principle of strategic autonomy.

1972

27. THE SIMLA AGREEMENT OF 1972

The hostilities born out of the 1971 War were officially brought to an end by the Simla Agreement, which was signed between Prime Minister Indira Gandhi and President Zulfikar Ali Bhutto on 2 July 1972. The purpose of this arrangement lay in its preamble, which declared that the two governments 'are resolved that the two countries put an end to the conflict and confrontation that have hitherto marred their relations', and to instead promote a 'friendly and harmonious relationship' to establish 'durable peace in the sub-continent', so that both nations can focus on 'the pressing task of advancing the welfare of their peoples'. The agreement acknowledged the ceasefire line from 17 December 1971 as the 'Line of Control', recognizing each side's position. It further stated: 'Neither side shall seek to alter it unilaterally… [and] refrain from the threat or the use of force in violation of this Line'. More broadly, both nations also recognized each other's sovereignty, political independence and territorial integrity; they agreed to the UN Charter governing the relationship and proclaimed that they would 'settle their differences through peaceful means, through bilateral negotiations or by any other peaceful means mutually agreed upon'.[16]

The understanding also committed to pushing for the development of friendly relations, through promoting travel, exchanges in science and culture, and resuming communications between the two nations. It further pledged that this delegation would 'meet from time to time to work out the necessary details', concluding that the two governments would meet again, while representatives would discuss the 'modalities and arrangements' for normalization of relations, resumption of diplomatic relations, durable peace, a final settlement of the Jammu and Kashmir issue, and repatriation of the prisoners of war from 1971. As an outcome of this initiative, India returned around 13,000 square kilometres of land it had captured from West Pakistan during the conflict. The agreement also laid the foundations for the negotiation and the signing of the Delhi Agreement in August 1973, in which Pakistan officially recognized Bangladesh, and under which India repatriated around 90,000 Pakistani prisoners of war captured in 1971.

The black box of negotiations that had underpinned the Simla Agreement received their fair share of both criticism and praise. The Jana Sangh objected to the 'unequal' exchange of territory, which could have instead been used for a favourable political settlement with regard to Kashmir. Far from reaching a favourable settlement, the agreement was seen to have delivered New Delhi a diplomatic defeat, from the military victory that had preceded it. Zulfikar Ali Bhutto saw the agreement as a political victory, stating that not only had Kashmir been included as an issue which awaited a 'final settlement', but Pakistan had also 'managed to have those territories vacated which were under Indian occupation…[and] repatriated 90,000 prisoners of war… without compromising [their] principles'.[17] K.N. Bakshi, a member of the Indian delegation at the signing of the agreement, recalls his dysphoric reaction when he first read the agreement, recounting during an interview, 'We [India] had all the cards. We had the POWs; we had the Pakistani territory; Pakistan was broken up;

world public opinion was very much with us. We had defied the Americans, the Soviet Union was supportive. Even then we could not achieve much. We were apologetic that we were the victors.'[18]

Bakshi further describes the outcome of the arrangement as a product of a 'Versailles Syndrome', in which New Delhi, viewing itself as the victor and the architect of a new peace in the subcontinent, was determined to steer clear of the mistakes committed by the allied powers, in which the humiliation inflicted on a defeated Germany led to its path-dependent militarization and the subsequent war. A month following the agreement, on 2 August 1972, Prime Minister Indira Gandhi addressed the Rajya Sabha, stating that 'there is a great change in Pakistan… regardless of whether they desire it or not', which President Bhutto also acknowledges by stating 'that the situation has changed today and that the need of the time is peace'.[19]

It appears that from New Delhi's perspective, its gains from the treaty were not strategic or territorial, but political. It had strengthened its legitimacy by eliminating any third-party interventionism in Kashmir, and had proved to the world its ability to shoulder this new responsibility of possessing power in South Asia, by engineering a solution for durable peace and demonstrating its genuine willingness for friendly relations based on equality and mutual respect. The juxtaposition of New Delhi's appeasement with the restored idealism, against the backdrop of its growing predilection for foreign policy pragmatism, has continued to represent a dissonance in its policy for detractors of the agreement. Critics further expose that the subscription to the ideals of the agreement remained unilateral, as Pakistan, far from subscribing to them, continued to exploit and take undue advantage of India's idealism.

The Simla Agreement has continued to remain a central tenet in bilateral relations, with nearly every agreement thereafter taking inspiration from its ethos. To this extent the arrangement has seen continued success, effectively resetting the relationship, which had seen three wars within the first twenty-two years of Independence. Notwithstanding the continued bilateral distrust and the Kargil War of 1999, the treaty has continued to symbolize an important milestone in India's foreign policy, as it ushered in a period of considerable peace.

1974

28. POKHRAN-I: OPERATION SMILING BUDDHA

On 18 May 1974, India carried out its first successful nuclear weapon test at the Indian Army's Test Range in Pokhran, Rajasthan—it was code-named Operation Smiling Buddha (also Pokhran-I). Led by physicist Dr Raja Ramanna and around seventy-five scientists and engineers, the test detonated a miniature nuclear device with an estimated yield of about nine kilotons. Pokhran-I was sanctioned by Prime Minister Indira Gandhi in 1972 and was developed in utmost secrecy. Notwithstanding the designation of the test as a peaceful nuclear explosion, the success of the test marked an important milestone not only for India but also for the rest of the world, as it was the first confirmed nuclear test outside of the five permanent members—US, UK, USSR, France and China—of the United Nations Security Council.

While it was domestically well received, fuelling a surge in Indira Gandhi's popularity, international reaction was marked by concern, as just four years prior to this India had refused to sign the Non-Proliferation Treaty (NPT), which was designed to restrain exactly this. As a reaction to the test, Canada claimed that a 1971 understanding had been violated, and revoked nuclear cooperation with India. Later, in 1978, the US administration under Jimmy Carter passed the Nuclear Non-Proliferation Act, after which the US ceased the export of nuclear assistance to India. The wider international community reacted by establishing the Nuclear Supplier Group (NSG)[20] in

1975, which aimed to take steps beyond the NPT to prevent nuclear proliferation, by controlling the export of materials, equipment and technology that can be used to manufacture nuclear weapons. The NSG had several meetings in London, making it known as the London Club, through which it decided, in 1992, that it would require a full scope of IAEA safeguards for any nuclear export deals. These restrictions continued to hamper India's ability to access nuclear material, until the Indo-US Civil Nuclear Agreement in 2008.

Despite the international censure, crossing the nuclear Rubicon had a material impact on New Delhi's status within the Asian and the wider international security apparatus. As mentioned earlier (see note on NPT), when the world turned a blind eye to its advocacy for nuclear disarmament and security concerns, India chose to take proactive steps to address its national security responsibilities, which had been impacted by the imbalances caused by the acquisition of nuclear weapons by China in 1964, and the consequent stratification of nuclear abilities that was attempted by the NPT in 1970.

However, its peaceful description was maintained, with the Indian Defence Minister stating, 'our armed forces know that its [sic] not for their use', and Prime Minster Indira Gandhi stating in a letter to her Pakistani counterpart that 'there are no political or foreign policy implications to this test'. Prime Minster Indira Gandhi justified it by saying, 'we had to do it to demonstrate our independent capability'.[21] The test was testament to not only India's nuclear capability but also its achievements, and its resolve to safeguard its strategic autonomy, which would have been forgone if it had simply aligned with an external security guarantor. New Delhi had broken the convention of the bifurcated world system divided into non-nuclear-weapon states and nuclear-weapon states, and had added to the mix non-nuclear-weapon states with the capability to manufacture nuclear weapons, providing the scope for non-weaponized deterrence.

Notwithstanding the peaceful underpinnings of Pokhran-I, India's feat had proved its technological ability, its self-reliance, and protected the safety and sovereignty of the nation against the backdrop of a nuclear-powered China. This event arguably also laid the groundwork for Islamabad to begin considering the nuclear question as it had marked an increment in India's nuclear policy, which had shifted from the advocacy for absolute global disarmament to the nuance of reciprocity, continuing with its long-held doctrine of a 'continued commitment to the goal of a nuclear weapon free world, through global, verifiable and non-discriminatory nuclear disarmament'. Following Pokhran-I, the Pokhran-II tests took place in 1998, after a gap of about two and a half decades. The event has continued to represent a moment of great significance for both New Delhi's position on the international stage and its ability to retain its strategic autonomy and guard its national security within the region. India, if not already after its victory in 1971, had by the end of 1974 become indisputably the paramount power within the subcontinent.

29. THE 1974 INDIA-BANGLADESH LAND BORDER AGREEMENT

On 16 May 1974, Prime Minister Indira Gandhi of India and Sheikh Mujibur Rahman, the first President of Bangladesh, signed the momentous Land Border Agreement, addressing the problem of unmarked borders and enclaves in each other's territories that had remained a continuing issue since 1947. This effort followed the Indo-Bangla Treaty of Friendship, Cooperation and Peace, signed between the same leaders in March 1972. The inheritance of several enclaves, on either side of the hastily marked border, had been a legacy of the accession of the erstwhile princely state of Cooch Behar to the Indian Union in 1949. These enclaves were landlocked parcels of land falling within the territories of the two nations and were characterized by the peculiarity of containing enclaves within them, known as counter-enclaves, which contained even smaller enclaves within them, known as counter-counter-enclaves. There were an estimated 113 Indian enclaves within Bangladesh, and fifty-three Bangladeshi enclaves within India. These enclaves were a continuing issue for both administrations, as their remoteness and lack of access had given rise to issues related to their development and security. These issues included those of undefined citizenship, healthcare challenges, constrained access to services, educational development, and other humanitarian challenges.

The agreement was built on the discussions that were initiated in 1958 between Prime Minister Jawaharlal Nehru of India and Prime Minister Feroz Khan Noon of Pakistan, in which both sides agreed to exchange the disputed territories without considering their own territorial gains or losses. Notwithstanding this attempt being stymied by nationalist protests on either side as well as legal challenges, it was symbolic, to the extent that both nations chose to negotiate with each other in an endeavour to find a peaceful resolution. This accord had continued to be shelved as a consequence of the deterioration of Indo-Pakistani relations. The 1974 Indira-Mujibur agreement succeeded this prolonged effort, in which Bangladesh abandoned Pakistan's claims to Berubari—a key challenge which had caused the 1958 agreement to fall through—and, in exchange, India allowed it to keep the Dahagram-Angarpota enclave, which was not completely landlocked like the other enclaves. The agreement further provided for the other enclaves to be exchanged as had been agreed upon in 1958. New Delhi further provided Dhaka with a lease in perpetuity of a small corridor of land known as the Tin Bigha, which would guarantee Bangladesh's access to the Dahagram-Angarpota enclave. Despite the two nations' success in restarting this exchange, New Delhi faced domestic protests over the leasing of Tin Bigha, and further constitutional hurdles which constrained the ratification of the agreement.

Although the agreement was not ratified, and it was only in 2015 that under India's Prime Minister Narendra Modi and his Bangladeshi counterpart Sheikh Hasina the agreement was finally adopted by both nations, the 1974 accord marked an important development in Indo-Bangladeshi relations. The relationship has stood the test of time, being not simply based on strategic necessities but also built on mutual benefits and their commitment to addressing mutually sensitive issues through peaceful dialogue. On the wider regional stage, this event showcased to India's neighbours that it was willing to shoulder the responsibilities of its position within the subcontinent and solve issues peacefully and mutually, even if it meant striking a compromise.

New Delhi's initiative had proved that it was not only its own strategic autonomy that it aimed to protect, but also that of the nations within the region, underscoring its commitment to its anti-imperial stance and its non-aggressive and non-expansionary foreign policy. This was particularly important after the 1971 War, which had raised accusations about an expansionary policy from Islamabad; instead, it exposed that it was indeed Islamabad that had proved unfit to take forward the 1958 discussion on bilateral border issues. More broadly, the agreement of 1974 cemented relations between Dhaka and New Delhi, and set them on a higher trajectory, affirming the willingness for cooperation, mutual benefits, and respect for each other's territorial integrity. While relations between the two nations have since ebbed and flowed, with the dynamic nature of the political landscapes of both nations, especially after a Bangladeshi coup d'état and the consequent assassination of Sheikh Mujibur Rahman in August 1975, the 1974 accord not only continues to represent a benchmark for relations between India and Bangladesh, but is also testament to India's regional position and its ability and disposition to maintain peace within its neighbourhood.

30. THE DECLARATION OF THE NEW INTERNATIONAL ECONOMIC ORDER

The United Nations General Assembly, in its Sixth Special Session on 1 May 1974, passed a resolution on the 'Declaration on the Establishment of a New International Economic Order'. It primarily aimed to address the 'gap between the developed and the developing countries [which] continues to widen in a system which was established at a time when most of the developing countries did not even exist as independent States and which perpetuates inequality'. Building momentum through the Non-Aligned Movement and the Group of 77 (G-77),[22] the creation of the New International Economic Order (NIEO) was a watershed moment for the Global South in its quest for an equitable international economic system.

The declaration not only presented the principles by which the economic system should be governed, it also shed light on the procedures for the establishment of this new economic order. It dealt with foundational issues in the trade and development of primary commodities and raw materials. The NIEO declaration also described the measures required for the alleviation of the chronic trade deficits endured by the Global South. The NIEO further deliberated on issues of transportation, insurance, industrialization and the transfer of technology. The principles of the NIEO, at a high level, included the sovereign equality of all nations, sovereignty over natural resources and other economic activities, an equitable relationship between the price of raw materials and other goods exported by developing countries, and international assistance to promote industrialization across the Global South. To achieve this end, the NIEO called for reforms which included an overhaul of the rules of international trade, a reform of the international monetary system, incentives for financial and technological transfers and assistance for industrialization, and the promotion of cooperation among countries of the Global South.

India's role in the NIEO cannot be understated as it was one of the driving forces behind the movement right from the time of its Independence, with its calls for economic self-sufficiency, to this declaration in the 1970s. The NAM, which had been thoughtfully orchestrated by India right from its genesis, was one of the main conduits through which it championed this economic mutiny through the ranks of the Global South. New Delhi had played a key part in sustaining and moulding the NAM, from its initial blinkered focus on just political independence to addressing the bifurcation which took place during the Cairo Summit in 1965, to eventually expanding its scope to include economic independence at the Lusaka Summit in 1970. New Delhi had played a pivotal role in advocating for the economic interests of the Third World, encouraging South-South cooperation and facilitating a North-South dialogue. Subsequently, the idea of a 'South-South Cooperation' has become one of New Delhi's longstanding foreign policy ideals. India had, from the beginning of the General Agreement on Tariffs and Trade (GATT)[23] in 1947, championed the cause and consistently represented the interests of developing nations in an unequal world.

The importance of economic self-sufficiency in combating imperial structures and systemic dependency is not novel for India, and has been deliberated upon right from its early experiences of colonialism, with Dadabhai Naoroji publishing the theory of the 'drain of wealth' less than a decade after the British had formally colonized India in 1858.[24] This idea of asymmetric economic structures was refined by Raúl Prebisch's Latin American experience, and formalized by Prebisch as the 'theory of dependency'.[25] Since its inception in 1949, though the idea has evolved significantly, it remains the sine qua non for a majority of critical theories which have questioned the existing global economic structures.[26] Accompanying this evolution of thought was the bifurcation of global economic ideas. The developing economies had rejected the essence of the classical liberalism of the Bretton Woods system established after the Second World War, and supported more state interventionist domestic economic policies. The NIEO was arguably rooted in the hypocrisy of Western economic structures, which supported the idea of international free trade through the reduction of tariff and non-tariff barriers facilitated through the GATT, whereas in fact these developed Western economies had used exactly these mercantilist policies to develop their own economies in different historical periods.[27]

Notably, the NIEO was declared subsequent to an oil price hike brought about by the Organization of the Petroleum Exporting Countries (OPEC), which shocked the global economy, quadrupled the price of oil in 1973, and strengthened the bargaining position of the Third World. At the time, Venezuela's President and OPEC leader Carlos Andrés Pérez stated that the aim was to 'take advantage of this opportunity when raw materials are worth just as much as capital and technology, in order to reach agreements that will ensure fair and lasting balances'.[28] Unfortunately, a lack of political will, coupled with a stiff Western ideological resistance, ensured that its demands were never met, and with time, its activism faded into relative obscurity. Although New Delhi, through the NIEO, did not achieve its desired reforms, it marked a significant milestone as it brought to the forefront a consolidated view from the Third World, representing a moment of solidarity and acknowledging the asymmetries of the global economic system. The activism and the call to action for a South-South cooperation that spread throughout the developing world through the NIEO has been a lasting legacy of India and its foreign policy, which has continued to subscribe to this idea as a fundament of its relationship with the rest of the Global South.

1976

31. RE-ESTABLISHING SINO-INDIAN AMBASSADORIAL RELATIONS

The appointment of K.K. Narayanan as ambassador to China by Indira Gandhi in 1976 reset the Sino-Indian relationship, which had rapidly deteriorated in 1959 and remained at its nadir since 1962. The foreign policy manoeuvre was a marked success, as Beijing reciprocated by appointing an ambassador to New Delhi. The significance of this diplomatic achievement was nothing short of extraordinary, as just a year before, in 1975, Sikkim had transitioned from being an Indian protectorate, which it had been since 1950, and finalized its accession to the Indian Union through a referendum. Beijing had consistently criticized New Delhi raising allegations about New Delhi's imperialism, asserting that it 'absolutely does not recognize India's illegal annexation of Sikkim'.[29] Along with this, tensions between the two nations were raised against the backdrop of the communist takeover in both Cambodia and South Vietnam, with New Delhi's concerns about Beijing-sponsored insurgencies along its northeastern frontier. Within this contextual framework, the 1976 diplomatic thaw orchestrated by New Delhi played a significant role in altering the trajectory of a relationship which had theretofore been characterized by mutual distrust and animosity.

The initial discussions which led to this decision began in 1970, catalyzed by Mao Zedong signalling his willingness to engage, to a senior Indian official Brijesh Mishra, stating that the two nations 'cannot keep on quarrelling like this. We should try and be friends again. India is a great country. Indian people are good people. We will be friends again someday'.[30] The decision was essentially a watershed for both nations and set in motion a significant period of Sino-Indian détente after 1976, during which they made a great deal of effort to address the mutual trust deficit. Although Prime Minister Indira Gandhi's government was replaced by the Janata Party under Morarji Desai's premiership, in the 1977 election, the trajectory of the Sino-Indian relationship continued with the enthusiasm of their 1976 diplomatic détente. Under the new government, the Minister of Foreign Affairs Atal Bihari Vajpayee paid a momentous visit to China in 1979, during which the border question was finally 'unfrozen', with both sides willing to deliberate on possible solutions to the issue.

China's relationship with the Soviet Union, arguably the cornerstone of its foreign policy, had been steadily unravelling since the late 1950s. Within a decade, the Sino-Soviet relationship had reached its lowest point with the Ussuri River crisis. The Ussuri clashes led to the rise of a nuclear rhetoric between the two former allies, which set the relationship into a decade-long period of 'intense antagonism'.[31] Acknowledging this situation, Mao Zedong noted in 1969, 'we are now confronted with a formidable enemy'.[32] Coupled with this development, the Soviet proposal to create an Asian collective security system in 1969, and the possibility of India joining it, heightened China's fears of being strategically encircled by its adversaries, with the Soviet Union to its east, north and west, Japan to its east, and India to its south. It appears that the stabilization of its relationship with its southern neighbour was pivotal in protecting its own national security.

The 1976 exchange proved, as Indira Gandhi also acknowledged, that it was not the Indo-Soviet Treaty of 1971 that had forestalled the improvement of Sino-Indian relations, but, instead, it was China's foreign policy strategies and its own behaviour that had stood in the way. She further commented on the treaty in an interview with *Le Figaro*, 'We will remain a non-aligned country and this friendship does not come in the way of our relations with other countries', further stating, 'our friendship with China depends on China's strategy'.[33] Affirming its subscription to the policy of non-alignment, India's Minister of External Affairs at the time, Y.B. Chavan, stated more generally that it was New Delhi's 'endeavour to develop amicable relations with all countries, notably our neighbours'.[34] Coincidentally, providing evidence of the independence of its foreign policy, on 15 April 1976, New Delhi also entered into an Indo-Soviet Trade Agreement to enhance commercial ties with the Soviet Union.

India's overtures, and the resultant restoration of Sino-Indian relations at the ambassadorial level, remain testament to India's policy of practising its autonomy on strategic matters. Apart from Beijing's strategic imperatives, New Delhi's achievement in restoring confidence and re-charting the course of its bilateral relationship remain remarkable against the backdrop of Beijing's negativity, its captious mindset and approach towards its neighbours. The event was symbolic in establishing the 'new normal', and laid the foundations for the development of Sino-Indian relations, with subsequent visits in 1979 and 1981. The latter visit in 1981 led to the start of bilateral Sino-Indian border negotiations. One of the key products of these negotiations was the solution of a 'package deal', offered by China to India to settle the border dispute.[35] The idea was that on the basis of the present Line of Actual Control, China would recognize India's claims with respect to the McMahon Line in the eastern sector, and in return, India should recognize China's claims in the western sector. Although the package deal was never realized, the relationship between the two nations continued to grow in other areas, the groundwork for which was laid by the 1976 reset.

1981

32. THE JOINT TECHNICAL-LEVEL BOUNDARY COMMITTEE BETWEEN INDIA AND NEPAL

India and Nepal share a boundary of about 1,880 kilometres, of which 1,240 kilometres comprise land and about 640 kilometres comprise river and rivulet boundaries. The historical antecedents of the border delineation between India and Nepal are rooted in the Treaty of Sugauli in 1816 and the subsequent Boundary Treaty of 1860.[36] Since 1816, the boundary had been continuously surveyed and divided into nine different sectors, with the construction of boundary pillars. Although, prior to Independence, regular surveys of the border and its maintenance were conducted, no joint boundary survey was conducted until 1981.

In November 1981, after a series of discussions, the two nations constituted the Nepal-India Joint Technical Level Boundary Committee (JTBC) for the maintenance of boundary pillars, re-establishing missing pillars, recording encroachment, and conducting periodic inspections. Later, in 1992, the JTBC was also mandated with the creation of a strip map with a 1:15000 scale, covering 500 metres from either side of the boundary, the numbering of all boundary pillars and exchanging their coordinates, and the construction of additional boundary pillars where required. The JTBC was efficacious, solving a majority of smaller disputes and completing the delineation of 98 per cent of the shared border in the twenty-six years of its functioning, before it was dissolved in 2008. The remaining two per cent of the unmarked border was a result of shifting river boundaries, and included the Kalapani-Limpiyadhura and Narsahi-Susta encroachments of about 17 and 20 kilometres, respectively. There are further encroachments, cross-holding occupation, disputes, claims and counter-claims in a total of seventy-one spots, constituting approximately 606 square kilometres of land.

Although the JTBC was never ratified due to the disputed two per cent of the border that remained unresolved, and was dissolved in 2008, its creation marked a significant step in bilateral relations, and its work and achievements represented the presence of a strong political will on both sides to maintain a peaceful border. The JTBC also furthered the cause of the bilateral relationship that had been built on the Peace and Friendship Treaty of 1950, which encouraged a well-defined and formally accepted 'open border' between the two nations that allowed for the free and unrestricted movement of people from either side. The JTBC was pivotal in maintaining and strengthening the principles of free movement established by the 1950 treaty, without which border hostilities between the two neighbours would be widespread and not limited to specific segments of the shared border. Nepal had already found considerable success in its treaties with China in 1960 and 1961, which effectively delineated a large part of its northern border. Realizing that the condition of its southern territory and a portion of its eastern and western segment are in an undesirable condition, and may create problems in the future, Kathmandu was keen to demarcate its borders and protect the provision for open movement, which would otherwise be threatened by any border dispute and the resultant hostilities.

The efficiency of the JTBC ensured that the boundary issue was limited to the two segments Kalapani and Susta on the border, preventing it from undermining the broader bilateral relationship. The Indo-Nepalese relationship has, since the JTBC, faced several significant challenges, which include the two border blockades of 1989 under Prime Minister Rajiv Gandhi and one in 2015 under Prime Minister Narendra Modi, and the frequent disputes over Lipulekh Pass in the Kalapani Valley in 2022. The legacy of the JTBC is visible in its functioning as guardrails against the escalation of bilateral border disputes, as it had successfully found mutual consensus for around 98 per cent of the shared boundary. The Indo-Nepalese border initiatives of 1981 displayed the willingness of both nations to be flexible and adapt to the challenging reality of fluid boundaries caused by the presence of rivers and rivulets. It displayed New Delhi's tendency to abstain from strong-arming its smaller neighbours, and instead reaching decisions based on mutual consensus. Notwithstanding the blockade of 1989, the collaboration born out of the JTBC in 1981 and its ability to protect the policy of 'open borders', built on the Treaty of Friendship between the two nations in 1950, have remained a central tenet of peaceful cooperation between the two historically friendly neighbours, representing a significant milestone in New Delhi's endeavours to establish the integrity of its territory, clear boundaries, and positive neighbourly relations.

1982

33. PRIME MINISTER INDIRA GANDHI IN THE UNITED STATES

Prime Minister Indira Gandhi made a ten-day visit to the United States in the months of July and August 1982—this was more than a decade since her last visit there. The visit was greatly publicized by the Indian press, who described the meet as a positive diplomatic development between the 'two largest democracies'. During this trip, apart from US President Ronald Reagan and his administration, the prime minister met several other dignitaries which included the UN Secretary-General Javier Pérez de Cuéllar, distinguished citizens, academics, intellectuals, scientists and businessmen.

This visit marked a significant change in US-Indian relations, which had trodden a precarious path so far, with occasional hostilities, right from President Lyndon B. Johnson's decision to politicize the grain shipments to India under Public Law (480) in the mid-1960s. The previous visit took place in November 1971 during the Pakistan-Bangladesh crisis, after the signing of the Indo-Soviet Treaty. With the subsequent war with Pakistan, and the Liberation of Bangladesh, the bilateral relationship between the US and India fell to a new low. However, several international developments took place in the meantime, which made amending the relationship important—these included the Soviet invasion of Afghanistan, the Revolution in Iran, the Gulf War, US presence in the Indian Ocean, the cessation of US funding to the International Development Agency (IDA), and the increasing supply of US arms and aid to Pakistan in an effort to bolster it as a 'frontline' state against the expansion of the Soviet sphere of influence.

The visit was widely described as a great success for Indian foreign policy, as it had reaffirmed its subscription to the non-aligned stance, secured military aid, expanded collaboration in science and technology, and secured the supply of nuclear fuel for its Tarapur reactor. India's share of interest-free loans from the IDA had been reduced due to cutbacks in US funding. President Reagan promised to support India in securing an IMF loan instalment of 2.3 billion special drawing rights (SDRs), and to enhance IDA aid to India. With New Delhi's gradual shift towards further liberalizing the private sector, deliberations were underway on expanding collaboration in trade, agriculture and technology. This included a broad set of agreements announced at the end of the visit, to enhance scientific, economic and cultural cooperation and conduct research on food production, resources, renewable energy and health.

The most significant of these agreements, however, was that on the supply of nuclear fuel. The US had supplied nuclear fuel for Tarapur under the thirty-year Indo-US nuclear cooperation agreement made in 1963. Subsequent to the peaceful nuclear explosion conducted by India in 1974, the US passed the 1978 Non-Proliferation Act which required the recipients of nuclear exports to subscribe to the safeguards mandated by the IAEA.

Consequently, the supplies were terminated in 1980 due to India's refusal to accept the conditions of the IAEA that were required for non-nuclear-weapon states, as they were designated by the NPT. During this trip, a pivotal agreement was made under which the US allowed France to supply uranium fuel, which was theretofore restricted.

The visit was monumentally symbolic for Indian foreign policy, as apart from reaffirming its adherence to non-alignment, which was being questioned because of its strengthening relationship with the Soviet Union, it both expressed its willingness to proactively engage in pragmatic relationships to address the rise of potential regional imbalances, and emphasized domestic growth and development as the sine qua non of its foreign policy. Prime Minister Indira Gandhi described, during the visit, that India's 'preoccupation is with building and development', further stating that its aim 'is not to influence others, but to consolidate our political and economic independence'. The visit was an integral part of New Delhi's efforts to consolidate its independence, stabilize its region, and re-energize its leadership of the NAM, with the prime minister stating, with regard to the inequities between the Global North and the Global South, that 'there are three main causes of the present disturbing situation: the growth of armaments; the increasing disparity between the rich and the poor, both between and within nations; and the thoughtless wounding of our Earth'. The prime minister further articulated: 'Our foreign policy is one of friendship for all, hence our nonalignment.'[37]

The visit marked the beginning of an era of enhanced trust and cooperation, playing a foundational role in reversing the negative image of India that the United States had, and set the stage for future partnerships with the US. The occasion has continued to represent the bedrock of not only Indo-US cooperation, but also India's closely guarded strategic autonomy that was crucial during the transition of its foreign policy into its next wave of 'opening up to the world', in the post-Cold War era.

1983

34. MAURITIAN SUSPICIONS AND OPERATIONS

In 1983, Prime Minister Indira Gandhi sanctioned Operation Lal Dora, a clandestine plan to intervene in the Indian Ocean Island of Mauritius with its military, to prevent a coup.[38] While the plan never actually materialized, the decision and the willingness of the Indian government to intervene, based on pragmatic necessities, marked an important development in New Delhi's growing confidence in its ability to provide stability within its neighbourhood. Mauritius and India have enjoyed a special relationship from before India's Independence, with most Mauritian politicians taking inspiration from India's anti-colonial struggle. Following the departure of the British Navy from the region, India shouldered the burden of Mauritius's security requirements, with the Indian Navy effectively becoming responsible for the Mauritian Coast Guard under the defence agreement of 1974.

Since Mauritius's independence from the United Kingdom in 1968, it had maintained a democratic system, which was dominated by Sir Seewoosagur Ramgoolam of the Mauritian Labour Party. This domination culminated in the electoral victory of the Mouvement Militant Mauricien (MMM), a left-wing socialist party led by Anerood Jugnauth and the more radical Paul Bérenger, in 1982. By early 1983, the relationship between Jugnauth and Bérenger fractured completely, with Jugnauth convinced that Bérenger would potentially lead a coup with the help of Libya and the Soviet Union. In February 1983, Jugnauth met with Prime Minister Indira Gandhi and requested military assistance in the event of a coup. At the time, several Indian Ocean islands, like the Seychelles, the Comoros and Madagascar, had been afflicted by coups supported by foreign interests.

Later, in March 1983, while Jugnauth was in New Delhi attending a NAM summit, Bérenger made several changes, converting the national language to Creole, and proposing constitutional changes that would strip power from the position of the prime minister, eventually causing the fall of the MMM government. As the Indian prime minister had promised support against a coup, the planning for a military intervention commenced under the code name Operation Lal Dora. Although this military intervention never took place for a variety of speculated reasons, New Delhi allegedly deployed the head of RAW, N.F. Suntook, in Mauritius. He reportedly worked with Jugnauth. Jugnauth later established a new party, the Militant Socialist Movement (MSM), and won the elections in August 1983 with a significant majority.

Operation Lal Dora was ideated as an amphibious exercise, based on the coordination between the Indian Navy and the Indian Army, to conduct a military intervention in the event of a coup orchestrated by Bérenger. The plan was sufficiently close to materialization—its initial steps had already begun, with the 54th Infantry Division being sent from Hyderabad to Mumbai to report to the Indian Naval ships. However, due to a variety of reasons, which included inter-services coordination, amphibious capability, and the prospect of a US military intervention from its nearby base Diego Garcia,[39] this plan was shelved and instead replaced by a more covert plan deploying Suntook in Mauritius.

New Delhi's concerns with Bérenger's coup included the potential ethnic targeting of people of Indian descent. Official discrimination had been faced across the Indo-Pacific, with the expulsion of Indians from Idi Amin's Uganda in 1972 and the contemporaneous communal tensions between Tamils and Sinhalese in Sri Lanka. Within the Indian Ocean, New Delhi also feared losing Mauritius from its sphere of influence, with the prospect of the widening links between Mauritius and the Soviet Union and Libya. Notwithstanding New Delhi's links with either Washington or a friendly Moscow, its ideology of non-alignment held the idea of the intrusion of either of the two great powers into the affairs of the developing world to be illegitimate. India had also, at the time, steadily expanded its own influence throughout the Indian Ocean, extending from Sri Lanka to the Seychelles, Maldives and Southern Africa, and had undertaken its first Antarctic expedition in 1981, signing the Antarctic Treaty in 1983.

The outcome of Jugnauth's electoral victory was a marked change towards a pro-West policy, along with stronger ties with New Delhi. While Operation Lal Dora did not go through, it embodied an important new symbolism in New Delhi's foreign policy, which had theretofore shied away from proactively protecting its interests externally and projecting its influence in its neighbourhood. The operation also proved New Delhi's commitment to protecting the interests of its diaspora. The event marked the start of a phase characterized by significantly more engagement on India's part in protecting the stability of the Indian Ocean Region, deploying its navy in 1986 under 'Operation Flowers are Blooming' near Seychelles to discourage a coup, sending peacekeeping forces to Sri Lanka in 1987 under 'Operation Pawan' to enforce a negotiated solution to the civil war, and sending a battalion of troopers to the Maldives under 'Operation Cactus' to avert an attempted coup.

Operation Lal Dora represents New Delhi's coming of age in its role as a net security provider in the Indian Ocean Region, and provides further proof of its ability to exercise strategic autonomy in its foreign policy, independent of either of the great powers of the Cold War period. The event also marked the beginning of a convergence between US and Indian interests in the Indian Ocean Region, something which has continued to expand exponentially after the end of the Cold War, with the establishment of the Indo-US Malabar naval exercises in 1992 and the eventual creation of the Quadrilateral Security Dialogue (Quad) among India, the United States, Australia and Japan in 2007.

1984

35. THE SIACHEN WAR

In April 1984, the Indian Army executed Operation Meghdoot through which it pre-emptively deployed a small company of troops on Saltoro Ridge, which overlooks the Siachen Glacier, and within a few days it secured three pivotal passes, Bilafond La, Sia La and Gyong La. This blitz resulted in the Indian forces successfully capturing the Siachen Glacier, its tributary glaciers, the heights of Saltoro Ridge as well as the aforementioned passes, amounting to about 2,600 square kilometres of territory. In response, Pakistani forces occupied the lower slopes of Saltoro Ridge. For the more tactical positions, the two sides engaged in skirmishes, and what began as a small operation developed into a major military confrontation between India and Pakistan. Within a year, forces on each side had expanded to over a brigade. The event became one of the key manifestations of the persistent and sustained hostilities between the two neighbours, with frequent military operations by both sides throughout the remainder of the twentieth century.

The cost of the conflict—in the form of men, money and material, due to the inhospitable conditions and the location—has been one of the key characteristics of this frozen war of attrition. The Siachen Glacier is not only one of the coldest places on the planet, with temperatures dropping to minus 67.8 degrees Celsius, but it is also the highest battlefield on earth, situated at a height of over 20,000 feet. These glacial conditions, with thin air, dangerously low levels of oxygen and deadly avalanches, have been the underlying reason for the casualties on both sides.[40] While the monetary impact of both the conflict and the maintenance of their bases has cost both sides exorbitant amounts, its environmental impact has also been significant, the conflict having detrimental effects on the glacier, which is one of the largest freshwater reserves of Asia.

Siachen remains yet another symbol of the legacy of un-demarcated borders for the two neighbours. The cause of the conflict is rooted in the 1949 Karachi Agreement, which established the ceasefire line. The Agreement's delineation of the border, unfortunately, concluded at Khor, and thereafter it simply stated that the line would run 'thence north to the glaciers'. This was done at the time as the terrain beyond was considered glaciated and uninhabitable, and of no value. Although the area had been under Indian jurisdiction since 1948,[41] exploiting the lack of clarity regarding its ownership, Pakistan allowed several mountaineering expeditions to it in the decades leading up to 1984. The history of hostility between India and Pakistan, the subsequent wars of 1949, 1965 and 1971, and Pakistan ceding the Indian-claimed territory Shaksgam Valley to China in 1963 had, unsurprisingly, left India concerned about this adventurism. This eventually developed into what has been described as 'oropolitics', or the politics of mountaineering, with India responding by sanctioning mountaineering expeditions and patrols in the area, beginning from 1978. It is reported that Indian intelligence intercepted large Pakistani orders of Arctic weather gear and, in response, made preparations and engaged in pre-emptive action before Pakistan's planned occupation.[42]

The strategic value of the Siachen Glacier has been questioned widely, with some arguing that the occupation remains a futile exercise, with little strategic or tactical value to add to either side. This proposition is based on the extraordinarily high requirement for men, money and material on both sides, in exchange for relatively little advantage. From an Indian security perspective, however, it was important to control glacier functions to ensure that Pakistani and Chinese links and connections were not attainable from the northeastern to the southwestern parts of the Karakoram Range. Sino-Pakistani links in these commanding heights are seen to potentially pose a strategic threat to Indian defensive positions.

The Siachen conflict that started in 1984 with Operation Meghdoot continued to provide fuel for hostility between the two nations, with several military operations taking place from each side throughout the remainder of the century. The success of the operation in 1984 marked an important transition in New Delhi's combat readiness in extreme terrains, building from gross unpreparedness for high-altitude warfare with China in 1962, to its expanding abilities through its Arctic programme beginning in 1981. Although the conflict finally abated, with a mutual ceasefire announced in 2003, the event impacted New Delhi's foreign policy significantly at the time, sustaining hostilities within the subcontinent for a considerably long period.

Prime Minister Atal Bihari Vajpayee visiting BSF troops stationed in the Kargil region during the 1999 conflict between India and Pakistan.

Source: PROBSFDelhi

Wave 3

1985–2004: Opening up to the World

PART I

The latter half of the 1980s saw a dramatic shift from regionalism to a broader global focus, as India opened its economy to the world and sought greater economic integration. India began to reorient its strategic outlook, forming new partnerships and reconfiguring its international relations to suit its evolving economic and political aspirations. This phase marks India's transition from an inward-looking posture to one of active global engagement.

1985

36. PRIME MINISTER RAJIV GANDHI'S VISIT TO THE SOVIET UNION

Rajiv Gandhi's first visit to the Soviet Union—from 21 to 26 May 1985—as India's prime minister was remarkable for several reasons. The trip enhanced economic ties between the two nations, with the signing of two significant agreements. The first provided a billion rubles (equivalent to about US$1.18 billion at the time) in Soviet credits, for supporting Indian energy-related projects. The second extended trade, scientific and technological cooperation for another fifteen years, till the year 2000.[1] More specifically, the visit proved to be an important conduit through which Rajiv Gandhi began positioning his government on key foreign policy issues. Furthermore, the visit cemented the continuance of the inherited relationship with the Soviet Union which had grown in leaps and bounds over the last two decades, since the Second Indo-Pak War in 1965. The *Times of India,* on 12 November 1984, quoted Rajiv Gandhi as affirming the following: 'Jawaharlal Nehru bequeathed to us a foreign policy which Indira Gandhi so creatively enriched. I shall carry it forward.'[2]

The trip came at a specifically precarious moment for Indo-Soviet relations, with not only a new Indian prime minster at the country's helm, but also a new Soviet General Secretary, with Mikhail Gorbachev ascending to the position just a couple of months before Rajiv Gandhi's trip, in March 1985. The Soviet Union had experienced significant changes since the death of General Secretary Leonid Brezhnev in 1982, and Gorbachev's ascendency in 1985 had come with varied speculation regarding changes in foreign policy and the existing Cold War dynamics. Amid this Great Game, Rajiv Gandhi's visit was crucial in determining how this new chapter in Indo-Soviet relations would play out. The outcome of this trip, quite clearly, proved that this relationship would endure, with successive trips and return trips taking place over the next few years.

The 1985 agreements of economic cooperation continued to grow in 1986, with expanding lines of Russian credit, joint technical exchanges and increased support for Indian energy projects. Military cooperation also intensified with India's Defence Minister P.V. Narasimha Rao's visit to Moscow in March 1985, and over the next few years, the two nations finalized agreements for supplies of Soviet military systems, including MiG-29 fighter aircraft transporters, helicopters and submarines. Later, in 1986, Rajiv Gandhi and Mikhail Gorbachev also signed the Delhi Declaration on the Principles of a Nuclear Weapon Free and Non-

Violent World, which played an important role in disarmament, occurring just a couple of years before the Reykjavik Summit between US President Ronald Reagan and Gorbachev, in which the Intermediate Range Nuclear Forces Treaty was signed.

The visit symbolized a step change in Indian foreign policy, which at the time was going through a process of reaffirming its strategic autonomy, practising its neutrality in the Cold War, and making its first voluntary attempt at liberalizing its economy, bolstering the private sector and opening up to the world. Rajiv Gandhi was acutely aware of India's security necessities, with Pakistan increasingly becoming a strategic ally for the US within the region, a development aimed to counterbalance the Soviet presence in Afghanistan, which had been building up since the Soviet invasion of Afghanistan and the subsequent war which begun in 1979. To enable this, the US had committed to providing Pakistan with military aid, valued at US$1.6 billion in 1985, and continued providing covert assistance to the anti-Soviet rebels in Afghanistan. Rajiv Gandhi had pointed out that this military aid had instead disturbed the regional balance, further accusing the US of turning a 'blind eye to the Pakistani nuclear program.'[3]

In this geopolitical context, Rajiv Gandhi had undertaken perhaps the single most intensive effort of upgrading the Indian armed forces, spending an average of 3.76 per cent of India's GDP on defence year-on-year between 1984 and 1989, with this spending reaching as high as 4.11 and 4.23 per cent in 1986 and 1987, respectively.[4] This is a significant spike in India's military expenditure, with this being the only instance in which it crossed the four per cent mark, with the average figure remaining 2.96 per cent between 1956 and 2022. It is not surprising that Soviet support had continued to be pivotal in achieving this modernization and re-establishing the balance of power in the region.

However, a now-declassified CIA report from November 1986 also indicates a visible diversification in Rajiv Gandhi's military procurement strategy, noting that since the beginning of 1985 until the time the report was written, the Soviet share of Indian purchases of foreign military equipment had declined to 55 per cent from 80 per cent.[5] And the West's share had increased from 20 to 45 per cent. It further stated that India had purchased $1.7 billion worth of arms from Western Europe, compared with $2.5 billion from USSR in the first eighteen months of Rajiv Gandhi's premiership. The US ambassador to India from 1985 to 1988, John Dean, understood Rajiv Gandhi's willingness to diversify military procurement, expand engagement with the West, and modernize India. Ambassador Dean continued to convey to Washington India's willingness to engage with the US, further substantiating that New Delhi's growing apprehensions about covert US activity in Afghanistan and its support for Pakistan had continued to promote Indo-Soviet collaboration.

Rajiv Gandhi's first visit to the Soviet Union was of marked importance, as it confirmed the direction of Indo-Soviet relations under the new leaders. The relationship reached new heights, beyond military and economic cooperation, with Gorbachev in July 1986 in Vladivostok openly lauding the Asian response of non-alignment to a world bifurcated into nuclear-armed blocs, further declaring that 'the acknowledged leader of this movement is great India, with its moral authority, and traditional wisdom, with its unique political experience and its enormous economic possibilities'.[6] Rajiv Gandhi's government had successfully managed to balance its security necessities with its aspirations for modernization, and increasing its engagement with the West, broadly maintaining its time-tested relationship with the Soviet Union and starting a new chapter in the Indo-Soviet relationship.

37. THE ESTABLISHMENT OF SAARC

The South Asian Association for Regional Cooperation (SAARC), which was signed into existence in Dhaka in December 1985, represents one of the first South Asian attempts at stimulating greater collaboration within the region in the post-Partition period. With its objectives of promoting the welfare and improving the quality of life of South Asian people, accelerating economic growth, social and cultural development within the region, providing all individuals with the opportunity to live in dignity, promoting mutual trust, strengthening cooperation among developing nations, and cooperating with international and regional organizations with similar interests, SAARC's ambitions for its vision of South Asian regionalism were remarkable. Headquartered in Kathmandu, SAARC initially consisted of Nepal, Bangladesh, Bhutan, India, the Maldives, Pakistan and Sri Lanka, with the more recent addition of Afghanistan as its eighth member in 2007.

Discussions about a regional organization began in the latter half of the 1970s, with the Bangladeshi President Ziaur Rahman's visit to the regional nations. Rahman's motivation for this proposal remains widely debated, and its cause has been attributed to a variety of factors. These include the Soviet invasion of Afghanistan in 1979, and the threat of the Cold War fostering instability across the region, Rahman's need for India's support to legitimize his coup d'état regime, an acute balance of payments crisis across South Asia exacerbated by the oil crisis of 1979, the lack of success in North-South dialogues with rising protectionism in developed economies, promises of economic assistance in 1978 from the Carter administration in the US for multilateral interstate projects for sharing water, and the willingness to set up a common forum for South Asian nations to help resolve conflicts. While ascertaining the *a priori* factors motivating Rahman's initial sponsorship remains challenging, his efforts were met with little enthusiasm initially from both India and Pakistan, who had fought no fewer than three wars in less than three decades since their Independence.

Pakistan's worries were centred around the possibility of India further cementing its political and economic domination of the region. India was concerned about its smaller neighbours uniting to disrupt its own regional interests. Ultimately an agreement was reached, as the thought of being 'on the menu' was perhaps significantly more perilous than being present 'at the table', with neither side wanting to be left out. The compromise made was in the wording of the draft created by Bangladesh which removed security issues and stated that only 'non-political and non-controversial areas of cooperation' would be covered. Subsequently, Rahman formally proposed the concept in May 1980, with the foreign secretaries of the South Asian nations meeting for the first time in April 1981 in Colombo to discuss topics of mutual interest. By the time the first summit was held in 1985, broad areas of mutual interest had been agreed upon, which included communication, connectivity, agriculture, public health, energy, environment and economic cooperation.

India's role in SAARC has been distinguished, being a founding member of the organization and hosting its summits thrice since its inception, in 1986, 1995 and 2007. With India's support, SAARC has seen several noteworthy achievements, like the creation of five SAARC regional centres focused on energy, agriculture, culture, health, and disaster management. India was later pivotal in the establishment of the South Asian University in New Delhi in 2010. In 2020, during the Covid pandemic India led the organization of the South Asian region's response, and on its initiative proposed an emergency SAARC fund with an initial offer of $10 million, and provided a broad range of humanitarian relief, set up the SAARC Disaster Management Centre in Gandhinagar, and developed a SAARC Covid-19 Information Exchange Platform to support the region as it battled the pandemic.

Notwithstanding SAARC's successes, South Asia remains one of the least integrated regions in the world, with intra-regional trade accounting for only five per cent of the region's total trade as of 2022, compared to the proportion of intra-regional trade being 50 per cent in East Asia.[7] SAARC has continued to face hurdles unique to its region, which include the lack of dispute-resolution mechanisms, the continuing antagonism between India and Pakistan, rise of bilateralism in the region, shortage of resources and apprehensive contributions from member nations, and widening trust deficit between member nations. Other initiatives of the SAARC, such as the much-celebrated South Asian Free Trade Agreement (SAFTA), have seen limited success in enabling wider economic interlinkages within the region. More pertinently, some have argued that in the latter half of the 2010s SAARC became 'practically defunct' with burgeoning hostilities within the region. While this hyperbole can be challenged, the rise in bilateralism and the creation of the Bay of Bengal Initiative for Multi-Sectoral Technical and Economic Cooperation (BIMSTEC) in 1997 by Bangladesh, Bhutan, India, Myanmar, Nepal, Sri Lanka and Thailand do raise questions about its obsolescence. BIMSTEC has seen significant success and has become the preferred conduit for regional collaboration—with the exclusion of Pakistan, India has been able to freely engage, without the apprehension of the zero-sum games and trust deficits that had spilled over into the workings of SAARC.

Regardless of its many imperfections, SAARC has continued to symbolize South Asian regionalism, representing the very first attempt for securing it in the contemporary period. While much has been said about SAARC, it has continued to provide the region with a useful forum for further negotiations, and its establishment in 1985 continues to represent a milestone in the institutionalization of cooperation within the region.

1986

38. THE SINO-PAKISTANI NUCLEAR ACCORD

In September 1986, the Pakistani Foreign Minister visited Beijing to sign the China-Pakistan Nuclear Cooperation Agreement, under which China agreed to expedite the transfer of civil nuclear technology by providing Islamabad with power reactors and a variety of nuclear-related products and services, which included research and technical support for uranium enrichment. Apart from bringing with it the promise of enhanced industrial capacity and bridging the energy requirements gap, this deal brought out into the open China's outright support for Pakistan to develop all things nuclear.

China used this opportunity to strengthen its credentials within the global community and dispel notions of its role as an enabler for global nuclear proliferation. Beijing saw the accord as underlining the 'peaceful nature of Sino-Pakistani nuclear cooperation', to check 'irresponsible rumours' and strengthen Beijing's credentials as a responsible nuclear power with a firm non-proliferation policy.[8] This agreement was monumental for Islamabad, which had theretofore relied primarily on Canada, with which it had initiated cooperation in 1959 and which came to a halt in 1976 after Canada reformed its nuclear policy. For both Islamabad and Beijing, this agreement was seen as a natural evolution of the relationship that had grown in leaps and bounds in the preceding two decades, since India fought successive wars with China in 1962 and with Pakistan in 1965.

Notwithstanding China's rhetoric about this exchange with Pakistan being strictly guarded by its nuclear proliferation policy, and Pakistan's consistent stand that it was only for peaceful purposes, this development was significantly concerning for India, as access to technology which could produce nuclear weapons threatened to destabilize the existing balance of powers within South Asia. This included not only the weaponization of nuclear power by Islamabad but also the potential permeation of this technology to other non-nuclear states and non-state actors. Notably, from New Delhi's perspective, Islamabad's close relationship with the American bloc and its growing alliance with Beijing foreshadowed the arrival of the globalized Cold War's localized manifestation right at New Delhi's doorstep. The region's access would be, in all likelihood, elevated from traditional weaponry to nuclear capabilities.

This agreement raised alarm bells even among Pakistan's allies in the West, which had diligently supplied the nation with aid in the form of finance and weaponry. Documents now declassified from the US National Security Archive reveal that this concern was justified, with a report from 1968 detailing the growing Sino-Pakistani collaboration, with Islamabad violating its agreement with the US and providing access to American-made systems, which included the US F-104 fighter aircraft. Later, in 1983, another US report confirmed that 'there is unambiguous evidence that Pakistan is actively pursuing a nuclear weapons development program', in which China played a significant part by helping in the production of fissile materials and potentially in 'nuclear device design'.[9]

However, for the US at the time, its Afghanistan policy was of far higher priority, due to which it had willingly both overlooked and changed its policies to continue supporting Pakistan. The Symington Amendment[10] in the US was replaced with the far less stringent Pressler Amendment in 1985, which allowed US economic aid and government military sales to continue as long as the president could certify that Pakistan had not assembled a nuclear device. This mechanism allowed the US to effectively express its concerns about Pakistan's nuclear status without jeopardizing the US-Afghanistan policy. Interestingly, a further correlation can be seen between the Pressler Amendment and the US-Afghanistan policy, as soon after the Soviet withdrawal from Afghanistan in 1989, the Bush administration declared in 1990 that it could not certify that Pakistan was compliant with the Pressler Amendment and suspended economic and military aid.

Later, in 2004, with a change in Libya's nuclear policy under Muammar Gaddafi, it was discovered that Pakistan had played the role of a super-proliferator of nuclear weapons. Islamabad had led a network that dispersed nuclear weapons designs to Libya which were created and provided by Beijing. US investigators also believed that this network enabled Iran and North Korea's access to their nuclear projects. Rajiv Gandhi's prognostication in 1986, of the US turning a 'blind eye to the Pakistani nuclear program' to protect its Afghanistan policy, was not only accurate in its calculations, but it also illustrated the obstacle which had continued to restrain India's closer cooperation with the US and the wider Western Bloc.

The Sino-Pakistan Nuclear Agreement, and the continued American patronage of Pakistan, had effectively limited Rajiv Gandhi's policy options and his ability to expand India's relationship with the West, and had instead reaffirmed the realities of a rapidly evolving Cold War within the subcontinent. The agreement also represented a major milestone in the relationship between China and Pakistan, both of which were nations that had individually represented India's key regional security challenges, and that together shared with India a land border running over 7,300 kilometres.

39. THE SINO-INDIAN STANDOFF AT SUMDORONG CHU

The nine-year-long military standoff between India and China began in June 1986, over Sumdorong Chu, a river flowing from west to east into Nyamjang Chu in the Thagla triangle, which had Bhutan to its west and Thagla Ridge to its north. Notably, an earlier confrontation at Thagla Ridge, in June 1962, was also one of the key events in the lead-up to the Sino-Indian War of 1962. The area had remained unoccupied after the war, until 1980, at which point the Indian Army decided to reinforce its positions in the forward areas. During the summer of 1984, India established an observation post on the banks of the river that was manned through the summer season and vacated over the winter. In June 1986, however, an Indian patrol found around forty

Chinese personnel working on permanent structures. Ignoring New Delhi's formal protest, Beijing reinforced its construction work, and by August had built a helipad there.

In September the Rajiv Gandhi government, in an attempt to diffuse the situation, offered to Beijing that if it agreed to withdraw its forces during the winter, Indian forces would not re-occupy the territory in the subsequent summer. As Beijing flatly declined this offer, in October the Indian Army set into motion Operation Falcon, under which an entire brigade was airlifted to Zemithang, the closest helipad north of Tawang. The Indian Army's blitz allowed it to take the strategically significant positions on Hathun La Ridge, across the Namka Chu River, and positions across the McMahon Line.

These positions overlooked the Sumdorong Chu River. Caught unawares, China upped the ante by reinforcing and strengthening its positions. The standoff continued to escalate, with New Delhi elevating the status of Arunachal Pradesh from a union territory to a full-fledged state on 20 February 1987.[11] China's response and rhetoric continued to escalate—right from the beginning of Operation Falcon—with growing belligerence. Both sides continued with heavy troop movements, with India conducting Operation Chequerboard, a largescale air-land exercise, along its northeastern border with China.

China's position on the incident, and its rhetoric throughout its development, remained antagonistic, with Chinese media and official communication repeatedly rejecting the 'so-called McMahon Line' as an outcome of colonialist aggression against it. In October 1986, Deng Xiaoping was troubled to the extent that he conveyed to the US Defence Secretary that China would have to 'teach India a lesson'.[12] Although a flag meeting took place in November 1986 to alleviate tensions, the standoff continued to trouble both sides, with the first steps to de-escalation being taken following the Indian Minister of External Affairs N.D. Tiwari's visit to Beijing on his way to Pyongyang, North Korea, in May 1987.

India's position on this incident has been hotly debated, with researchers pointing out the disagreements between the Indian military and its political establishment on how to deal with the issue. It appears that while Rajiv Gandhi's government was keen to resolve the issue through diplomatic channels right from the beginning, India's then Chief of Army Staff (CoAS) General Krishnaswamy Sundarji's counsel had held that New Delhi should stand firm on its position. While Operation Falcon's success in occupying strategic positions has been attributed to General Sundarji's planning, others have noted that it created a gridlock in the Sino-Indian position, with each side now unable to back down from the fear of losing face. Furthermore, others have noted that both Operations Falcon and Chequerboard were considerable gambles, as they involved the maintenance of about 21,000 tons of equipment around 80 kilometres ahead of existing roads. In actual warfare, this would have translated to battling China with little logistical support, apart from limited air maintenance.

Notwithstanding the situation, the Rajiv Gandhi government's strong political willingness to resolve the issue diplomatically allowed for the initial breakthroughs that prevented further escalation. The visit by India's Minister of External Affairs was an important development, as it affirmed the willingness and desire of both New Delhi and Beijing to continue their ongoing discussions over resolving the border issues. Others have pointed out that New Delhi's decision to continue on its path with firmness regarding its positions paved the way for Rajiv Gandhi's visit to Beijing in 1988, giving New Delhi the confidence to detach the border issue from the need to develop better relations with Beijing. New Delhi's firm stance encouraged Beijing to agree on an equitable regime of confidence-building measures that were ultimately included in an agreement in 1993 to maintain peace on the border, ultimately bringing the crisis to an end in 1995.

The Sumdorong incident holds an important place in the

evolution of India's foreign policy, as it set the tone for the realities of the Sino-Indian relationship which would come to characterize the post-Cold War period. India had stood strong and firm in its stance, without the support of any extra-regional balancer. During this period, the Soviet Union was in the process of disintegrating and India's relations with the US were cold, with the US's continued patronage of Pakistan to support the US-Afghanistan policy. Added to this, New Delhi's domestic economy was also in turmoil, with a severe balance of payments crisis. In the face of these challenges, and the lack of any external support, India's response to China's obduracy and belligerence was remarkable, and set a powerful precedent that built on its achievements during its successful actions at Nathu La and Cho La during the Sino-Indian border clashes of 1967. The conversion of Arunachal Pradesh from a union territory to a state further underscored New Delhi's resolve on its uncompromising willingness to protect its borders, against the backdrop of a strengthened military and a wider modernization of its armed forces.

1987

40. THE INDO-SRI LANKAN ACCORD OF 1987

Amidst a civil war in Sri Lanka, fought between the northern Tamil groups and the Sri Lankan government, India under Prime Minster Rajiv Gandhi and Sri Lanka under President J.R. Jayewardene signed the Indo-Sri Lanka Peace Accord on 19 July 1987. This agreement mandated an immediate ceasefire, the merger of the Northern and Eastern Sri Lankan provinces into a single administrative unit with an elected Provincial Council, a referendum in the Eastern province to decide if the merger would be continued, to be held by December 1988, and elections for the Northern and Eastern councils, under Indian observation, to be held before December 1987.

Further, the agreement had India commit to providing military support to the Sri Lankan government, if requested. In another annexure to the agreement, both the parties aligned their foreign policies closer to each other than ever before, with India committing to repatriating Sri Lankans engaged in terrorist activities, and Sri Lanka agreeing not to allow any other country to access Trincomalee or any other port of military use and thereby threaten India's interests. Notably, this bilateral agreement only consulted the Tamil groups, like Velupillai Prabhakaran's Liberation Tigers of Tamil Eelam (LTTE), ex post facto—they never truly accepted the agreement, and only made a token surrender to the Indian Peace-Keeping Force (IPKF). Later, in October, the LTTE declared war on the IPKF, claiming that it was incapable of protecting the Tamils from Sinhalese brutality.

In response to the LTTE, the IPKF launched Operation Pawan, which managed to occupy the LTTE stronghold of Jaffna Peninsula, but at a significant cost over a fierce three-week battle with the support of heavy artillery and tanks. Although this feat was theretofore not achieved by the Sri Lankan government, which had tried to do it several times in the years leading up to the accord, India's success, given the cost it had to pay in the form of lives lost, has been widely questioned. Perhaps one of the greatest fallouts of IPKF's operations in Sri Lanka was the assassination of Rajiv Gandhi in 1991 by a member of the LTTE, after which the LTTE was formally designated as a terrorist group by India, further reducing India's involvement in the civil war. The Sri Lankan government continued to battle the group, with its final decimation in May 2009.

India's involvement in the Sri Lankan civil war began after the anti-Tamil pogroms that occurred in 1983. Indira Gandhi's government was not only sympathetic to the humanitarian concerns, but was also compelled to help them due to the Indian state Tamil Nadu's concern for the plight of the Sri Lankan Tamil population. The civil war that ensued fractured Sri Lanka causing an ethnic divide, with Tamil groups like the LTTE in the north and the east of the island fighting for the creation of a separate state, the 'Tamil Eelam', and the southern Sinhalese-majority Sri Lankan government fighting to rein in the separatism. New Delhi, during the course of the successive governments under Indira Gandhi and Rajiv Gandhi, had attempted to play the role of a mediator at several points, although with limited success. The Tamil groups refused to accept anything less than the creation of a separate state, and the Sri Lankan government's scepticism about India's role only continued to mount, given the asymmetry in the relative sizes of the two countries and the fact that many of the Tamil separatist organizations had their bases in Tamil Nadu.

Rajiv Gandhi's government saw comparatively more success in the mediation process, with its crackdown on Tamil militant bases and renewed efforts to formulate a compromise. However, matters deteriorated with the Sri Lankan government using an iron fist to extinguish Tamil insurgency and separatism in its northern territories, carrying out military activities and imposing an economic blockade on the LTTE-controlled Jaffna Peninsula. Concerned by the plight of the Tamil community, and with Sri Lanka's refusal to lift the blockade, India carried out Operation Poomalai on 4 June 1987 which violated Sri Lankan airspace and airdropped supplies over the besieged city of Jaffna, using five An-32s escorted by five Mirage 2000H fighter jets. It was ultimately the pressure put on Colombo with this manoeuvre that brought it back to the table for negotiations, after which the Indo-Sri Lanka Accord was signed. Unfortunately, the LTTE's refusal to comply with the accord and its subsequent declaration of war against the IPKF dragged India into one of its most brutal actions. The IPKF was finally withdrawn with the fall of Rajiv Gandhi's government and the discretion of the new Indian Prime Minister V.P. Singh.

India's eagerness to play a larger role as a humanitarian and security provider in the violence that pervaded its southern neighbour was part of a broader transition in its foreign policy, under which it increased its engagement with key regional issues of the time. Domestically, the Rajiv Gandhi government had also undertaken an overhaul of its internal security, with several key accords being signed in the first few years of his premiership in addition to the Sri Lankan Accord. These included the Longowal Accord and the Assam Accord in 1985, and the Mizo Accord in 1986.

Right from the beginning of the Sri Lankan civil war, India had been well aware of its policy constraints vis-à-vis its Tamil population, and the possibility of some form of intervention in its own backyard carried out by extra-regional powers like the US, Britain, Pakistan, Israel and Bangladesh. Interestingly, the United States, with which India continued to have a frosty relationship during the 1990s, appeared to have trusted New Delhi's management of the Sri Lankan situation, with the Deputy Assistant Secretary of State informing the Solarz subcommittee of the House of Representatives about the Sri Lankan civil war in March 1987, that 'we have been gratified in the last year or two that our policies and the policies of the Government of India are very much running in parallel'.

Notably, in 1988, India carried out another manoeuvre known as Operation Cactus, at the request of the Maldivian President Maumoon Abdul Gayoom, to prevent a coup d'état by a Maldivian group led by Abdulla Luthufee and assisted by a Sri Lankan Tamil separatist group, the People's Liberation Organisation of Tamil Eelam (PLOTE). India deployed a contingent of paratroopers which successfully rescued President Gayoom, secured the capital Malé, and averted the PLOTE coup. New Delhi's actions were commended across the Western nations for upholding the Maldivian civil administration. New Delhi's involvement in both Sri Lanka and the Maldives illustrated its willingness to own its role in the region as a net security provider. Fundamentally, India's foreign policy had transitioned, with its growing confidence in projecting its own power to its wider neighbourhood and presenting itself to the international audience as a trustworthy and stabilizing factor within the region.

41. OPERATION BRASSTACKS

Between November 1986 and January 1987, the Indian Army conducted a military exercise, known as Operation Brasstacks, on an extensive scale involving nearly half a million troops which included three armoured, three mechanized, nine infantry and one air assault divisions. The exercise was conducted in the desert of Rajasthan, just a few hundred miles from India's border with Pakistan. The Indian forces were issued with live ammunition for the exercise, and conducted war simulations along the border. In response to this sudden military build-up with no prior warning, Islamabad, feeling existentially threatened and fearing it was preparation for a large-scale attack, responded by carrying out similar exercises along the border of the Indian state of Punjab.

The heightened tensions fuelled by the two armies within firing distance of each other stimulated frantic diplomatic activity in New Delhi and Islamabad to address the perilous military build-up on each side. The situation continued to deteriorate, reaching its nadir in late January 1987, with the director of the Pakistani nuclear programme stating to an Indian journalist that Pakistan not only possessed nuclear weapons, but was also willing to use it if its existence was threatened. Tensions began to gradually abate post-February 1987, after President Zia-ul-Haq's visit to India and his meeting with Rajiv Gandhi on the sidelines of an India-Pakistan cricket match.

From a Pakistani perspective, the sudden Indian military build-up and the lack of any warning were seen as a clear indication of an imminent Indian invasion. This perspective included an Indian plan to bifurcate Pakistan by attacking the Punjab province of Pakistan and cutting off its access to the Sindh province. The rationale behind this reasoning was that India would use this opportunity to subdue Pakistan in conventional warfare, before the latter's nuclear capabilities would have a chance to materialize and afford it a nuclear deterrent to war. Other pessimistic observers interpreted the Indian manoeuvre as an attempt to provoke Pakistan into some action, which would give the Indian military an excuse to launch an offensive. The reasons for this offensive ranged widely, from the willingness to simply impress Pakistan with its modernized military capabilities, destroying the supposed Pakistani nuclear capabilities, eliminating anti-India terrorist camps on Pakistani soil, to the complete invasion and bifurcation of Pakistan. However, India's vehement diplomatic efforts to quell the hostile military build-up across the border challenged the core assumption of these pessimistic perspectives.

From an Indian perspective, as was insinuated by its Chief of Army Staff at the time, General Krishnaswamy Sundarji, this exercise was a regular event that need not have startled Islamabad. For Gen. Sundarji, the operation was conducted to test key strategic concepts like the RAPIDS,[13] newly acquired weaponry, and the coordination of the three services. However, more practically, other interpretations point at the failure of military intelligence on both sides, and the great misrepresentation of one another's actions on the part of each nation, as the fundamental reason for the escalating antagonism between them. The US Association for Diplomatic Studies and Training (ADST) reports that the 'more alarmist reports from their [India and Pakistan] own intelligence services were exaggerated', and these encouraged an escalation of military deployment along the borders in Rajasthan, Punjab and Kashmir.[14]

While each of these perspectives competes with others, with their various versions of Indian intent, what remains unambiguous is the simple causal relationship between Operation Brasstacks and the military build-up along the India-Pakistan border. While these consequences may have been unintended, general opinion has remained divided regarding Gen. Sundarji's decision-making and planning that led to this diplomatic crisis. Gen. Sundarji's modernization drive for the Indian armed forces has been widely commended, and described by some as being ahead of its time. Others have argued that his hawkish approach to defence had driven military brinkmanship, which spread the military perilously thin and added to its fatigue, with the late 1980s seeing active deployment of the armed forces in the form of Operation Pawan in Sri Lanka, Operations Falcon and Chequerboard in the Indian state of Arunachal Pradesh, in Siachen after Operation Meghdoot, and Operation Cactus in the Maldives. Referencing Operation Brasstacks, a senior cabinet minister at the time is quoted by *India Today* as having said, 'I am sorry to say that the man [Gen. Sundarji] almost led us to war. The prime minister had not been adequately briefed.'[15]

Operation Brasstacks was a pivotal moment for Indo-Pakistani relations, as it cemented Pakistan's suspicions of India and ensured that the existing Indo-Pakistani trust deficit continued to expand. In an effort to bridge this gap, the two sides made attempts at implementing confidence-building measures, like the bilateral signing in December 1988 of the Agreement on the Prohibition of Attack against Nuclear Installations and Facilities. However, Brasstacks encouraged Pakistan to increase its military expenditure, and strengthen its focus on securing nuclear weapons to gain the capability of deploying a credible nuclear deterrent against India in the future.

1988

42. THE INDO-NEPALESE CRISIS OF 1988–90

The relationship between India and Nepal has evolved immensely since the bilateral treaty signed in 1950. Notably, the core tenets of the treaty have broadly been sustained, which include a 'special relationship' under which citizens of each nation would be accorded open borders and special privileges. Subsequently, in 1965 the two nations signed the bilateral Security Cooperation Agreement, under which they accepted India's role as the sole supplier of arms to Nepal. The UK and the US were stipulated to supplement defence assistance to Nepal if India fell short. Nevertheless, the relationship had its fair share of highs and lows, with the period between 1988 and 1990 seeing an unprecedented spike in antagonism. At the root of this was the lapse of the Trade and Transit Treaties of 1978. The disagreement lay in Nepal's refusal to accommodate India's call for a single commerce and transit treaty. Following their inability to reach an agreement, after two extensions the treaty expired on 23 March 1989, which resulted in the halting of commerce and trade that lasted until April 1990.

The outcome of this was far-reaching for Nepal's economy, which almost immediately faced a growing political and economic crisis. This developed into an economic blockade, and Nepal faced a dire shortage of key commodities like petroleum, coal, medicines and spare parts, and this brought its economy to a standstill, with its gross domestic product (GDP) growth rate dropping from 7.7 per cent in 1988 to 4.3 per cent in 1989.[16] Internally, Nepal's panchayat system, backed by its monarchy,[17] faced mounting pressure for reforms, with the outbreak of riots stimulated by its dire economic condition. Finally, in April 1990, through a mass movement for multiparty democracy, the panchayat system was overthrown by the Nepali Congress and the United Left Front, and replaced by an interim government led by Prime Minister Krishna Prasad Bhattarai.[18] Following this, Prime Minister Bhattarai visited India in November and signed a joint communiqué which restored the status quo ante, vis-à-vis April 1987.

Although trade and transit had been agreed upon under a single treaty before 1978, Kathmandu outwardly expressed its unwillingness to go back to the pre-1978 formula, in an effort to reduce its dependence on New Delhi. Nepal's Foreign Minister, in an interview in 1989, affirmed that its special relationship with India had become one of economic dependence, further stating that it was in Nepal's 'interest to let interdependence grow', but it was also in its interest 'to see that our dependence on one country does not grow'.[19] The fear of dependence was rooted in the fact that trade and transit were seen as distinctly separate matters. While trade was seen as an evolving bilateral matter with India, transit was seen as a right for landlocked countries under international law. For Nepal, transit was seen as pivotal for engagement, not only with India but also with the rest of the world.

However, from New Delhi's perspective, although the fifteen existing transit points were reduced to two with the lapse of the treaty, international law had not been violated as it required landlocked countries to be given one transit point. India had provided two, which gave Nepal access to the Kolkata and Haldia ports. Further, New Delhi maintained that it had not enforced any blockade or carried out any retaliation, and since the treaties had lapsed, Nepal was simply being treated on a most-favoured-nation basis, on a par with Bangladesh and Pakistan at the time. However, what was certain in this instance was the deadlock that both the governments had reached, and their inability to back down from their positions. The joint communiqué signed in 1990 was not only a result of a change in the Nepalese regime, but also an outcome of the willingness to re-engage, with a new government in India under Prime Minister V.P. Singh.

New Delhi's evolving threat perception has also been tabled as an explanation for this diplomatic fallout. After the Sino-Indian War of 1962, the known-to-be impregnable Himalayan border with China had been compromised by modern technology and Beijing's expansionist political will. Beijing had begun making inroads into Kathmandu with the building of the Kathmandu-Kodari Road in 1965, connecting Nepal to China. New Delhi had, in 1965, entered a security treaty with Kathmandu. Later, in 1970, Nepal further reduced its security alignment with New Delhi, requesting Indian personnel to be withdrawn from the Nepal-Tibet border check posts and demanding that the trade and transit treaties be separated. This was the first instance of a disagreement on the treaty and a de facto blockade being placed, which was lifted with a combined treaty being signed in 1971.

Right before the 1988 disagreement, Nepal had taken a step to completely disregard the security treaty of 1965, by importing arms from China which included anti-aircraft guns and assault rifles, among other things. The insistence of Rajiv Gandhi's government on combining the treaties was viewed by Nepal as a retaliation against this activity. Other pressures which mounted on New Delhi's decision to combine the two treaties included the perceived dilution of not only the 1965 security treaty but also the goodwill that was embedded in the 1950 treaty, with Nepal placing tariff barriers against Indian imports, lifting import duties from Chinese imports, instituting work permits for Indians in certain Nepalese regions, and the potential disenfranchisement of the minorities in the Teri region of Nepal,[20] among other things.

The consequences of the 1989–90 Indo-Nepalese crisis were far-reaching for the relationship between the two countries. Although mass Nepalese support saw the rise of a multi-party system, there was also sown the seed of widespread resentment against India's high-handedness. While New Delhi was able to wield its economic whip, which eventually saw Kathmandu yield to its pressure, the political cost and the loss of goodwill have continued to shadow the relationship. The relationship has since continued to navigate a complex landscape, which include the decade-long civil war between the Nepalese state and the Communist Party of Nepal (Maoist Centre) which began in 1996, the evolving Sino-Indian relationship, China's increasing interest in Nepal, the rise of new Indo-Nepalese territorial disputes like that over the Kalapani region in 1998, and a similar bilateral economic crisis in 2015.

43. PRIME MINISTER RAJIV GANDHI'S VISIT TO BEIJING

From 19 to 23 December 1988, Rajiv Gandhi paid an official visit to Beijing that proved to be historic, not only because it averted the recent Sumdorong Chu impasse but also because it represented a watershed moment in the wider Sino-Indian relationship. This was the first visit by an Indian prime minister in thirty-four years, with the last being made by Rajiv Gandhi's maternal grandfather Jawaharlal Nehru in 1954, at the height of Sino-Indian diplomatic ties. Rajiv Gandhi's five-day visit was made at the invitation of the Chinese Premier Li Peng, during which he also met the Chinese President Yang Shangkun and the Chairman of China's Central Military Commission, Deng Xiaoping. The outcomes of the visit included an affirmation by both governments of their subscription to the Five Principles and Peaceful Coexistence, the call for a more equitable international system, an understanding that both nations were keen to develop bilateral relations, and a joint press communiqué issued by both governments.

Notably, both sides agreed to de-link the border dispute with broader bilateral relations, and decided to address both areas in terms of independent frameworks. For the border issue, a joint working group was set up which met annually at the foreign secretary or vice foreign minister level. For broader bilateral collaboration, a joint group on the economy, trade, and science and technology was set up. Further agreements were made on cooperation in science and technology, civil aviation transportation and culture. Crucially, after reiterating that Tibet was an autonomous region of China, Rajiv Gandhi also reaffirmed that anti-China political activities by Tibetans were not permitted on Indian soil.

One of the key criticisms of this visit is the lack of a concrete time-frame for the resolution of the border issue. However, others propose that this visit was less about major breakthroughs, and more about resetting diplomatic ties. As Rajiv Gandhi stated, 'I take a more pragmatic view… I see it as a new beginning.'[21] Prudently, the expectations and optimism both during and after this visit remained guarded by most observers, who noted the continuing existence of substantial differences. These included not only the border issue but also nuclear weaponry, India's policy towards Sri Lanka, and wider foreign policy misalignments over Afghanistan and Cambodia.

Rajiv Gandhi's outreach was underscored by a distinct change and a transition in the geopolitical stage, with the Cold War beginning to diminish under General Secretary and President Mikhail Gorbachev. New Delhi had begun expanding its engagement with the wider world beyond the Soviet Union, and had become acutely aware that in this new and dramatically changing era, amidst a thaw in the Sino-Soviet relationship, it had to chalk out its own relationship with China. China, for its part, had already considerably improved its relationship with the US and the wider West, with the help of Kissinger's Cold War manoeuvring since the 1970s. Bending backwards on the Tibet issue has since been interpreted as a key concession to engage and influence a policy change in China vis-à-vis India. Furthermore, prior to Rajiv Gandhi's government, in the early parts of the 1980s New Delhi had already begun to secretly explore the possibility of resetting its relationship with China. Normalizing the Sino-Indian relationship was also seen as an important factor in moderating the Sino-Pakistani entente.

From Beijing's perspective, this diplomatic thaw benefitted it in a variety of areas including its internal security issues, the bolstering of its economy, and its international profile. Beijing's territorial integrity had been questioned with the ongoing unrest in Tibet that began in 1987 and would continue till 1989. Securing New Delhi's confirmation of its support for Beijing's control of Tibet was pivotal, as India was seen to have been a haven for anti-China activities. China's economy at the time was also going through significant turmoil, with uncontrolled inflation, a spike in unemployment, and droughts that had severely impacted its agricultural output. A decrease in hostility and expanding economic ties with India were seen as an important step in addressing China's internal economic challenges. On the global stage, China's socialization into the wider international system had only recently commenced, with patronage from the US in the 1970s. Engaging with India and resetting its relationship promised to bolster its credentials as a responsible member of the international community.

In retrospect, Rajiv Gandhi's visit served as a significant step change in the Sino-Indian relationship. The momentum built from this visit instigated a growth in leader-level interactions, a growth in bilateral business, and the bilateral signing of the Agreement on the Maintenance of Peace and Tranquillity along the Line of Actual Control (LAC) in 1993, in which both sides agreed to maintain the status quo until the border dispute was mutually resolved. Notwithstanding the importance of this visit, the wider Sino-Indian relationship, however, has continued to face challenges.

The post-1990 period saw a significant change in Beijing's foreign policy, which has continued to limit the spirit of the 1988 Rajiv Gandhi-Deng Xiaoping modus vivendi. Unfortunately, the trust deficit between the two nations has only grown since the turn of the century, catalyzed by China's unilateral decisions, which include its rapid construction of infrastructure along the LAC and in Tibet after 2000, and the continued support and the provision of access to lethal weapons to Pakistan, among others. Although this relationship has gradually grown into one of hostility, Rajiv Gandhi's efforts went a long way in establishing a mutually agreed-upon framework that has continued to underpin the rules of engagement for the wider relationship between the two nations.

44. PRIME MINISTER RAJIV GANDHI'S PROPOSAL FOR GLOBAL NUCLEAR DISARMAMENT

India's call for disarmament is strongly rooted in its diplomatic history, right from Prime Minister Nehru's response to the Castle Bravo detonation by the US in 1954, proposing to the UN and nuclear-armed states a 'Standstill Agreement'. India's support for nuclear disarmament had matured significantly since then. In 1978, it called for negotiations towards an international convention prohibiting the use, or the threat of use, of nuclear weapons. However, on 9 June 1988, addressing the Third Special Session on Disarmament of the UN General Assembly, Rajiv Gandhi asserted that 'the champions of nuclear deterrence argue that nuclear weapons have been invented and therefore, cannot be eliminated. We do not agree. We have an international convention eliminating biological weapons by prohibiting their use in war. We are working on similarly eliminating chemical weapons. There is no reason on principle why nuclear weapons too cannot be eliminated.'[22] Subsequently, the Rajiv Gandhi government tabled the most comprehensive proposal for nuclear disarmament. The action plan had a built-in time frame that envisaged 2010 as the year by which the complete elimination of nuclear weapons would be realized.

The action plan was built on four essential features. First, there should be a binding commitment from all nations to eliminate nuclear weapons in staged phases, at the latest by 2010. Second, all nuclear-weapons states must participate in the process. All other countries must also be a part of the process. Third, there must be tangible progress at each stage towards the common goal, to help demonstrate good faith and build the required confidence. Fourth, since changes are required in doctrines, policies and institutions to sustain a world free of nuclear weapons, negotiations should be undertaken to establish a Comprehensive Global Security System under the aegis of the UN. The plan also included two working papers on new technologies and the arms race, and the disposal of warheads. The action plan, in its essence, broke down the period between 1988 and 2010 into three stages, with the final stage culminating in the 'elimination of all nuclear weapons from the world', and a 'universal adherence to the comprehensive global security system'.

Unlike the 1968 Non-Proliferation Treaty (NPT), Rajiv Gandhi's action plan was inherently non-discriminatory in nature. Unlike the NPT, which did little to limit vertical proliferation and focused on only eliminating horizontal proliferation, India's action plan was designed to induce both vertical and horizontal disarmament. The action plan did this by making both nuclear-weapon states and non-nuclear-weapon states equal participants in the process of achieving universal disarmament. With the luxury of hindsight, we can see that India's action plan failed to deliver this vision in practice, as the international community has not only crossed the time frame of the planned twenty-two years, but it has also seen nuclear proliferation continue largely unchecked. Partly, the reason for its failure was that it did not receive the requisite attention from the recognized NWS.[23] A majority of the initiatives it recommended were not accepted by the NWS, which continued to maintain their arsenals and perceived them as essential to their security.

The action plan was presented to the UN General Assembly at what was a particularly precarious period not only for India but also for the rest of the world. The early 1980s had seen the Reagan administration in the US up the ante, with promises of developing new weapons systems, increasing US defence preparedness, development of new missile systems, and deployment of nuclear weapons in Europe to counter the Soviet build-up there. Closer to home, Pakistan had just entered into a nuclear agreement with China in 1986, securing Islamabad power reactors and a variety of nuclear-related products and services, which included research and technical support for uranium enrichment.[24] Although China had reaffirmed its policy of non-proliferation, it was now but a matter of time till Pakistan weaponized this capability. It was precisely these challenges of the international system's reliance on deterrence, without a non-discriminatory framework, that Rajiv Gandhi's action plan was designed to address. Rajiv Gandhi, in fact, went a step further and confirmed that deterrence had no place in the action plan, describing it as the 'ultimate expression of the philosophy of terrorism'.[25]

In this, Rajiv Gandhi was further encouraged by the signing of the Intermediate-Range Nuclear Forces Treaty between the US and the Soviet Union in 1987, which banned both nations' nuclear and conventional ground-launched ballistic and cruise missiles with the ranges of 500–5,500 kilometres.[26] Later, in December 1988, Rajiv Gandhi signed the bilateral Non-Nuclear Aggression Agreement with the Pakistani Prime Minister Benazir Bhutto, which affirmed that the two nations would not attack each other's nuclear installations.[27] Unfortunately, with the lack of a buy-in for the action plan, India reluctantly went nuclear in May 1998 and declared itself a NWS. As an NWS, India also declared its doctrine of nuclear deterrence, the heart of which has remained its policy of 'no first use' of nuclear weapons.

While Rajiv Gandhi's action plan failed to achieve its desired outcome, it both set a precedent for future disarmament endeavours and socialized a non-discriminatory framework that could be adapted and adopted by the international community. The action plan's fundamental goal of 'ushering in a non-violent world free of nuclear weapons' has continued to underscore New Delhi's aspirational objective and its goal of disarmament. This initiative was visionary and has remained unmatched, as it not only foresaw the dangers of proliferation but also described a realistic path to universal disarmament.

PART II

1991

45. THE BUDGET OF JULY 1991

On 24 July 1991, the P.V. Narasimha Rao government presented a budget which brought a colossal change to India's economic policy. Presented by the finance minister at the time, Dr Manmohan Singh, the budget introduced a slew of policy changes which included reforms in India's fiscal, monetary and financial sectors, its capital markets, industrial policy, trade policy, and currency exchange rate policy, and fundamentally focused on promoting foreign investment in India. These changes essentially translated into the devaluation of the Indian rupee, a cut in public expenditure and fiscal deficit, the free flow of foreign capital, the privatization of public sector undertakings (PSUs), and broadly the reduction of state interventionism in the Indian economy in a bid to stimulate the free market.

The budget declared in July 1991 has been widely acknowledged to have successfully initiated the process of India's economic liberalization, overhauling the economic structures and ideas that had broadly characterized it throughout the Cold War. The new policies steered the economy to become more market-oriented, expanding the role of private and foreign investment, and did away with the infamous 'licence raj', reducing tariffs, ending public monopolies, and encouraging foreign direct investment in many sectors. The reforms were a significant milestone for both Indian economic and foreign policy, marking India's reducing reliance on centralized planning and its shift towards liberalization, privatization and neoliberal globalization, which was precipitated by the end of the Cold War and the dissolution of the Union of Soviet Socialist Republics into fifteen independent states.

Although 1991 is often perceived as the watershed for India's economic liberalization, the epoch of economic liberalization is rooted deeper in the evolution of its economic ideas. The relationship between the state and the market, and the idea of finding the perfect balance in their interaction, have been subject to extensive debate in the field of political economy. On the one extreme exist minimum state intervention and the preservation of a free market, and on the other extreme exist heightened state interventionism and the regulation of the market. While the perfect formula remains hotly debated, put simply, the former functions to protect against the concentration of power and the capture of the economy by interest groups, and the latter is designed to prevent market failure and protect wider public interests. Though the relationship between the market and the state in India had evolved considerably since 1947, from the perspective of the state-market continuum, the Indian economy had continued to be dominated by state interventionism.

New Delhi had at several points in its history attempted to give its market a freer rein, however with limited success. Attempts were made during the First Five-Year Plan (1951–56), then again in 1966, and finally during the 1980s. In the first attempt, import controls were relaxed through the expansion of the open general licensing list (OGL), in what Bhagwati and Desai describe as 'progressive liberalization.'[28] Unfortunately a foreign exchange crisis in 1956–57 put a stop to this, with import controls restored and maintained till 1966. In the second attempt, facing high fiscal deficits and low foreign exchange reserves, and under pressure from the World Bank, New Delhi devalued its currency and reduced import tariffs and export subsidies. However, due to a variety of reasons, this change was also short-lived, with the reversal of all liberalizing initiatives and the restoration of import controls in 1968 (see Note 20[*]). Finally, in the 1980s there

*Note number corresponds to event with same number; for example, Note 20 refers to event number 20 as mentioned in this book.

began a gradual transition of policies which ultimately facilitated the policy overhaul of 1991. Often described as 'liberalization by stealth', the 1980s and specifically the period between 1985 and 1988 saw significant policy changes, which included the expansion of the OGL, the decline in the share of canalized imports,[29] the increasing incentivization of exports, the relaxation of industrial controls, and the development of an exchange rate policy.

Building from this foundation, several internal and external factors catalyzed the final push towards liberalization in 1991. Internally, India was facing a severe economic challenge in the form of a foreign exchange crisis. With foreign exchange reserves of barely two weeks of imports, New Delhi was increasingly unable to control inflation and it faced high fiscal deficits, an extreme disequilibrium in its balance of payments, and was burdened with considerable external debt. Coupled with this, external factors like the Gulf War, which had caused a spike in oil prices, along with the loss of export markets for India due to the instability in the Middle East, exacerbated New Delhi's balance of payments crisis. As an immediate measure to bolster its foreign exchange reserves, the Reserve Bank of India had to literally airlift more than 45 tons of gold bullion to secure loans of over $400 million from the Bank of England and Bank of Japan.

In the broader geopolitical sphere, the fall of the Berlin Wall and the precipitation of the end of the Cold War had reduced the policy options for New Delhi. The Washington Consensus model of structural adjustment policies (SAPs), sponsored by the World Bank and the International Monetary Fund (IMF), had come to represent the only way out of India's economic crisis. Alternative models of aid and financing, which had been offered by the Soviet bloc theretofore, had now ceased to exist. The victory of the West over the Soviet bloc had propelled a wave of neoliberalism that engulfed the world with its unique form of neoliberal globalization.[30]

The new economic policy of 1991 had far-reaching positive effects for bolstering the economy, reviving it from its continuous balance of payments challenge, stabilizing the economy, and building the foundations from which the economy continues to soar to new heights. The ratio of the total exports of goods and services to its GDP doubled from 7.3 per cent in 1990 to 14 per cent in 2000. The services sector saw a significant boost, increasing its annual average growth rate from 6.9 per cent between 1981 and 1991, to 8.1 per cent between 1991 and 2001. The most lacklustre change in performance has been in its industrial sector, decreasing from 6.8 per cent during 1981–91, to 6.4 per cent between 1991 and 2001.[31]

While the 1991 policy changes were crucial in reviving India from the dire straits of economic crises, some have also pointed out the negative side effects of the wave of neoliberalism that New Delhi continues to grapple with. These include its inability to control capital accumulation, the spiralling rise of income and wealth inequalities, which have only continued to widen in the decades following 1991, and the plethora of problems attached with the current neoliberal international system.[32]

Notwithstanding the different perspectives, the policy changes of 1991 and the consequent economic liberalization of India have continued to represent a key milestone in both its domestic and foreign policies. The neoliberal norms and ideas that New Delhi formally subscribed to, with the implementation of the 1991 budget, have only driven it closer in alignment to the West and the wider international community. This change was crucial as sans the Soviet Union, New Delhi's foreign policy strategy had to adapt and manoeuvre with respect to the new realities of the international system. India had effectively responded to the dawn of a new age, described prematurely by Francis Fukuyama as the 'end of history'.

46. THE INITIATION OF THE LOOK EAST POLICY

The end of the Cold War precipitated a major foreign policy transition for New Delhi. Its engagement with key geographies within its neighbourhood had finally been able to break from its dogmatic over-emphasis on idealistic concepts which supported non-alignment—faced with new challenges and presented with new opportunities, the geopolitical arena had evolved considerably. Amidst these geopolitical vicissitudes, the P.V. Narasimha Rao government launched the Look East Policy (LEP) in 1991, which has since become a key feature of Indian foreign policy. The LEP of the Narasimha Rao government essentially aimed at expanding economic engagement with Southeast Asia, developing relations with nations like Cambodia, Laos, Vietnam, Myanmar and Indonesia. The economic rationale was fundamental in the LEP, with New Delhi aiming to bolster the economic reforms and the processes of liberalization that were recently initiated, sustain its rate of economic growth, strengthen regional economic integration, and provide an economic boost to India's northeastern states.

The immediate outcomes of this initiative were markedly successful, with India rapidly expanding its relationship with the Association of Southeast Asian Nations (ASEAN),[33] becoming a sectoral dialogue partner in March 1993 in trade, investment and tourism, attaining a full dialogue partnership in 1995, then becoming a member of the ASEAN Regional Forum (ARF) in July 1996, and obtaining a summit level partnership in 2002. New Delhi's economic engagement with the region has correspondingly grown, with its trade with ASEAN and the wider Southeast Asian region growing in leaps and bounds in the following decades. Between 1990 and 2005, the former grew from $2.4 billion to $23 billion, while the latter burgeoned from $8 billion to $67.6 billion.[34] In July 1996, the Minister for External Affairs I.K. Gujral, in an ASEAN Post-Ministerial Conference in Jakarta, accurately asserted, 'What Look East really means is that an outward looking India, is gathering all forces of dynamism, domestic and regional, and is directly focusing on establishing synergies with a fast consolidating and progressive neighbourhood to its East...'[35] The

LEP has continued to receive broad domestic and cross-party support, with the successive governments of I.K. Gujral, Atal Bihari Vajpayee and Manmohan Singh progressing its agenda over the following decades.

India's engagement with its Southeast Asian neighbours had a notable antecedent in its efforts of moulding a collective pan-Asian identity to act as a bulwark against the divisive Cold War and support the Asian nations in their bid to maintain non-alignment. The Narasimha Rao government's aggressive push for economic liberalization lifted key policy obstacles that had previously hindered the expansion of India's collaboration with Southeast Asia. India's pre-1991 development model was characterized by an effort to industrialize through import substitution. This focus on self-reliance and reducing external dependencies necessitated the deployment of tariff and non-tariff barriers to imports, which included licences, high tariffs, and quotas designed to control foreign investment and develop indigenous industry.

India's economic liberalization in 1991 had effectively broken these shackles and integrated India into the neoliberal system in which further engagement with Southeast Asia was not only incentivized but also became an important part of its new economic strategy. Fundamentally, the new neoliberal paradigm and its unique development model had swept the globe, and the success story of the Southeast Asian nations, referred to as the 'Asian Tigers', in achieving development through this model had made stark the importance of increasing India's engagement with them. While the neoliberal narrative and its role in facilitating the success of the Asian Tigers remains greatly debated, the East Asian nations had indeed come a long way, and now presented India with an opportunity to complement its existing interlinkages with the West and expand its regional engagement.

The end of the Cold War facilitated the elimination of bloc alignments, which had functioned to keep India and the wider East Asian nations at a distance from one another. The Philippines and Thailand had been a part of the US-sponsored Southeast Asia Treaty Organization (SEATO), which also included Pakistan and presented a security challenge for India. The end of the Vietnam War in 1975 marked the beginning of the region's development, and while China had remained a constant security concern for India, balancing China was not an important factor in India's initial LEP—this was true for at least the first phase that lasted about a decade. India's relationship with China had developed considerably since the Sumdorong Chu incident in 1986, and following Rajiv Gandhi's visit in 1988. In fact, with the LEP, trade and economic engagement with China grew, eventually becoming India's largest trading partner with the trade between the two nations amounting to $41.8 billion in 2008–09.

The LEP has had far-reaching consequences for Indian foreign policy, as New Delhi effectively committed itself to furthering its interlinkages with its Asian partners and the rest of the world. The LEP has since evolved greatly with the extension of its coverage in the early 2000s from Australia to East Asia, with ASEAN continuing at its core. This extension was not only in terms of geographical area, but also in terms of the topics considered, which expanded from just trade cooperation to include wider economic and security cooperation, political partnerships and physical connectivity. With this development, Prime Minister Manmohan Singh asserted that the LEP was 'not merely an external economic policy, it is also a strategic shift in India's vision of the world and India's place in the evolving global economy.'[36] Later, in 2014, the Modi government's rebranding of the LEP into the Act East Policy (AEP) further enhanced the importance of East Asia for India. Beginning as a simple framework to expand trade cooperation within the region, the LEP has gradually grown to form a cornerstone of Indian strategic doctrine, working to expand economic and security integration within the region, and will continue to be critical for India for its evolving position on the international stage.

1992

47. INDIA TRANSITIONS ITS STRATEGY TOWARDS THE GLOBAL ECONOMIC ORDER

India's approach to the global economic order evolved considerably in the first five decades after Independence. The post-Second World War global economic order was initially established under what John Ruggie describes as an 'embedded liberalism', which was designed to support multilateral trade liberalization, while also permitting limited state intervention in domestic markets to prevent market failure. The General Agreement on Tariffs and Trade (GATT) was established within this ideational framework in 1947, and was designed to find a balance between the binaries of free trade and protectionism. Although India joined the GATT as a founding member, its proclivity towards protectionism broadly characterized its first four and a half decades. The embedded liberal compromise eventually gave way in the 1970s with the rise of stagflation,[37] as Keynesian supply-side solutions to counter a fall in unemployment could no longer function alongside the rising inflation.[38] Led by the Thatcher and the Reagan governments in the 1970s–80s, the embedded liberal compromise was replaced by a purer form of liberalism, which called for decreased state intervention coupled with a strong focus on market forces.

The Uruguay Round (1986–94), the GATT's eighth and final round of multilateral trade negotiations, is viewed by many to have marked this transition in the global economic system. The role of the GATT had transformed from being focused on just reducing tariff and non-tariff barriers to trade, to focusing on 'new issues', which included services, investment, and intellectual property. The new issues required the subscribing governments to make substantive changes to their economic policies and domestic legislation. The Uruguay Round, starting in 1986, was completed with the signing of the Marrakesh Agreement in 1994, leading to the establishment of, and the GATT's replacement by, the World Trade Organization (WTO) in 1995. The creation of the WTO was a remarkable departure from its antecedent, with its dispute-settlement mechanism and the principle of 'single undertaking' strengthening the failing institutional structures of the global economic system, which were deteriorating under the GATT.

However, the expanded scope of the global economic system and its increased control in domestic legislation, initially proposed by the Uruguay Round, was also met with great protest from India and the rest of the developing world. The inclusion of new issues like services (GATS),[39] Trade-Related Investment Measures (TRIMS),[40] and Trade-Related Aspects of Intellectual Property Rights (TRIPS)[41] was widely criticized by India as being unfair and designed to protect the continuance of the high-value knowledge economies of the developed world. These agreements were designed to inhibit the infringement of copyrights in the developing world, an aspect that would ultimately retain the existing unequal interstate relationships between the Global North and the Global South. TRIPS was also criticized for its limiting effect on the access of medicines in the Global South, and its inhibiting effect on the transfer of technology from the developed to the developing nations.

The WTO had not simply evolved as a natural consequence of the GATT, but it was far more engineered and intrinsically different from the latter. Nitsan Chorev describes the Uruguay Round and the eventual creation of the WTO as a 'turning point in the governance of trade under neoliberal globalism, from a "trade liberalization" project, in which governments were allowed to compensate those suffering injuries due to the process of free trade, to a trade "neo-liberalization project", where such compensation was no longer permitted.'[42] Right from the initiation of the Uruguay Round in 1986, India had firmly opposed the inclusion of substantive norms and standards for the protection of intellectual property rights within the negotiating mandate. Although New Delhi remained committed to this stance against the 'development deficit' facilitated by the Uruguay Round throughout the remainder of the 1980s, the early 1990s saw a significant shift with New Delhi's eventual subscription to the WTO in 1995.

The rationale for India's policy shift and its benefits have remained disputed. While a majority of scholars view this shift in economic policy as a consequence of India's economic liberalization after the July 1991 budget, others perceive this as a submission to the principle of the single undertaking, under which states could no longer pick and choose what they would like to subscribe to. According to this perspective, the benefits of being integrated in the international economic system simply outweighed the disadvantages of subscribing to agreements like TRIPS.

A.V. Ganesan[43] notes that other factors that also encouraged this policy change included the pressure exerted by the United States. The US had placed India on its priority list from 1989 and moved it to the even worse status of Priority Foreign Country due to the lack of pharmaceutical patent protection in India. Ganesan notes that the fear of punitive and retaliatory action by the US against India, and its garment and other exports to the US, was prevalent. Added to this, against the backdrop of a new unipolar world under American supremacy, New Delhi had been actively cultivating its relationship with the US, which was growing in a positive direction with several scientific and technical collaborations already in place. Ganesan also proposes that a palpable change had taken place across the developing world with many nations facing pressures from a new unipolar system, similar to those faced by India.

Furthermore, with the demise of the Soviet Union and the end of the Cold War, it was crucial for India to be on the right side of what was then expected to be the end of history. The neoliberal world was seen as one without an alternative and an enduring reality in the new post-Cold War era. Notwithstanding why India chose to change its policies, its decision to join the WTO reverberated across its foreign policy. Although there were trade-offs, India's participation in the WTO has, in the decades that followed, boosted its integration into the global economy, helping its economic interlinkages proliferate and its economy grow rapidly. Its participation was also crucial to cement its place in the post-Cold War global order, and socialize itself into the new US-led unipolar world system that had been created.

48. INDIA ESTABLISHES FULL DIPLOMATIC RELATIONS WITH ISRAEL

In January 1992, the P.V. Narasimha Rao government took the momentous decision of establishing full diplomatic relations with the state of Israel. The decision overturned decades of New Delhi's strategy, and its effects reverberated through the sinews of India's foreign policy. Although New Delhi had announced its recognition of Israel as far back as September 1950, and the two nations engaged in significant covert collaboration over the succeeding decades, formal diplomatic relations had still not been achieved. The significance of this was far-reaching for both nations. The relationship rapidly blossomed, with defence and agriculture at the vanguard of their bilateral engagement. Economic relations between the two nations have since proliferated, with merchandise trade diversifying and increasing from $200 million in 1992 to $10.77 billion in 2022–23 (excluding defence).

For New Delhi, the enhancement of this relationship was critical to its geopolitical and regional security calculus, especially against the backdrop of the dismemberment of the Soviet Union. For Israel, India's diplomatic approval and the enhancement of the ties between the two nations were perceived as critical for its bid to socialize itself in the milieu of the wider Global South, which had generally remained sympathetic to the Palestinian position. This change also took place against the backdrop of significant developments in the Israel-Palestine peace process, with Israel and Palestine signing two interim agreements, known as the Oslo Accords, in 1993 and 1995. In retrospect, while Tel Aviv's growing relationship with New Delhi did not help it break into the ranks of the Global South, the developing bilateral relationship has remained geopolitically important for Tel Aviv's bid for wider international engagement.

New Delhi's forty-five-year delay in establishing full diplomatic relations with Israel was primarily caused by its historical sympathies for the Palestinian cause. There has been significant policy continuity vis-à-vis India's support for the Palestinian cause, with its more recent co-sponsorship at the United Nations General Assembly in 2012 for a resolution upgrading its status as a 'non-member state'. India was a founding member of the Non-Aligned Movement and a global champion of decolonization and the anti-colonial movement that spread after the end of the Second World War. The plight of the Palestinian people could simply not be overlooked. New Delhi's principled stance and domestic political conditions at the time also made it impossible for it to accept the creation of a state based on religious grounds, as it was perceived to be congruous to the justification given for the creation of Pakistan.

Growing from its initial stance of principled idealism, New Delhi's anti-Israel stance also soon became part of a more pragmatic strategy to neutralize Islamabad's influence across the Arab world. The latter had increasingly become an important stakeholder in India's foreign policy, with not only India's growing interlinkages with it for reasons of energy security, but also because of significant foreign remittances from India's diaspora that was vital in maintaining its foreign exchange reserves. Subsequently, India was the first non-Arab nation to recognize both the Palestine Liberation Organization (PLO) in 1974 and the state of Palestine in 1988, as proclaimed by the PLO. The era of the Cold War did not help either, with the US's patronage of Israel and India's growing sympathies for the Soviet Union. Notwithstanding India's official position on Israel, the two nations had continued to engage covertly, with Israel supporting India with provisions during its conflicts with China and Pakistan in the 1960s and 1970s.

Within this context, this significant transition in India's diplomatic strategy was remarkable. While initial probes for greater collaboration were made by the Rajiv Gandhi government in the late 1980s, complex exogenous and endogenous transformations in the early 1990s provided it with its critical mass. India's expanding interest in the West in the late 1980s, accompanied by its worsening economic conditions and the eventual liberalization of its economy in 1991, had seen it 'open up' to the rest of the world. Geopolitically, the fall of the Berlin Wall, the subsequent end of the Cold War, and the wave of neoliberalism, as well as the rise of American hegemony had shaken the international order to its core. Faced with these significant internal and external disruptions, New Delhi had little choice but to recreate its foreign policy. India's new external strategy naturally prioritized the development of its relationship with Washington, coupled with its engagement with nations within its region through the Look East Policy. The end of the Cold War had also brought an end to India's Third World project and made the ideas of non-alignment irrelevant. Given the close relationship between Israel and the US, Israel's developed defence industry, and its mature economy, the establishment of relations and greater cooperation seemed simply necessary for India.

The decision taken by the Narasimha Rao government remains a landmark one, signposting a significant development in India's external strategy. The relationship has gradually grown to be pivotal for India, with expanding cooperation in trade, counter-terrorism, defence, agriculture, research and health, among others. Although the succeeding governments continued to patronize these expanding interlinkages, New Delhi's foreign policy has also continued to tread a careful line in the wider Gulf region, between the GCC,[44] Israel and Iran. Notably, between 1998 and 2014, the highest level of visits between India and Israel that took place were at the foreign minister level in 2000 and 2001. Since 2014 the relationship has grown significantly, and has become more publicized, with the Narendra Modi government's effort to de-link the Israel and Palestine equation and maintain an independent policy towards both.

1996

49. INDIA ABSTAINS FROM SIGNING THE COMPREHENSIVE NUCLEAR-TEST-BAN TREATY

The Comprehensive Nuclear-Test-Ban Treaty (CTBT) was introduced and opened for signatures in September 1996, at the UN General Assembly, as a multilateral treaty urging each party 'not to carry out any nuclear weapon test explosion or any other nuclear explosion, and to prohibit and prevent any such nuclear explosion at any place under its jurisdiction or control', and 'to refrain from causing, encouraging, or in any way participating in the carrying out of any nuclear weapon test explosion or any other nuclear explosion.'[45] The CTBT had gone a step further than its precursor, the Partial Test Ban Treaty (PTBT) of 1963, by prohibiting nuclear tests in all environments including those carried out underground.[46]

Article IV of the treaty states that it is to enter into force 180 days after its ratification by all Annex 2 states.[47] Unfortunately, out of the Annex 2 states, as of 2024,[48] ratification is still awaited from China, Egypt, Iran, Israel, Russia and the United States. India, Pakistan and North Korea are yet to become signatories to the treaty. This has meant that the CTBT has not yet entered into force, and has remained unimplemented heretofore. India's decision to exclude itself from the CTBT has remained a contentious issue that has permeated discussions around the nuclear question beyond New Delhi's strategic circles, and into the realms of public debate.

India's stance on nuclear disarmament has remained unambiguous since Prime Minister Nehru's internationally trailblazing call for a 'standstill agreement' on testing in 1954. By the 1970s, the efficacy of the Non-Proliferation Treaty (NPT) and PTBT in controlling nuclear weapons became increasingly questioned, against the backdrop of an unprecedented and continuing nuclear arms race, the deterioration of relations between the two Cold War blocs, and the newer doctrines of a 'winnable' and 'limited' nuclear war. Later, in 1988, India participated in the Six Nation Initiative, which requested the UN to convene a special conference to consider amending the PTBT to make it comprehensive. While this conference failed to reach an agreement on the PTBT, the UNGA in 1993 unanimously adopted a resolution calling on the Conference on Disarmament (CD)[49] to negotiate a CTBT at the earliest.

The CD was expanded to include sixty-four members and began negotiations on the CTBT in January 1994. While India enthusiastically participated in the process, in August 1996, due to serious differences in the final CTBT text, India along with Iran blocked consensus. Disregarding the general norm of only draft texts being adopted by consensus, and despite India's strong protests, the president of the CD made the decision to forward the disputed text to the UNGA in September 1996, which was subsequently adopted and made open to signatures later that month.

The rationale for India's protest and abstinence from supporting the resolution has remained complex, with several competing and complementary factors. This disagreement is in line with India's steadfast position on the importance of the linkage between CTBT and nuclear disarmament, maintaining that a genuine CTBT should be linked to a time-bound nuclear disarmament programme. India's position on this has remained constant, right from the 1970s to Rajiv Gandhi's proposed nuclear disarmament plan of 1988 (see Note 44). At the plenary meeting of the CD to discuss the CTBT in August 1996, Arundhati Ghose[50] stated:

> We have always believed that the objective of a CTBT was to bring about an end to nuclear weapons development.

> We are all aware that nuclear explosion technology is only one of the technologies available to the nuclear weapon states. Technologies relating to sub-critical testing, advanced computer simulation using extensive data relating to previous explosive testing and weapon related applications of laser ignition will lead to fourth generation nuclear weapons, even with a ban on explosive testing. It is a fact that weapons related R and D in these technologies is being promoted. Our objective therefore was a truly Comprehensive Test Ban Treaty rather than merely a nuclear test explosion ban treaty... Today underground explosion technology has the same relevance to halting development of nuclear weapons by the nuclear weapon states as banning atmospheric tests did in 1963. A truly comprehensive treaty should have fossilised the technology of nuclear weapons. Despite our efforts, these concerns were not addressed and nor did India's proposals receive adequate consideration... As a result we were obliged to reiterate that India could not subscribe to the Chairman's draft Treaty text [...] Our commitment to nuclear disarmament by continuing to work towards achieving the objective of a nuclear weapon-free world, remains undiminished.[51]

Fundamentally, India's inability to subscribe to the treaty stemmed from the treaty's incapacity to address the global nuclear disarmament in a more comprehensive manner, as seen from India's principled stance. Added to this concern, others point out, was also the fact that the text of the treaty included considerable ambiguities regarding the meaning of technical terms and phrases that left it open to interpretation.[52] N.D. Jayaprakash proposes that this was not due to oversight but specifically designed by the US, which, being the predominant power at the time, held considerable sway during the drafting phase in the CD.

A document sent by the US President to the US senate in September 1997, explaining the US interpretation of the treaty, described that 'the US decided at the outset of negotiations that is was unnecessary, and probably would be problematic, to seek to include a definition in the Treaty text of a "nuclear weapon test explosion or any other nuclear explosion" for the purpose of specifying in technical terms what is prohibited by the Treaty'. He further stated that the treaty does 'not prohibit any activities not involving nuclear explosions that are required to maintain the safety, security, and reliability of the US stockpile, to include: design, development, production, and manufacture of nuclear weapons'.[53] The purpose of the CTBT had transformed considerably, from its initial goal of universal nuclear disarmament to a discriminatory focus on just horizontal nuclear proliferation, similar to the NPT (see note 23).

Others note that New Delhi's motivations included more pragmatic considerations of losing its nuclear option against the backdrop of an entente between a nuclear-powered China and Pakistan, which had just a decade ago in 1986 completed the Sino-Pakistani nuclear accord (see note 38). More importantly, the discussion regarding CTBT and the wider nuclear question had entered the public domain, due to which internal domestic political pressure was faced across the political spectrum including from its scientific community, with security analysts like Brahma Chellaney stating that India's 'security interests demand that either India live in a world moving toward complete nuclear disarmament or it build nuclear weapons [sic]'.[54]

India's decision to remain removed from the CTBT, and consequently obstruct its implementation, has remained an important landmark of the continuity in its nuclear policy that demanded that any agreement to end testing must be linked to the global elimination of nuclear weapons. The debate and controversy around the CTBT arguably also reignited the debate around the wider nuclear question for India's own internal security, with it ultimately making the decision to go ahead, in 1998, with the Pokhran-II tests, finally announcing itself as a full-fledged nuclear state.

1997

50. THE BISTEC IS BORN

At a ministerial meeting held in Bangkok in June 1997 under the aegis of New Delhi, a regional organization called BISTEC was formed, consisting of Bangladesh, India, Sri Lanka and Thailand. In December that year, the grouping was expanded to include Myanmar and it was renamed BIMSTEC.[55] The core purpose of the grouping was to cater to greater socio-economic cooperation and expand interlinkages for nations dependent on the Bay of Bengal. Being sector-driven, BIMSTEC initially focused on six sectors, which included trade, technology, energy, tourism, transport and fisheries. At the outset, the creation of BIMSTEC was an attempt to capture the synergies of land and maritime contiguity amongst the people of the region who historically had close cultural and commercial ties. The initial hope was that this grouping would facilitate enhanced ties between the two ASEAN[56] and three SAARC[57] nations.

The decade after the end of the Cold War had seen a growing trend of regionalism, with regional organizations going from strength to strength. The creation of organizations like the World Trade Organization (WTO) in 1995 and the European Union (EU), formally established with the signing of the Maastricht Treaty in 1992, were representative of this shift. The neoliberal triumph, and the narrative of there being no alternative, had pervaded the international system. Regional integration and the expanding trade interlinkages with more open economies had underpinned the BIMSTEC initiative. At the first summit held in 2004, the member nations signed a framework agreement to create a free trade area by 2017.

The creation of BIMSTEC was an important moment in the evolution of New Delhi's foreign policy. The end of the Cold War, coupled with domestic economic turmoil and the subsequent restructuring, had precipitated a profound transformation in how New Delhi approached the world. Launched in 1991, India's Look East Policy was now well underway, with New Delhi becoming a full dialogue partner of ASEAN, participating in the ASEAN Post-Ministerial Conference and the ASEAN Regional Forum (ARF) in 1996. The BIMSTEC initiative was a natural evolution of this broader strategy, also marking a significant achievement of the first stage of the Look East Policy in which New Delhi aimed to rebuild its economic relations with Southeast Asia, to diversify its trade away from its main trading partners in Europe and North America. In its second phase, which started around 1998, India sought to forge stronger relationships with Cambodia, Laos, Myanmar and Vietnam (CLMV) and further expand its engagement with ASEAN.

While one of the two principles of BIMSTEC states that 'cooperation within the BIMSTEC will be complementary to and not be a substitute for bilateral, sub-regional, regional or multilateral cooperation involving the Member States', several scholars point out its de facto replacement, in function, of the consistently hamstrung SAARC setup in 1985 (see note 37). With the historically antagonistic relationship between India and Pakistan, the exclusion of the latter in BIMSTEC effectively removed one of the key obstructionist and persistent impediments to regional cooperation. More importantly, BIMSTEC was also an outcome of what has, in retrospect, been termed as New Delhi's Gujral Doctrine.[58] Inder Kumar Gujral heavily influenced Indian foreign policy between 1996 and 1998. He was India's minister of external affairs between 1989 and 1990, and again in 1996, and then India's prime minister from 1997 to 1998, during which time he also held the portfolio for external affairs. The Gujral Doctrine, as described by himself in 1997, proposed:

> First, with its neighbours like Bangladesh, Bhutan, Maldives, Nepal and Sri Lanka, India does not ask for reciprocity, but gives and accommodates what it can in good faith and trust. Second, we believe that no South Asian country should allow its territory to be used against the interests of another

> country of the region. Third, that none should interfere in the internal affairs of another. Fourth, all South Asian countries must respect each other's territorial integrity and sovereignty. And finally, they should settle all their disputes through peaceful bilateral negotiations.[59]

Further explaining this approach in his autobiography, Gujral states that 'the logic behind the Gujral Doctrine was that since we had to face two hostile neighbours in the north and the west, we had to be at "total peace" with all other immediate neighbours in order to contain Pakistan's and China's influence in the region'.[60] This doctrine was pivotal in redirecting India's focus away from Pakistan, for which it has received considerable criticism in retrospect, and intensified its focus beyond its immediate borders. BIMSTEC was, in essence, one of the achievements of this doctrine. I.K. Gujral was able to better India's relations with Nepal, Sri Lanka and Bangladesh. The relationship with the first two had been strained with the economic blockade with Nepal (see note 42), and its intervention in the Sri Lankan civil war (see note 40).

The creation of BIMSTEC was symbolic of the rapprochement, rekindling, and reconfirmation of solidarity amongst India's key neighbours, in a bid to strengthen regional security and prevent being strategically encircled by a potentially expanding Chinese influence. BIMSTEC continues to be New Delhi's favoured platform for regional cooperation, with the collaboration among the nations strengthening in the decades to follow.

1998

51. POKHRAN-II: INDIA CROSSES THE NUCLEAR RUBICON

> Today, at 15:45 hours, India conducted three underground nuclear tests in the Pokhran range. The tests conducted

> today were with a fission device, a low yield device and a thermonuclear device. The measured yields are in line with expected values. Measurements have also confirmed that there was no release of radioactivity into the atmosphere. These were contained explosions like the experiment conducted in May 1974. I warmly congratulate the scientists and engineers who have carried out these successful tests.[61]

With this announcement on 11 May 1998, the recently elected prime minister, Atal Bihari Vajpayee, publicly declared that India had finally crossed the nuclear Rubicon. Following this, on 13 May the tests were completed, with the setting-off of a total of five underground nuclear devices of advanced weapon design in Pokhran, Rajasthan. Occurring twenty-four years after India's first test, also conducted in Pokhran (see note 28), the May 1998 tests, commonly referred to as Pokhran-II, profoundly and irreversibly transformed India's nuclear policy, security environment and broader foreign policy. Subsequent to this, on 28 and 30 May, Pakistan detonated five nuclear devices and followed India to become the seventh nation to successfully develop and test nuclear weapons.

While both sets of tests were received with widespread domestic celebration in their respective countries, they received equally widespread international condemnation. Sanctions were levied on both India and Pakistan by the United States and Japan. Fourteen countries, including Australia, Germany, Japan, Denmark and Sweden, suspended bilateral aid programmes for both nations. The Group of Seven (G7) nations, along with several non-G7 nations, joined the US in opposing any new non-humanitarian lending to India and Pakistan by the World Bank, the International Monetary Fund (IMF), and the Asian Development Bank (ADB).[62]

Considering the extent of the diplomatic and economic fallout of these tests, and given that India ostensibly had the ability to weaponize its nuclear capability right from its first test in 1974, the test's timing and rationale have been greatly debated. Ever since 1974, India had proved its willingness to reserve the right to weaponize its nuclear capability, but it had not since overtly declared its intent to do so. Later, in the mid-1990s, the Narasimha Rao government permitted the preparations for carrying out a test in December 1995, which was allegedly detected by American reconnaissance satellites and subsequently stopped under US pressure.[63]

Deterministically, New Delhi's security environment had fundamentally transformed since the beginning of the 1990s, with domestic separatist challenges, economic and political instability, and the fall of the Soviet Union, which had removed an important balancing factor for China within the Asian security environment. Against the backdrop of China's overt patronage of Pakistan, a general consensus exists that one of the immediate triggers for India weaponizing its nuclear capability lay in Pakistan testing a North Korean-made intermediate-range ballistic missile, named Ghauri, on 6 April 1998.[64] This strengthened perceptions of the deterioration of New Delhi's security, as the new missile, with a range of 1,500 kilometres, gave Islamabad the capability to target twenty-six Indian cities.

New Delhi's official stance also admitted that its perceptions about its own security were an important driver in its decision to go nuclear. Just about a week before Pokhran-II, the Indian defence minister at the time, George Fernandes, described China as 'potential threat No. 1' and urged India to abandon its 'careless and casual attitude', and further stated that 'Chinese military activities and alliances, especially those involving Pakistan, Burma, and Tibet, are encircling India'.[65] Notably, after the event, in a letter to the US President Bill Clinton, Prime Minister Vajpayee explained the rationale of the tests, declaring:

> I have been deeply concerned at the deteriorating security environment, specially the nuclear environment, faced by India for some years past. We have an overt nuclear weapon state on our borders, a state which committed armed aggression

> against India in 1962. Although our relations with that country have improved in the last decade or so, an atmosphere of distrust persists mainly due to the unresolved border problem. To add to the distrust that country has materially helped another neighbour of ours to become a covert nuclear weapons state. At the hands of this bitter neighbour we have suffered three aggressions in the last 50 years. And for the last ten years we have been the victim of unremitting terrorism and militancy sponsored by it in several parts of our country, specially Punjab and Jammu & Kashmir.[66]

Others have also pointed out the dire instability of India's economic and political situation since the early 1990s as an exacerbating factor in the nation's perceived deterioration of its security milieu. Notwithstanding domestic precarity, undeniably several external factors contributed to this strategic vulnerability. Pakistan's weapon expansion and its nuclear programme had continued over the preceding two decades, unhindered by any international censure. With the Sino-Pakistani nuclear accord of 1986, Beijing's support for Islamabad's nuclear ambitions no longer remained covert (see note 38). Initially, the US turned a blind eye to these activities, as Pakistan was a crucial part of the US-Afghanistan policy. Concerningly for India, the end of the Cold War removed the Soviet Union as a key balancer for China in the region. Furthermore, a Sino-US rapprochement, and the strengthening of their relations that had begun in the 1970s, only continued to develop in the 1990s. India found itself, in the 1990s, to have become a 'lonely' and 'friendless' power.[67] The passing of the Brown Amendment in 1995 under the Clinton administration in the US only worsened India's apprehensions about its increasing regional vulnerability.[68]

Others have pointed out that India's options for engaging the nuclear option had significantly narrowed with considerable international pressure, led by the US. At the twenty-five-year review for the Non-Proliferation Treaty (NPT) in 1995, the

US sought and successfully manoeuvred its 'unconditional and indefinite extension'.[69] The discussions and negotiations over the Comprehensive Nuclear-Test-Ban Treaty that went on for two years before its adoption by the UN in 1996, had continued to strain India's policy manoeuvrability (see note 49). Both these treaties provided for a discriminatory ban on proliferation and testing, respectively, and did little to address a universal nuclear disarmament or provide any guarantees to non-nuclear states.[70]

Notwithstanding the plethora of reasons that motivated India to cross the nuclear Rubicon, an undeniable outcome was Pakistan's decision to follow suit. In 2003, India published its Official Nuclear Doctrine which confirmed its position of 'No First Use', corroborated that it would 'maintain a credible minimum deterrent', and declared that 'nuclear weapons will only be used in retaliation against a nuclear attack on Indian territory or on Indian forces anywhere'.[71] The decision to develop and weaponize its nuclear capability has had an extraordinary impact on not only India's foreign policy, but also the broader area of Asian security. It irreversibly transformed the security dynamics of the continent, and has continued to be a core part of India's security strategy.

1999

52. THE LAHORE DECLARATION

The Lahore Declaration was signed between Indian Prime Minister Atal Bihari Vajpayee and Pakistani Prime Minister Nawaz Sharif on 21 February 1999, around eight months after both nations weaponized their nuclear capabilities. The summit was, quintessentially, a breakthrough in the Indo-Pakistani relationship, which had remained strained since both nations conducted the nuclear tests in May 1998 (see note 51). Notably, the declaration stated that both nations were 'committed to the objective of universal nuclear disarmament and non-proliferation'.

The summit concluded with the announcement of the Lahore Declaration, the release of a joint statement by both prime ministers, and the issuing of a memorandum of understanding by the foreign secretaries of the two nations.[72]

The accord concluded a variety of confidence-building measures, which included a mutual understanding on the development of nuclear arsenals, the prevention of incidents at sea, and an agreement on providing each other with advance notice of ballistic missile flight tests and accidental or unauthorized use of nuclear weapons. The joint statement also included decisions taken by both sides on the coordination of their approaches to the World Trade Organization (WTO), collaboration in the field of information technology, liberalizing the bilateral visa and travel regimes, periodic discussions about all mutual concerns and nuclear-related issues, and the creation of a ministerial-level two-member committee to examine humanitarian issues relating to missing prisoners of war and civilian detainees. The summit was received positively by both nations, and has been described as an important step towards normalizing the relations between them.

The relations between the two nations had remained tense in the previous decades, with limited progress between 1990 and 1994, and some attempts made in 1997, but all to no avail. The nuclear weapon testing that both the nations conducted in May 1998 only exacerbated bilateral tensions. Subsequently, on 23 September later that year, the prime ministers of both nations met on the sidelines of the UNGA in New York and issued a guarded joint statement. Although it did not mention any nuclear-related issues, it did declare that both leaders believed that 'an environment of durable peace and security was in the supreme interest of both India and Pakistan, and of the region as a whole'. Against this backdrop, the thaw of 1999 and its profound breakthrough in terms of the commitments that were made demonstrated the presence of considerable political will on both sides. The accord realized the promise of finally normalizing relations and, for a short period, evidenced the effectiveness of nuclear deterrence[73] in diminishing hostilities and bringing historical antagonists to the negotiating table.

Strong political will on both sides drove the agreement, with both nations making significant concessions in their positions. Notably, Pakistan consented to the inclusion of terrorism and India to the inclusion of Kashmir in the agreement's text.[74] Amit Baruah writes in *The Hindu,* on 3 April 1999, that an agreement was reached in which 'Mr A.B. Vajpayee will not refer to Kashmir as an integral part of India in public, Mr Nawaz Sharif will reciprocate by not mentioning the US resolutions on Kashmir.' [75]

Notwithstanding the political will on both sides to better relations, the Pakistani prime minister's inability to garner the support of his military chiefs in this effort was notable, with the conspicuous absence of the latter at the reception for the Indian prime minister. Pakistani military chiefs did not support the peace process, and just three months later organized an infiltration into Indian territory, with Pakistani troops crossing the Line of Control in Kargil, dampening any chances of further rapprochement and beginning a brutal three-month war. Later, on 14 October 1999, with a coup d'état, the Pakistani army replaced Pakistani Prime Minister Sharif with Gen. Pervez Musharraf. Umair Khalil concludes that an important lesson from the failure of the Lahore Declaration is that 'the Government of Pakistan cannot make substantial progress in terms of relations with India without seeking approval of the [Pakistani] military'.[76]

The Lahore Declaration is viewed as one of the most transformational agreements in the pursuit of peace between India and Pakistan. The impact of the accord on the foreign policy of both nations is compared with that of the Tashkent Agreement of 1965 (see note 19), and the Simla Agreement of 1972 (see note 27). In spite of its short duration, with the three-month-long Kargil War breaking out in May 1999, the Lahore Declaration laid out the basic framework of cooperation known as the composite and integrated dialogue process, which has since continued to be used to engage on matters of mutual concern.

Although New Delhi was deeply disillusioned with the turn of events after the Lahore Declaration, as the Kargil War broke out, the accord continues to remain an important reference for engagement between the two nations, extending the spirit of the Simla Agreement and keeping aflame the potential for greater rapprochement and enhancement of relations. The event remains a key landmark, symbolic of New Delhi's political will and the complex and medieval relationship between the Pakistani military and its civil authorities, which continue to hamstring any movement in a positive direction.

53. THE KARGIL WAR

The Kargil War took place in the Kargil district of Kashmir and along the Line of Control (LOC), and lasted about three months, beginning in May 1999, just three months after the signing of the Lahore Declaration. This was the fourth, and most recent, war fought between India and Pakistan, succeeding the wars of 1948, 1965 and 1971. Pakistan had been waging a proxy war in Kashmir since 1987, cultivating a growing militancy within the region by supporting infiltration. In the beginning of the summer of 1999, Pakistan began occupying Indian forward posts on the Indian side of the LOC.[77] The overt purpose of this manoeuvre was to occupy the high-altitude areas of Kargil and facilitate the interdiction of National Highway 1A, a key highway connecting Srinagar (in Kashmir) with Leh (in Ladakh). Strategically, this would bolster anti-India militancy and force India to vacate the Siachen Glacier, which had been occupied since the Indian Army's Operation Meghdoot in 1984 (see note 35).

Following a wholescale retreat by the Pakistani forces, the war culminated in July 1999, with India successfully defending its territory and maintaining the status quo of the LOC. New Delhi's strong yet restrained response, along with the large-scale international censure of Pakistan's actions and US pressure on Islamabad, prevented any further escalation. Throughout the war, in the course of India's response its army and air force did not cross the LOC, and refrained from entering Pakistani territory or its airspace. The Indian Air Force's Operation Safed Sagar, the Indian Army's Operation Vijay, and the Indian Navy's Operation Talwar provided the necessary firepower and strategic manoeuvring required to contain and repel any further Pakistani adventurism.

The international community widely criticized Pakistan for its unliteral aggression, which had completely derailed the three-month-old Lahore Declaration's significant contribution to the peace process. India's diplomatic standing and its decision to show restraint in its response was widely commended, and backed by nations across the globe, like Russia, Israel, Chile and France, as well as groups like ASEAN.[78] The Kargil War has continued to represent a profound moment for South Asian security, removing the likelihood for regional stability which the Lahore Declaration had envisioned, enhancing New Delhi's diplomatic position, transforming the Indo-US relationship, and shaping the debate around nuclear weapons in South Asia.

From a Pakistani perspective, its delinquency and egregious miscalculations continue to exist in a complex web of explanations and justifications. Islamabad initially reacted with plausible deniability, maintaining that the infiltrators were not a part of its armed forces, and were instead the Mujahideen. While this position was soon withdrawn, Prime Minister Nawaz Sharif claimed that he had not been informed of this action, and actually learnt of it from an urgent call with his Indian counterpart in May 1999. Sharif alleged that nearly all senior commanders and officials were kept in the dark about the 'ill-conceived, ill-planned and ill-executed misadventure of army chief Gen Pervez Musharraf'.[79]

Musharraf, on the other hand, claimed that Sharif had been

informed of the plans on 5 February 1999.[80] Benazir Bhutto alleged that during her premiership (1993–96), Musharraf, as Director General of Military Operations, had presented the Kargil plans which were vetoed by her. Bhutto further stated that the 'Taliban regrouped under Musharraf's watch, [and] militants started dictating' Pakistani foreign policy.[81] No commissions or inquiries were carried out by Pakistan to review the war. Notwithstanding the competing narratives about the roots of this decision, the political fallout for Islamabad was far-reaching, with the ascendency of Gen. Musharraf through the fourth coup d'état in the nation's fifty-two-year history.

For India, its defence of the LOC in Kargil was wholly successful, and the restraint it showed thereafter was testament to the status it strived for as a responsible nuclear power state. The war was significant for New Delhi's security strategy, as it exposed the clear inefficiencies in its military preparedness and intelligence capabilities. On 29 July 1999, New Delhi commissioned the Kargil Review Committee under K. Subrahmanyam, which ran a wholesale review of the sequence of events of the Kargil War. The Committee found inefficiencies in inter-agency coordination and recommended a complete review of the national security system in its entirety.

The Kargil War remains a pivotal event in Indo-Pakistani relationship, and an important landmark for Indian foreign policy. Academic discourse around South Asian nuclear proliferation has also been rooted in the events of the Kargil War. Proliferation optimists argue that the possession of nuclear weapons helped in restraining further escalation, as the nations were dissuaded by the fear that war may escalate to the nuclear level.[82] Others like S. Paul Kapur argue more pessimistically that nuclear weapons had only further destabilized the region. This happened because nuclear weapons shielded Pakistan from an all-out Indian retaliation while also bringing the India-Pakistan dispute into the international spotlight, emboldening Pakistan to adopt a more aggressive stance.

Furthermore, Pakistan's new low-intensity conflict strategy had forced India to make significant changes in its conventional military capabilities and postures, creating the foundation for increased security competition and further instability.[83]

A significant outcome for India's foreign policy was New Delhi's strengthened relationship with Washington.[84] In a summit between Sharif and President Bill Clinton on 4 July 1999, instead of extending the support that was expected, President Clinton affirmed that unless Islamabad withdrew its forces to the previous status quo behind the LOC, Washington would blame Islamabad for the war. Clinton further threatened to speak of Islamabad's relationship with the Al-Qaeda and Osama Bin Laden. This was representative of a significant shift in US policy towards the subcontinent.

General Musharraf's coup d'état only further cemented US misgivings about Pakistan's inclination towards supporting regional instability. The ongoing dialogue on nuclear proliferation that had begun between the US and India in June 1998 expanded to include broader economic and strategic cooperation. The dialogue was led by the US Deputy Secretary of State Strobe Talbot and the Indian Minister of External Affairs Jaswant Singh, who met fourteen times between June 1998 and September 2000. The stage was set for President Clinton's multi-day trip to India, and a few hours-long stopover at Pakistan. Clinton's trip in 2000 broke the decades-long absence of US presidential trips to India, and set a new precedent for his successors.

2001

54. THE ATTACK ON THE INDIAN PARLIAMENT

After the Kargil War India and Pakistan restarted the peace process, at the heart of which was the Agra Summit held in July 2001. A wide variety of topics were discussed here which included cross-border terrorism, the Kashmir issue, and the reduction of nuclear arsenals. Although no agreements were reached at the end of the summit, the initiative was important to symbolize the intent and the willingness of both governments to engage on key bilateral issues. Unfortunately, much like how Pakistani infiltration and the subsequent Kargil War undid the progress of the Lahore Declaration in 1999, a series of terrorist attacks on Indian soil put paid to any further progress after the Agra Summit in 2001.

On 1 October 2001, terrorist groups trained and funded by Pakistan,[85] namely Lashkar-e-Taiba (LeT) and Jaish-e-Mohammed (JeM),[86] organized a terrorist attack on the Kashmir state legislature. A couple of months later, on 13 December, the groups went a step further and carried out another terrorist attack on the Indian parliament. Frustrated with diplomatic routes to address the cross-border terrorism, the Vajpayee government responded by deploying its armed forces under Operation Parakram. This operation was the first full-scale mobilization of the armed forces since the 1971 war, with the Indian Army readying for engagement and concentrating its forces towards the Line of Control and the rest of its shared border with Pakistan.

With significant US and Western pressure, General Musharraf gave a crucial televised address on 12 January 2002, in which he declared that 'no organizations will be able to carry out terrorism under the pretext of Kashmir.'[87] Musharraf further announced a ban on LeT, JeM and several other designated terrorist organizations. Other measures mentioned in the speech included the reform of Pakistani religious schools to curb extremism, and it further denounced any kind of religious intolerance from groups that supported the Taliban in Afghanistan.

Although the Vajpayee government remained sceptical of these empty promises, it decided to hold back with regard to its planned armed action and tactical strikes against terrorist outfits. However, Indian troops were not withdrawn, as the Indian Defence Minister George Fernandes wanted to first see concrete steps to end cross-border terrorism and also be assured of the extradition from Pakistan of any Indian nationals suspected of terrorist activity.[88] Unfortunately, far from these conditions being met, an increase in Pakistani infiltration from April onwards demonstrated to the Indian government that Musharraf's speech was disingenuous and mere rhetoric to pacify the US.

On 14 May 2002, terrorists brutally massacred twenty-three people, including women and children from army families, at the Kaluchak army base in Kashmir. This diabolical act led to another period of high tension in which the Pakistani ambassador was expelled, and later, on 22 May, Vajpayee declared that it was 'now time for a decisive fight'.[89] Pakistan upped the ante on 25–26 May with the testing of nuclear-capable ballistic missiles. There was widespread belief that an Indian invasion was imminent, with invasion plans that were far more significant than during the January tensions. Musharraf addressed the nation again on 27 May in which he conciliatorily stated that Islamabad wanted peace in the region, and did not want, or would initiate, war, making further assurances that 'Pakistan will never allow the export of terrorism anywhere in the world from within Pakistan'.[90]

Although heavy shelling continued on both sides, by the beginning of June, under heavy international pressure and on the basis of confirmations secured by the US that Musharraf would 'permanently' end cross-border infiltration,[91] both nations inched away from the brink of conflict. While the period of 'twin tensions' had come to an end, India continued its heightened presence on its borders with Pakistan. The extent and the duration of the mobilization from December 2001 to June 2002 had impacted both sides significantly, in terms of men, money and material.

Throughout this period, Pakistan had refused to accept responsibility for these attacks or any support given to these groups. Realizing the seriousness of New Delhi's intent to wage war and given its superior military-fiscal machine, stronger economy, and superior conventional capabilities, Islamabad had at several points threatened the use of nuclear weapons. The military standoff and the nuclear rhetoric had escalated to the extent that it was not only the first nuclear standoff of the twenty-first century, but its scale and seriousness were also widely compared to the Cuban Missile Crisis of 1962 between the US and the Soviet Union.

From the Vajpayee government's perspective, the Kargil War and the twin terrorist attacks had removed the remnants of faith that existed with regard to improving relations between New Delhi and Islamabad. Militarily, New Delhi also took away lessons regarding its deployment and its military strategy. Operation Parakram was commonly seen to have been unsuccessful in its bid to neutralize terrorist targets due to its slow mobilization of the strike corps and the inability of its defensive positions to execute the required strikes. By 2004, India's generally defensive military strategy, defined by the Sundarji Doctrine, had transformed into a more aggressive one with the development of a Cold Start Doctrine.[92] The new doctrine was purposed with deploying smaller-scale, quicker, and more decisive conventional operations to deter and counter terrorist attacks on Indian soil. While the existence of such a doctrine remains debated, what cannot be disregarded is India's changing approach to its military strategy, from its historically defensive inclinations.

The pressure placed by the US and the rest of the international community was pivotal in restraining an escalation into conventional, or perhaps even nuclear, war. Notably, with the recent 11 September attacks by the Al-Qaeda in New York, the US had launched a war on terrorism in Afghanistan, which was ruled by the Taliban.[93] Although the US was keen to prevent nuclear conflict, it was significantly driven to maintain peace in the region, as Pakistan had once again become a strategically important ally in its Afghanistan policy.[94] As mentioned earlier, US mediation was critical in de-escalating the situation in both January and May 2002.

The debate around nuclear proliferation in South Asia developed considerably with these events. While some have argued that deterrence proved its mettle in constraining the two nations, others have noted that it created a wholly new genre of violence inflicted by Pakistan, in the form of asymmetric terrorist activities which were low-cost and high-impact. Contrary to the many promises and affirmations about limiting terrorist activities and infiltration into India, between September 2001 and June 2004, there were forty-seven instances of terrorist attacks inflicted on India by Pakistan-based groups.[95]

The attack on the Indian parliament remains one of the most significant moments for Indian foreign policy, triggering transformations in its defence strategy, Pakistan policy, Asian security strategy, and relationship with the West. For the Vajpayee government, rapprochement from this point onwards was impossible given that it was betrayed more than thrice in less than two and a half years, in the form of the Lahore Declaration, the Agra Summit, and the successive duplicitous pledges by General Musharraf to rein in his proxies in 2002. India's restraint had enhanced its global standing and its image as a responsible nuclear power, but it was a victim to the same terror that had profoundly impacted the West. Post-9/11 US and post-13 December India had visible alignments and synergies that could be unlocked in their battle against this new global crisis. However, while referring to the US war on terror, the Indian Foreign Minister Jaswant Singh stated that it had led the US to 'excessive militarisation',[96] which, he thought, was not the answer.

2003

55. PRIME MINISTER VAJPAYEE MAKES AN OFFICIAL VISIT TO CHINA

Between 22 and 27 June 2003, Prime Minister Atal Bihari Vajpayee made a momentous visit to China, after more than a decade since the previous prime ministerial visit by Narasimha Rao in

1993. Despite occasional tensions, the interlude saw diplomatic relations incrementally develop and bilateral visits continue.[97] Using this momentum, on 24 June, Prime Minister Vajpayee and Premier Wen Jiabao signed the historic 'Declaration on Principles for Relations and Comprehensive Cooperation'.[98] The agreement enacted a profound change, resetting Sino-Indian relations, forging a consensus on a variety of bilateral, regional and global issues, and supported both sides' core interests around development, modernization, and their aspirations for great power status.[99]

Along with this declaration, the two sides also signed a memorandum of understanding on expanding border trade. The highlights of this visit were the formation of a border trade protocol to add a border crossing between Sikkim and the Tibet Autonomous Region (TAR), and the appointment of Special Representatives to explore a framework for a boundary settlement from a political perspective. While continuing with Indian policy on Tibet, initially expressed in the Panchsheel Agreement of 1954, which described it as the 'Tibet region of China' (see note 5), and the 1988 Sino-Indian Joint Communiqué, which stated that 'Tibet is an autonomous region of China' (see note 43), the declaration reiterated in unambiguous terms India's official stand on the issue. The document declared that New Delhi 'recognizes that the Tibet Autonomous Region is part of the territory of the People's Republic of China and reiterates that it does not allow Tibetans to engage in anti-China political activities in India'.

From Beijing's perspective, this agreement was greatly significant in both economic and geopolitical terms. The resumption of trans-Himalayan trade had become one of China's priorities in the region, as it would enable the development and modernization of its southern provinces, specifically the TAR, in which the Qinghai-Tibet railway line had only recently been opened to enhance access to the region.[100] Until then, TAR only had border trade with Nepal, which represented more than 70 per cent of its regional foreign trade. The reopening of the

Sikkim border would greatly boost Chinese trade in South Asia, and crucially, take the first few steps at opening up the Indian economy, one of the fastest growing with an enormous consumer base, to greater collaboration and engagement. Enabling economic development has remained inexorably linked with Beijing's regime stability, territorial integrity and domestic stability, and bridging the development gap between the coastal cities and interior regions remains a profound challenge.

Geopolitically, the growing Indo-US entente posed a dangerous development for China, which had traditionally feared encirclement or containment by competing powers.[101] With references in New Delhi to a 'China threat' also being a major rationale for the 1998 tests, strengthening Indo-US relations was a potential future challenge. However, others also point out that at the time, given China's relatively strong relationship with the US, India's threat perception would have probably not been high.[102]

For India, reopening the historical trade links between Sikkim and Tibet would be a great lift for the economy of the Sikkim state, and a powerful instrument to stimulate the wider region's development, including the northeastern Indian state of Arunachal Pradesh. More importantly, the quid pro quo of the 2003 agreement was an important step for protecting India's territorial integrity. While India had once again recognized Tibet as a part of China, the trade border agreement was seen as a tacit recognition of India's 1975 annexation and the status of Sikkim as an Indian state. In October 2003, when Prime Minister Vajpayee and his Chinese counterpart met on the sidelines of a South Asia summit in Indonesia, China deleted all references to Sikkim from its websites.[103] In 2004, China revised its cartographic depictions of Sikkim, excluding it from TAR.[104] However, others have criticized the Vajpayee government for recognizing China's position on Tibet in such absolute terms, while accepting the absence of an explicit Chinese recognition of Sikkim as an Indian state.

For New Delhi, an outcome of this was also checking the Sino-

Pakistani axis, which had gone from strength to strength since 1965. With the successive diplomatic crises that had taken place since 1998, the Kargil War, and the 2001–02 military standoff, enhancing relations with China would potentially translate into controlling the persistent cross-border terrorism that Pakistan had waged against India for over a decade.

The transformative nature of the 2003 declaration can be seen in the fact that by 2005, Sino-Indian trade had grown by more than 40 per cent annually, amounting to ₹79,000 crore by 2005–06. Estimates showed that with the reopening of the trade route through Nathu La, trade with countries of South and Southeast Asia was expected to improve the economy of the entire region, with the trade turnover increasing at least five times.[105] The declaration's importance lay in facilitating enhanced economic cooperation between the two nations, engaging in a new sphere of diplomatic activity which was inaugurated by Rajiv Gandhi's visit in 1998 (see note 43).

This event has continued to remain a landmark for Indian foreign policy, seeing China and India finally leverage and unlock the glaring synergies between the two massive economies, creating the potential for a formidable Asian alliance. The developments arising from this agreement continued to enhance bilateral relations right until the latter half of the 2010s, when China finally cast aside its veneer of a peaceful rise, forsaking its policy to 'abide time and wait', and instead transitioning to its belligerent 'wolf warrior diplomacy', aggressively advocating for its own interests and strategies like the Belt and Road initiative (BRI). China found, with its strong economy and military, that it was perhaps time to finally question American hegemony and overtly revise the rules-based global order.

Prime Minister Manmohan Singh with leaders of the BRICS nations during the summit in New Delhi in March 2012.

Source: PIB

Wave 4

2004–Present: On the Path to Global Leadership

PART I

Since the turn of the millennium, India has increasingly sought to assert itself as a key player on the global stage, reflecting its growing economic strength and strategic ambitions. This phase represents the achievement of India's long-standing quest for a prominent role in the international arena, as it balances its global leadership ambitions with its regional interests.

2004

56. THE INDIAN OCEAN TSUNAMI

On 26 December 2004, a massive tsunami struck twelve Indian Ocean countries, killing over 225,000 people and displacing 1.7 million, with the worst affected being Indonesia, Malaysia, the Maldives, Myanmar, Sri Lanka, the Seychelles, Somalia, Thailand and India. In response, the international community, comprising governments, the UN, and other multilateral agencies and NGOs, immediately mobilized relief and rescue measures for the affected population.

While dealing with the destruction caused by the tsunami on its own shores, India remained confident in its capabilities to manage the fallout in terms of both resources and providing relief. It politely refused international aid, instead suggesting that it should be rerouted to the other affected countries. While this decision was initially criticized for 'false or misplaced pride', the international community later appreciated this gesture of solidarity towards the wider region.

India became the first responder in the affected countries. It was the first country to send the navy to provide disaster relief to Sri Lanka, and announced assistance of about ₹100 crore. About 40 tons of relief supplies and three tons of medical supplies were carried by the Indian Navy to Indonesia. India also provided a relief package of ₹5 crore to the Maldives, and the Indian Navy set up medical camps and drinking water facilities there.

India's efforts to provide disaster relief to South and Southeast Asian countries were not only for humanitarian reasons, but also motivated by its historical and socio-cultural ties with the region. It was also seen as implementing its Look East Policy from the early 1990s, wherein India sought increased political, economic and security cooperation with the region, especially through ASEAN. During the tenure of the Modi government, this Look East Policy was transformed into an Act East Policy by injecting greater action and dynamism in the effort.

India's capabilities in disaster relief and its maturity in providing immediate international assistance gained international recognition. Australian security analysts described it as India's emergence as a naval superpower in the region. US President Bush called on PM Manmohan Singh to be part of a coordinated disaster response, called the Tsunami Core Group, composed of the US, Japan and Australia. The Group would identify and plug gaps in the relief processes and prevent the duplication of efforts. This Group contributed more than 40,000 personnel, in addition to helicopters, cargo ships and transport planes. It also worked closely with the

UN to channel relief efforts.

According to the then US Under Secretary of State for Political Affairs Marc Grossman, this ad hoc coalition experimented with 'transformational diplomacy', where nations came together because they had 'the resources and the desire to act effectively and quickly'.[1] This new kind of diplomacy implies an active response to new challenges that nations face, by breaking old habits and partnering with countries who share values and wish to improve people's lives.

It is important to note that the then US Secretary of State Colin Powell declined UN Secretary-General Kofi Annan's request to include China in the Tsunami Core group. Together with the 1992 Indo-US Malabar exercises, and increased maritime cooperation during 'Operation Enduring Freedom' of 2002, US efforts in the aftermath of the tsunami could be interpreted as laying down the ideational construct for what would later be referred to as the US 'rebalancing' or 'pivot to Asia'.

With the emergence of the geopolitical construct of the 'Indo-Pacific', the above-mentioned 'transformational diplomacy' of the Tsunami Core Group was revived in the form of the Quadrilateral Security Dialogue (Quad), comprising the four original members. Although it is argued to have been formed as a counter to the rising assertiveness of China in the region, the Quad commits to actively supporting an open, inclusive, stable and prosperous Indo-Pacific. Currently, the Quad partners with other countries in the region to tackle pressing challenges including climate change, humanitarian assistance and disaster relief, maritime security, and cyber security.

The lessons learnt from the tsunami led to the establishment of an Indian Tsunami Early Warning System (ITEWS) in 2007, at the Indian National Centre for Ocean Information Services (INCOIS), Hyderabad. The system detects seismic activities and disseminates advisories to all Indian Ocean rim countries, as part of the UNESCO-Intergovernmental Oceanographic Commission framework. In 2005 India also brought in the Disaster Management Act, wherein the National Disaster Response Force (NDRF) has functioned as 'Samaritan Diplomats', bringing relief to cyclone-hit Myanmar in 2008, tsunami-affected Japan in 2011, and earthquake-affected Nepal in 2015. The latest in a series of humanitarian support missions was Operation Dost in earthquake-hit Turkey and Syria in 2023. Coupled with the Vaccine Maitri Initiative during Covid, India has attained a global reputation in disaster management, resilience and relief, and humanitarian assistance.

2005

57. THE INDO-US CIVIL NUCLEAR AGREEMENT

The Indo-US Civil Nuclear Agreement emerged from the joint statement issued by Prime Minister Manmohan Singh and President Bush on July 18, 2005. While underlining India's credentials as a responsible nuclear state, the US agreed to adjust its laws and policies when working with friends and allies around international regimes, to enable civil nuclear energy cooperation and trade with India. In return, India agreed to identify and separate its civil and military nuclear facilities, and place its civilian nuclear facilities under IAEA safeguards. India also agreed to continue its unilateral moratorium on nuclear testing and refrain from the transfer of nuclear technology to other non-nuclear states.

The agreement was a significant milestone in Indo-US relations. It implicitly recognized India's status as a nuclear-weapon state, and ended years of nuclear isolation. It was a concrete step towards implementing the 'Next Steps in Strategic Partnership' (NSSP) initiative, signed by President Bush and Prime Minister Atal Bihari Vajpayee in 2004. Without giving up its nuclear weapons programme, the deal enabled India to access nuclear power for its energy security while being environmentally sustainable. Other nuclear powers, such as the UK, France and Russia, were allowed to sell nuclear fuel, reactors and equipment to India. However, China expressed its displeasure with the agreement and, in a not-so-subtle message to India, decided to sell six to eight nuclear reactors to Pakistan.

Critics in the US argued that such a policy of 'exceptionalism' towards India would undermine the existing non-proliferation regime, and other countries such as France, Russia and China may relax their own rules in favour of Iran, Pakistan and Syria. Moreover, they were concerned that India might continue to develop nuclear weapons, since the new fuel supply would free up India's existing capacity to increase its nuclear stockpile. It is also because India's PM categorically asserted that the 2005 deal did not constrain India from building any future nuclear facilities, civilian or military.

Proponents of the deal in the US argued that it gave them the opportunity to use India's growing power for the US's own geopolitical and geo-economic interests in the region. The US had begun to view India not only as a potential counterweight to China and terrorism, but also as a responsible rising power that needed to be accommodated into the global order. By doing so, the US removed the nuclear impediment to improve India-US relations. The Bush administration also showed that India's commitment to keeping strict export controls, aligned with IAEA protocols, would strengthen the anti-proliferation network. This led to a waiver from the Nuclear Suppliers Group in 2008, and after a few weeks, the US Congress approved the 2005 deal.

On the Indian side, the atomic energy community was deeply suspicious of American motivations, and argued that the separation of civilian and military facilities would have serious repercussions for research and development and for strengthening nuclear deterrence. This issue was also raised by the BJP, led by former PM Vajpayee. The leftist parties voiced concern that India would end up being a regional 'client state' of the US against China and, hence, lose its strategic autonomy. The Communist parties even threatened to pull away support from the coalition government. PM Singh had to reassure his communist partners that India would not align against China, and that the nuclear deal meant cooperation not just with the US but also with the international system.

The Indian proponents saw the US commitment to the deal as helpful in improving the image of the latter. According to Ashley Tellis, the deal 'becomes the vehicle by which the Indian people are reassured that the United States is a true friend and ally responsive to their deepest aspirations'.[2] During his trip to India, President Bush claimed that the United States and India were 'closer than ever before and this partnership has the power to transform the world'.[3] This has become true in the present context, when the Indo-US relationship has transformed into a comprehensive global strategic partnership, spanning almost all areas of human endeavour including defence, technology, and vibrant people-to-people contacts. Besides high-level exchanges, an increasing convergence of interests on a range of global issues has led both countries to evolve arrangements, such as the G20, Quad and the I2U2, to tackle emerging challenges.

58. AGREEMENTS BETWEEN INDIA AND CHINA

During Chinese Premier Wen Jiabao's visit to India in April 2005, the two countries signed two important agreements towards resolving the boundary question. The first agreement pertained to the 'Political Parameters and Guiding Principles for the Settlement of the India-China Boundary Question', while the second was a 'Protocol on Modalities for the Implementation of Confidence Building Measures in the Military Field Along the Line of Actual Control'. Rooting the agreements in the five principles of peaceful coexistence and the commitment to abide by the 1993 and 1996 agreements, both parties agreed to seek a political settlement to the boundary question through peaceful and friendly consultations.

Through the first agreement, India and China shared their confidence in the Special Representatives mechanism to continue consultations and arrive at an agreed framework for a boundary settlement. Both sides agreed to give due consideration to each other's strategic and reasonable interests, and safeguard the interests of their settled populations in the border areas. However, pending an ultimate settlement of the boundary question, it was emphasized that the two sides would strictly respect the LAC and maintain peace and tranquillity in the border areas.

The second agreement—'Protocol on Modalities'—was essentially built on the 1996 'Agreement on Confidence Building Measures in the Military Field along the Line of Actual Control'. Under this agreement, both sought to avoid holding large-scale military exercises in close proximity to the LAC, and required that they send prior intimation to each other about small-scale exercises through flag meetings. In case of a face-to-face situation, both sides agreed to cease their activities in the area and enter into immediate consultations through border meetings or diplomatic channels. Moreover, both sides agreed to hold additional border meetings at Spanggur Gap, Nathu La Pass and Bum La.

In the context of broad bilateral relations, both agreements represented a significant development. For China, the agreements sought to build a peaceful neighbourhood, so that it could concentrate on its economic development and, more specifically, tap into the giant Indian market. Seeing India's strengthening relations with the US at the time, and fearing that India might be used to contain China, the latter sought to engage India in a long-term strategic relationship. It, therefore, wished India and China to speak with one voice on multilateral issues, and push for a multipolar order to reduce American dominance.

For India, a peaceful border was desired, and the sentiment prevailed that increased trade would build an atmosphere that reduced differences on other issues. China recognized Sikkim as part of India; the latter wanted both countries to look at the boundary question from long-term and strategic perspectives, rather than as a mere territorial issue. Another line of thought was that India did not see China as a competitor or rival. Rather, it believed that there was enough space in Asia for the rise of both India and China, and that both could contribute together to the development of Asia. Although China's 'all-weather friendship' with Pakistan continued to be a sore point with India, both governments had agreed to establish a strategic and cooperative partnership for peace and prosperity.

Despite the commitment to peace and to each other's interests that the two countries demonstrated during Wen Jiabao's visit, China continued to antagonize India. In November 2006, Sun Yuxi, the Chinese ambassador to India, said on CNN-IBN that all of Arunachal Pradesh was a part of China.[4] It was no longer interested in giving up its claims to Arunachal Pradesh, in exchange for India withdrawing its claim to Aksai Chin in Ladakh, as suggested by Zhou Enlai in 1959. The chill in their relations was attributed to India's increasing tilt towards the US through the 2005 nuclear deal, and the US Secretary of State Condoleezza Rice's statement to 'help make India a major world power in the twenty-first century'.[5]

In the present context, India views the border clashes with China in Eastern Ladakh since 2020 as a violation of the 2005 agreements, and those signed in 1993 and 1996. While border standoffs in the past were resolved peacefully, the recent clashes point to a different reality. Bullets have been fired, and clashes have resulted in the death of soldiers on both sides. China wishes to continue its engagement with India, citing the provisions of the 'Political Parameters' agreement, and mentioning that the differences on the boundary question should not affect the overall development of bilateral relations. However, India cites the same provision stating that the agreement also prohibited the use of force in resolving the issue. Hence, the 2020 clashes in Galwan reflect China's violation of the agreement. India has clearly stated that the departure of China from what was agreed upon in 1993, 1996 and 2005, is the cause of 'the difficult phase' in the relationship, and that the state of the border will determine the state of the relationship.

2007

59. MALABAR AND THE BIRTH OF QUAD

The Malabar exercise began in 1992 as a bilateral naval exercise between the US and India, off the Malabar Coast in the Arabian Sea. In 2007, two Malabar exercises took place. The first took place in April off the Japanese Island of Okinawa in the Philippine Sea, marking their first venture into the Western Pacific Ocean. The second exercise was held in September 2007, involving the navies of the US, India, Japan, Australia and Singapore in the Bay of Bengal, thereby increasing the scale and complexity of the maritime operations. This exercise is deemed as the first step towards initiating the Quadrilateral Initiative involving the US, India, Japan and Australia.

The Malabar exercises aim to increase naval interoperability and enhance cooperative security relationships among partner countries. The exercises concentrate on the maritime domain of warfare and include sea control operations such as interdiction and responding to threats and challenges such as terrorism and piracy, the proliferation of weapons of mass destruction, pandemics and natural disasters. The September 2007 Malabar exercise was held 350 km southwest of the Andaman Islands, close to the Malacca Strait, indicating the purpose of protecting international sea routes from terrorism and piracy. While executing these operations, this exercise also grounded the idea of the Quadrilateral Initiative—envisioned by the Japanese PM Shinzo Abe in March 2007, during US Vice President Dick Cheney's visit to Tokyo.

While the September 2007 exercises generated significant international interest due to the multinational nature of the exercise, the efficacy of the Malabar exercises in promoting India's security in general was questioned. However, its proponents asserted that stability and tranquillity in the Indian Ocean Region are imperative to ensure India's national security. They showed how the threats of piracy, organized crime and terrorism could harm India's sea-borne trade, and given the limited capability of India's maritime security forces, it was crucial that security partnerships were created with major naval powers having mutual interests in the region. They emphasized that operating 'solo' was impossible even for a major naval power like the US. Hence, joint exercises such as the Malabar enabled the interoperability of their assets, which could be used in response to common challenges and contingencies. This was exemplified during the 2004 tsunami in the Indian Ocean, when the navies of the US, India, Japan and Australia collaborated to provide disaster relief.

Achieving interoperability through these exercises provides immense benefits. It not only ensures familiarity with the procedures and technologies of the partners, but also widens the horizons of the personnel and the decision-makers in terms of doctrines, strategies and best practices developed over time to counter different security scenarios. These exercises also help assess the effectiveness of India's own weapon platforms and ascertain the need to upgrade its military hardware and technology.

The strategic rationale also necessitates a security partnership with major naval powers. China's development of strategic 'nodes of influence' in the Indian Ocean Region was already noted in its economic and maritime security ties with Myanmar, Sri Lanka and Pakistan, which were concretized through the Gwadar and Hambantota port construction deals. Thus, it became imperative for India to counter China's 'string of pearls' strategy by developing its own naval capabilities. Joint exercises like Malabar would be critical, and provide the necessary 'hedge' against any power whose interests ran counter to India's. The fact that Malabar 2007 and Quad attracted the attention of China's political leadership shows that security partnerships such as these build strategic deterrence, and point to their success.

The September 2007 Malabar Exercise indeed realized the idea of the Quad. However, it was short-lived. After the first meeting of the Quad on the sidelines of an ASEAN Regional Forum meeting in Manila in May 2007, China expressed its displeasure with the group members, perceiving it as an 'Asian NATO'. Shortly after the Malabar exercise, Japan's PM Abe resigned. In November 2007, Australia's new PM Kevin Rudd committed to a more conciliatory approach towards China. In India, the left parties protested against antagonizing China and the apparent loss of strategic autonomy due to partnering with the Quad. Hence, the idea lost momentum, and for the next few years, Malabar reverted to its original form of bilateral US-India naval exercises.

However, with the change in the geopolitical circumstances of the Indo-Pacific, Japan permanently re-joined the Malabar exercises in 2015. Australia, too, re-joined in 2020, against the backdrop of the revival of the Quad in November 2017. Malabar is now one of the cornerstones of Quad military cooperation. It reflects the desire to ensure the freedom of navigation in the Indo-Pacific—one of the principles of the Quad's charter. It also sends a strong message to China, which has antagonized all members of the Quad through its military assertiveness and adventures.

2008

60. THE INDIA-FRANCE NUCLEAR PACT AND THE INDO-US NUCLEAR DEAL

India's long-standing nuclear apartheid ceased with the signing of the Indo-US Civil Nuclear Agreement during PM Manmohan

Singh's visit to the US in 2005. The deal is also known as the '123 Agreement', due to Section 123 of the US Atomic Energy Act 1954, under which the US can trade nuclear material or equipment with a country if it meets its nine-point non-proliferation criteria, thereby guiding nuclear cooperation between the US and its partners. As a result, before commencing nuclear commerce with the US, India had to stand the test of US domestic law, which it did, owing to its strong non-nuclear proliferation credentials. Subsequently, President George W. Bush pursued unprecedented exemptions from the international nuclear regime guidelines, to allow India access to civil nuclear perks without having to ratify the NPT.

After securing an India-specific IAEA safeguard and the NSG waiver, the US House of Representatives passed a bill to cement the deal in October 2008. Soon, France inked a similar nuclear agreement with India. India and France agreed to cooperate in areas of nuclear safety and the prevention of the trafficking of nuclear material. In this way, the pact was a landmark in ending India's decades-old nuclear isolation. The agreement laid the foundations for the present-day participation of France in India's nuclear power programme, including the 2018 decision to assist in the development of six nuclear reactors in Jaitapur in Maharashtra.

On 1 October 2008 the US Senate approved the bill, setting the stage for the Indo-US nuclear deal. Subsequently, George W. Bush signed the legislation, giving force to the law now called the United States-India Nuclear Cooperation Approval and Non-proliferation Enhancement Act. Consequently, the Indian Minister of External Affairs Pranab Mukherjee and US Secretary of State Condoleezza Rice sealed the bilateral 123 Agreement at the US State Department, calling it a 'historical event' in the Indo-US strategic partnership, changing the narrative of 'estranged democracies', and becoming 'engaged democracies' for the twenty-first century.

Despite a strong bipartisan sentiment in the US towards strengthening relations with India, the non-proliferation lobby was highly critical of the bill. Voices in the US arose demanding amendments to the bill, urging the government to terminate nuclear trade with India if the latter resumed nuclear testing, and to explore applicable export control authorities for US nuclear exports to other nuclear supplier nations that engage in nuclear trade with India. However, the Indo-American community leveraged their strong relationship with critics like Senator Howard Berman to accept the Senate version of the bill.

Critics also problematized the distinction between 'good' and 'bad' proliferation, underlying India's potential to be an unstable and irresponsible nuclear power. Robert Einhorn, former Assistant Secretary of State for Nonproliferation, called out American double standards in carving out a niche for India among the other NPT cheaters like North Korea and Iran. Strobe Talbott, the former deputy secretary of state who advocated for India-US strategic partnership, also rebuked the Bush administration for 'giving too much'. Nevertheless, its proponents, with a not-so-myopic view, emphasized the importance of strengthening US's partnership with an India that shared its democratic values, and which could 'exert increasing influence on the world stage'.[6]

On the Indian side, a major contention was posed with regard to the limit imposed by the deal on the size of India's nuclear arsenal. India's political opposition, like the BJP, criticized the deal on grounds of a cap on nuclear testing which would have implications for India's military programmes. However, as per scholars like Ashley Tellis, the Indo-US deal has limited bearing on India's nuclear capabilities as 'India has sufficient natural uranium reserves to sustain the largest nuclear weapons program that can be envisaged relative to its current capabilities; it also possesses enough uranium to sustain more than three times its current and planned capacity as far as nuclear power production involving pressurised heavy water reactors (PHWRs) is concerned'.[7]

Similarly, apprehensions surrounded India's over-dependence on the US for nuclear fuel. To mitigate this, India has tried to diversify its sources of nuclear imports in the recent past.

The agreement holds multiple strategic connotations for India, apart from just being an enabler of nuclear energy security. It is a recognition of the enhanced role of India in the strategic calculus of the US in Asia, especially to counter China, patrol the Indian Ocean, counter terrorism, and provide disaster relief. India's status as a major nuclear power in the region has helped it strike similar deals with major powers like France, Russia, the UK, South Korea, Australia and others. It also gave a fillip to military cooperation, defence trade, access to critical technology, and energy collaboration between the two countries. The deal outlined India's strategic autonomy vis-à-vis a major power, and secured nuclear energy for India to meet the growing domestic demand thereof. The agreement established the present nature of the relationship, which has only grown stronger. In spite of changes in governments, the idea of shared prosperity has remained a priority on both sides, not guided by the impediments of the past.

61. THE NSG WAIVER

The Nuclear Suppliers Group (NSG) is a multilateral export control regime. This forty-eight-member group seeks to contribute to the global non-proliferation order by monitoring nuclear trade for peaceful purposes, so as to check the proliferation of nuclear explosives. The 1974 peaceful nuclear explosions by India acted as a trigger for the NPT regime (London Club) to draft stringent rules and expand the nuclear non-proliferation regime to curb the policy of 'nuclear ambiguity' pursued by some states, giving birth to the NSG the same year. In 1992, the NSG brought export mechanisms in congruence with IAEA's full-scope safeguards, barring non-NPT states from having trade relations with NPT states. Countries like India suffered a huge setback since they were now forced to acknowledge the consortium of nuclear powers, which it had earlier deemed inequitable for the developing world. India's second nuclear test (Operation Shakti) in 1998 invited a major backlash from the international community. The US imposed sanctions and NSG denied fuel to the Tarapur Atomic Power station, while the Missile Technology Control Regime (MTCR) guidelines were cited to prevent the transfer of cryogenic engine technology from Russia to India. This left a major dent in India's self-proclaimed 'nuclear power' status, as it was considered an outcast overall.

What came as a relief was the US's intention to finally engage in civil nuclear cooperation with India using a comprehensive strategy, but it was plagued by multiple conditionalities. American interests heavily relied on ensuring that the civil nuclear assistance rendered to India was not diverted to its military programmes. To ensure this, certain concessions to the separation of India's civil and military nuclear facilities were sought, along with the agreement to place its civil nuclear installations under IAEA safeguards. Simultaneously, India reciprocated by synchronizing its export control mechanism with the NSG and the MTCR guidelines, by passing the 'Weapons of Mass Destruction and their Delivery Systems (Prohibition of Unlawful Activities) Act, 2005', despite not being a member of either organization.

Because of India's strong commitment to nuclear non-proliferation and its voluntary unilateral moratorium in the same direction, at the NSG meeting in Vienna it achieved the US-brokered NSG waiver to commence civil nuclear trade with other countries. India became the first country ever, outside the NPT regime, to achieve a 'clean waiver' from the existing rules, allowing it to resume the import of critical technology to enrich uranium and reprocess plutonium.

Washington was firm in its attempt to facilitate international nuclear trade with India. However, major debates around the waiver still afflicted the American political landscape. A contention was raised on the eight nuclear projects kept outside IAEA safeguards, alleging that it left major production capacity available for India. Some senators also opposed India's right to enrichment and reprocessing (ENR) technology. Nevertheless, President Bush clarified that India would be prohibited from accessing the critical ENR technology, in his overriding 123 Agreement. Thus, unlike popular belief, the NSG waiver was not unconditional or absolute.

Countries like China strongly opposed the waiver because they wanted India to become a signatory to the NPT. The Chinese delegation to the NSG said, 'the group should address the aspirations of other countries too'.[8] Chinese resistance was influenced by the non-admission of its close ally Pakistan in the club. Consequently, China abstained from the final voting process, asserting the 'non-discriminatory' principle of the regime. Moreover, what differentiated India from Pakistan was its strong non-proliferation credentials, which bestowed on it the title of a 'responsible nuclear power'. The French, American and Russian championing of India's 'merit-based approach' generated intense pressure on the holdout countries, eventually leading to a unanimous consensus for an India-specific NSG waiver.

The NSG waiver allowed France, a keen supporter of India's membership, to sign a civil nuclear agreement with India; eventually the US followed. It paved the way for India's membership in other export control groupings like the Australia Group, the Wassenaar Arrangement, and the MTCR in a 'phased manner'. The waiver has the potential to underpin India's case for permanent membership at the UNSC. In the present context, it can contribute to India's commitment to reducing dependence on fossil fuels and ensuring that 40 per cent of its energy is sourced from renewable and clean sources.

India's successful inclusion in the group urged the US to present a paper titled 'Food for Thought' in 2011, to stimulate a conversation on accommodating newer members into the non-proliferation arrangement. However, 'The waiver came in the form of concession without according to India the status of a full member and therefore had an element of unpredictability and attendant risks in the long run for India's long-term nuclear power programme remained', recalled Jitendra Singh, former minister of atomic energy and space.[9] To address this, India is committed to pursuing a full membership in the NSG, further solidifying its position as a major player in the global nuclear order. The French precedent of being a member of the elite group without ratifying the NPT served as a major boost to India's ambitions. During his Republic Day visit to India in 2015, President Obama gave a green flag to India for NSG membership. Similarly, Russian president Vladimir Putin has also offered unconditional support to India's entry into the NSG. Several other countries, such as Switzerland and Japan, have expressed a similar desire for backing India. This strong support for India reflects its diplomatic rigour, giving it the ability to influence the popular narrative and win 'friends and foes' alike.

2009

62. THE SHARM EL-SHEIKH PACT

On 16 July 2009, PM Manmohan Singh held talks with his Pakistani counterpart Syed Yusuf Raza Gilani at the Egyptian resort Sharm el-Sheikh, on the sidelines of the NAM summit. A joint statement was issued at the end of these talks which considered the entire gamut of bilateral relations. However, two issues in the statement became points of concern—delinking the Composite Dialogue from Pakistan's action on terror, and the mention of Balochistan.

In the joint statement, both leaders agreed on the threat posed by terrorism to their countries and resolved to cooperate in fighting it. Pakistan agreed to bring the perpetrators of the 26/11 attacks in Mumbai to justice. While both the PMs recognized the importance of a dialogue, it was agreed that Pakistan's action on terrorism should not be linked to the Composite Dialogue process, which started in 1998 and covered eight subjects including Siachen, Sir Creek, terrorism, and Jammu and Kashmir. Both leaders agreed to create an atmosphere of mutual trust and confidence, and hold foreign secretary-level talks as often as necessary. Additionally, the statement mentioned that Pakistan had information about threats in Balochistan and other areas.

PM Manmohan Singh's assent to delink Pakistan's action on terrorism from the Composite Dialogue process became a subject of immense controversy. The joint statement was seen, on the part of India, as having agreed to start the Composite Dialogue and discuss the Kashmir issue with Pakistan without expecting concrete actions from the latter on the 2008 Mumbai terror attack perpetrators—giving a clear advantage to Pakistan. Foreign policy analyst Sushant Sareen argued that 'diplomatic and political naivety' caused the joint statement to be 'full of concessions, compromises and climb-downs by India'.[10] Sareen also contended that India made a mistake by focusing only on Pakistan's actions on the 2008 Mumbai attacks, and giving up its advantage of calling on Pakistan not to allow the territory under its control to be used for spreading terrorism.

The joint statement faced severe criticism from the opposition parties, particularly the BJP, which dubbed the statement 'surrender by India'. Besides some coalition partners, members of Singh's Congress Party also saw it as India going soft on the 26/11 diplomatic campaign against Pakistan, even though this issue had helped them win the 2009 general election. The news media also reported that India succumbed to pressure from the US to resume talks with Pakistan.

Moreover, the mention of Balochistan in the joint statement was seen as legitimizing years of accusations levied by Pakistan against India, of fomenting terror in the province and using the Indian consulates in Afghanistan for this purpose. No sooner did Pakistan's PM Gilani return to Islamabad after the Sharm el-Sheikh talks than he accused India of interfering in Balochistan. The statement was called a 'diplomatic blunder', and a 'foolhardy act', which shifted the responsibility for the problems in Balochistan from Pakistan to India. BJP leader Yashwant Sinha said, 'All the waters of seven seas will not wash the shame at Sharm-el-Sheikh.'[11] Moreover, it was argued that this statement gave Pakistan the legitimacy to equate Balochistan with Kashmir in all bilateral discourses, thereby giving it the right to shape the agenda on terrorism as a reciprocal issue.

However, Prime Minister Manmohan Singh and Foreign Secretary Shiv Shankar Menon defended the reference to Balochistan, arguing that they have 'nothing to hide'. US Special Representative for Afghanistan and Pakistan, Richard Holbrooke, came in support of India by asking Pakistan for credible evidence against India on its involvement in Balochistan. In addition, some argued that it was Pakistan's blunder which gave India the opportunity to internationalize Pakistan's persecution of the Baloch population, which was already well documented in Western media. Hence, it was suggested that when Pakistan accused India in the international forum of violating human rights in Kashmir, India could turn the mirror around by highlighting Pakistan's actions in Balochistan.

Responding to the criticism, PM Singh said in parliament, 'Unless we want to go to war with Pakistan, dialogue is the only way out.' Defending the statement, Foreign Secretary Shiv Shankar Menon said, 'Pakistan can no more say that they would not act on terror because the Composite Dialogue is not on.' However, due to the severity of the criticism, PM Singh had to backtrack from the Sharm el-Sheikh commitment, and talks continued to be suspended. Foreign Secretary Menon said that the Composite Dialogue would resume only after Pakistan informed India about the credible actions it had taken on the 26/11 terrorists. Because of this, Pakistan's High Commissioner Shahid Malik accused India of not fulfilling its commitment and relinking the talks with action against terrorism.

In 2015, PM Modi met with Pakistan's PM Nawaz Sharif in Ufa and agreed to delink the talks and terror, while resuming what came to be known as the Comprehensive Bilateral Dialogue. However, due to continued provocation in the form of terrorist attacks, such as those in Pathankot, Uri and Pulwama, India openly called Pakistan the 'epicentre of terrorism'. New Delhi has now declared that it has made irrelevant Pakistan's game of using cross-border terrorism to bring India to the table. It has clearly maintained that for any dialogue to begin, Pakistan-sponsored terrorism has to stop.

2012

63. INDIA HOSTS THE BRICS SUMMIT

In March 2012, the fourth BRICS Summit was convened in New Delhi under the theme 'BRICS Partnership for Global Stability, Security and Prosperity'. The outcome of the summit was the Delhi Declaration, which stated the shared position of the BRICS nations on global issues, and the Delhi Action Plan, which outlined the roadmap for further cooperation. The importance of the summit was reflected in two aspects—consideration of a new development bank and conducting intra-BRICS trade in local currency, which reflected the aspirations of this bloc of emerging economies to convert its economic might into collective diplomatic influence.

The idea of BRIC (Brazil, Russia, India and China) was conceived by Jim O'Neill (an economist at Goldman Sachs) in 2001 to forecast global economic trends. The group acquired political value with the meeting of the BRIC foreign ministers in 2006 on the sidelines of the UN General Assembly, and was upgraded to a summit-level meeting in 2009. In 2010, South Africa joined the group and BRICS, as we know it, was formed.

Beginning as a forum for cooperation on economic issues of mutual interest, such as overcoming the 2008 financial crisis, the agenda of BRICS has expanded to include global issues such as reforming the United Nations and other international economic and financial institutions, climate change, meeting the Millennium Development Goals, and addressing food and energy security. The transcontinental dimension of the BRICS members' cooperation holds immense significance as, by 2012, they accounted for roughly 40 per cent of the world population, 18 per cent of the world's GDP, and 40 per cent of global currency reserves.

The fourth summit was held against the backdrop of a faltering global recovery after the 2008 financial crisis and market instability in the eurozone, concerns about sustainable development and climate change, and geopolitical instabilities in the Middle East and North Africa. Deliberating on these issues, the member countries resolved to cooperate in addressing these global challenges.

The Declaration called for better representation of developing countries in the international financial architecture, underlining the urgent need to implement governance and quota reforms at the IMF. In addition, they also called for the World Bank to reform itself into a multilateral institution that promoted equal partnership among all countries and mobilized resources for meeting the needs of development finance. In this regard, the Delhi Declaration considered setting up a new development bank to mobilize resources for infrastructure and sustainable development projects in BRICS and other developing countries. The respective finance ministers were directed to set up a joint working group to examine the feasibility and viability of such a bank.

The idea of a new development bank is seen by analysts as a potential counterweight to existing institutions such as the World Bank. However, the Declaration mentioned that the intended role of the bank would be to supplement the existing efforts of multilateral and regional financial institutions for global growth and development. In this respect, the bank could be considered a key response to the economic necessities of the times, and could serve as a lending platform during future financial crises.

At this summit, two key agreements were signed—one on extending credit facility in the local currency under the BRICS Interbank Cooperation Mechanism, and the second, a credit confirmation facility between the member-states' EXIMs or development banks. While these agreements would enhance intra-BRICS trade in the following years by reducing the demand for fully convertible currencies, they were also perceived to be challenging the supremacy of the US dollar as the world's reserve currency. According to estimates provided at the time by Dilma Rousseff, president of Brazil, intra-BRICS trade was to rise to $250 billion in 2012, and to $500 billion by 2015.

While the key agreements reached at this summit hold economic significance, the nature of such a coalition of emerging economies is seen as a hurdle to its ambition of influencing global policies. Hence, it is often referred to as a grouping of 'disparate countries' with little in common. Besides the radical political and economic differences among its members, mutual suspicion and disagreements also mar the relationship between them. Ties between India and China remain strained due to pre-existing issues, and it has been argued that the competition between the rivals would be one of the biggest stumbling blocks that the BRICS grouping would have to overcome.

The establishment of BRICS prompted the debate of a rising 'non-Western order'. However, the 2012 Delhi Declaration sees the BRICS platform as key to enhancing 'security and development in a multipolar, interdependent and increasingly complex, globalising world'.[12] BRICS also holds immense significance for India, especially in its ability to shape international narratives about its rising global profile and its capacity to reshape the international order. Hence, serving as a platform for facilitating a multipolar order, BRICS allows India to take the lead in voicing the concerns of the Global South. While countries such as China wish BRICS to be an anti-Western group, India views it as a 'non-Western' one, underlining its strong relations with the West, especially the US, and its desire not to be perceived in terms of an alliance with, or against, a particular country.

PART II

2014

64. ACT EAST AND THE SAGAR POLICY

At the 12th ASEAN Summit on 12 November 2014, in Naypyidaw, India's Prime Minister Narendra Modi declared that India's Look East Policy of 1992 had been upgraded to an Act East Policy to underline India's desire to boost its ties with Southeast and East Asian (SEEA) countries. While the Look East Policy focused on boosting economic ties with the SEEA countries, the Act East Policy underscored PM Modi's action-oriented stance, not only in terms of economic policy but also in the political, strategic and cultural domains. The policy even envisioned the improvement of relations with Australia, encompassing the Asia-Pacific region.

The influence of the US can also be gauged in the launch of India's AEP. Given the changing security dynamics of the Asia-Pacific region, especially due to the rising assertiveness of China, and the economic potential of the countries in the region, US Secretary of State Hillary Clinton encouraged New Delhi 'not just to look East, but to engage East and act East',[13] during her visit to India in July 2011. During PM Modi's visit to the US in September 2014, both countries also agreed on a joint vision for the Indo-Pacific, where the security and stability of the region were considered paramount for economic prosperity. After the launch of the AEP, the Obama administration welcomed it (in line with its own Asia-Pacific rebalancing strategy), and in the 2015 US-India Joint Strategic Vision for the Asia-Pacific and Indian Ocean Region, it called for India's membership in the Asia-Pacific Economic Cooperation forum.

As with the Look East Policy, ASEAN is central to the AEP. At the 12 November summit, PM Modi suggested the establishment of a special purpose vehicle for financing infrastructure projects, and invited ASEAN countries to invest in India's economic transformation—in sectors such as manufacturing, skill development, urban renewal, and connectivity projects. India's northeastern states have been accorded priority in the AEP. Commerce, culture and connectivity were the three domains in which bilateral and regional ties with ASEAN were to be boosted. Major works already in the pipeline include the Kaladan Multi-Modal Transit Transport Project with Myanmar, the India-Myanmar-Thailand (IMT) Trilateral Highway Project, the Rhi-Tiddim Road Project, and Border Haats. In the cultural domain, Buddhist linkages between India and ASEAN nations were to be harnessed as a foreign policy tool. In this respect, one of the associated aims was to neutralize China's soft power advantages.

Maritime cooperation with ASEAN, regarding search and rescue and managing accidents or incidents, was another domain of cooperation through the Expanded ASEAN Maritime Forum (EAMF). In this regard, ASEAN welcomed India's 2015 Security and Growth for All in the Region (SAGAR) policy. The elements of the SAGAR policy—in terms of economic security and maritime cooperation, sustainable development of the countries through striving towards a blue economy, together with the congruence of their views on the importance of a rules-based order in the region—resonated well with ASEAN countries, and provided an opportunity to link South Asia with SEEA and the Indo-Pacific.

According to Ashok Sajjanhar, a former diplomat, the AEP's launch has lent greater vigour to India's multidimensional ties with ASEAN. This is reflected in an increasing number of high-level visits, to not only ASEAN states but also to Australia in November 2014 (the first visit by an Indian PM after twenty-eight years) and Fiji in the same month (the first visit by an Indian PM after thirty-three years). Renewed energy and focus were given to projects, such as the IMT Trilateral Highway. At the 2015 Kuala Lumpur Summit of ASEAN, India allocated $1 billion to promote connectivity projects. Moreover, India's relations with ASEAN have encompassed strategic dimensions, including defence collaborations with Singapore and Vietnam. Due to the AEP, Japan accelerated the signing of a civil nuclear deal with India (eventually signed in 2016), and committed to invest $35 billion in India over five years.

However, C. Raja Mohan argued that India needed to show tangible results under the AEP—for example, fast-tracking India's accession to the ASEAN-led Regional Comprehensive Economic Partnership (RCEP) to boost trade ties. V.S. Seshadri, India's former ambassador to Myanmar, also suggested setting up a high-level bilateral mechanism between India and Myanmar to review the progress of infrastructure projects, and expand their ties to include 'soft infrastructure' projects on transit and transport. Additionally, analysts pointed out that there was a lack of an overall foreign policy framework interconnecting various policies, such as 'Act East', 'Neighbourhood First', 'Link West' and 'Sagarmala', because of which these disparate policies did not form an integrated foreign policy strategy. Moreover, India needed to account for the political uncertainties within Myanmar and Thailand, which could pose challenges for the AEP.

As AEP completes ten years, credit must be given to its role in boosting India's rise as the third largest economy in the world, and its status as a net security provider in the Indo-Pacific region. Given the rising aggression of China in the South China Sea, India has increased its strategic cooperation with ASEAN and, through QUAD, has made a stand for a rules-based order in the Indo-Pacific. This was seen in the visit of the Indian Minister of External Affairs S. Jaishankar to the Philippines, where he supported the latter's right to protect its territorial sovereignty and integrity against China's incursions. Discussions are also underway to review the India-ASEAN Free Trade Agreement due to the trade imbalance of $43.57 billion in favour of ASEAN.

2015

65. THE INDIA-BANGLADESH BOUNDARY DEAL

During PM Modi's state visit to Bangladesh on 6–7 June 2015, three important agreements were signed: first, the conclusion of the land boundary agreement (LBA), the process for which had started in 1974; second, the launch of bus services connecting India to the Northeast through Bangladesh, and the commencement of negotiations on a multi-modal transport agreement; and third, the renewal of the bilateral trade agreement of 1972 that envisaged the promotion of trade through land, waterways and railways between the two countries.

The LBA resolved decades-long border disputes by settling the issues of enclaves, adverse possessions, and an undemarcated land boundary of approximately 6.1 km in three sectors. Through the agreement, the land boundary was demarcated, 111 Indian enclaves were exchanged with fifty-one Bangladeshi enclaves (territories deep within each other's boundaries), and recognition was given to adverse possessions (territories contiguous to the border and within the control of one country but legally a part of the bordering country).

The boundary problem between India and Bangladesh (erstwhile East Pakistan) was created in 1947 by a flawed partition process, leaving some Indian territories within Bangladesh, and some Bangladeshi territories within India. Around 51,200 people lived in these territories without legal rights, access to basic facilities like healthcare and electricity, and proper law and order. In 1974, a land boundary pact was signed between India and Bangladesh but was not fully implemented. The pact was reviewed in 2011 and a protocol was agreed upon by both countries, but it could not be implemented due to political opposition within India. The issue was resolved with the 2015 LBA, and people living in these territories were given full legal rights. The Indian government also sanctioned a ₹1,005.99 crore rehabilitation package for the enclave dwellers who came to India from Bangladesh. The agreement represented a success of the 'Neighbourhood First' policy of the newly elected Modi government.

In a joint statement, both PMs noted that seamless, multi-modal connectivity through roadways, railways and waterways was fundamental to an interdependent and mutually beneficial relationship among the countries of the region. Therefore, they launched two bus services connecting Dhaka-Shillong-Guwahati and Kolkata-Dhaka-Agartala. Both these bus services would reduce the travel distance and promote people-to-people contact. Both PMs agreed to commence negotiations on a multi-modal transport agreement between the two countries and constitute a joint task force for this purpose. Moreover, the 1972 Protocol on Inland Waterways Transit and Trade (PIWTT) was renewed to allow the use of the waterways of both countries for commerce between them, and the passage of goods to other countries through each other's territory.

The third significant achievement of PM Modi's visit was renewal of the 1972 bilateral trade agreement. The agreement would enable trade between the two countries through land, waterways and railways, and would boost development in the northeastern states. It would not only improve bilateral trade, investment and economic cooperation in a balanced and sustainable manner for mutual benefit, but also open up opportunities for regional trade. In this regard, India agreed to give Nepal and Bhutan access to Bangladeshi cargo. Both countries also agreed to eliminate technical barriers to trade, to facilitate and enhance the reciprocal market access to products in each other's countries. In addition, an agreement on coastal shipping was also signed to promote two-way trade through ports, which until then was conducted through Colombo and Singapore.

The LBA would certainly check illegal migration and drug and arms trafficking, and help in tightening security along the border. However, the major concern that arose was the resettlement and rehabilitation of the people who became citizens of India, and how the central and state governments would coordinate with each other for this purpose, given their political differences. Another issue was the politicization of these 'new citizens', to gain votes during elections. The renewal of the bilateral trade agreement and the associated agreements led to rapid growth in bilateral trade. However, due to poor preparation for the new situation, there was road congestion at the border and at customs checkposts such as Petrapole and Benapole. Because of this, exporters and importers on both sides faced undue hikes in transportation costs.

Nevertheless, the implementation of the LBA showed how the central and the state governments can depoliticize their differences and cooperate to achieve substantive benefits for the nation. The agreements signed in 2015 paved the way for further development of ties between India and Bangladesh. Both the countries have now signed defence cooperation agreements, whereby they regularly conduct military exercises aimed at ensuring maritime security and humanitarian assistance and disaster relief (HADR) efforts. Trade and connectivity have improved between the two nations, and their relationship serves as a model for bilateral relations in the entire region and beyond. Bangladesh has also emerged as a strong supporter of India's leadership initiatives, such as the Voice of the Global South Summit.

66. INDIA NOT TO BE A PART OF BRI

The colossal Chinese project of 2013, the One Belt One Road Initiative (now called the Belt and Road Initiative), is an ambitious infrastructure development project and investment programme aiming to create a network of maritime and land trade routes, connecting China to Europe, Africa and beyond. It delineates two major components: the land component, China's Silk Road Economic Belt (SREB), and the Maritime Silk Road (MSR), which proposes to link China's coast with Southeast Asia, the Indian Ocean, the Arabian Sea and Africa, extending to Europe. From an economic standpoint, the BRI is China's response to the Trans-Pacific Partnership (TPP) and the Transatlantic Trade and Investment Partnership (TTIP), with a vision to replace the liberal economic world order led by the US and 'rejuvenate' China as a global power. It is also seen as an attempt by China to rebuild its economy, which was negatively impacted by the 2008–09 financial crisis. From a diplomatic point, the BRI is China's grand strategy based on its policy of 'peripheral diplomacy' to shape the regional order.

Though India has repeatedly shown its tacit reluctance about the project since its inception, a strong rejection was meted out when China announced the initiation of its geographical corridors—the China-Pakistan Economic Corridor (CPEC) and the Bangladesh-China-India-Myanmar Corridor (BCIM)—under the BRI. Since the project (aiming to connect Kashgar with Gwadar) passes through the Gilgit-Baltistan region of the Pakistan-occupied Kashmir, the Indian side deemed it a violation of the universally recognized international norms of sovereignty and territorial integrity. It urged China to embrace the principles of openness, transparency and financial responsibility in a manner that respects and promotes other nations' sovereignty, equality and territorial integrity. India's position on the BRI has been unequivocally endorsed by other nations, namely the US, Japan and the EU, in their respective joint statements titled 'Prosperity through Partnership'. Surely enough, acting against India's interests, China dropped the BCIM project via a communiqué during the second BRI Forum in 2019, and replaced it with the China-Myanmar Economic Corridor (CMEC). However, the CPEC still continued.

India's apprehensions about the CPEC were also shaped by the perceived notions of the Chinese intention to convert this alleged 'economic' cooperation into a military front against India, if need be. Furthermore, India feared an obvious intrusion by China in the domestic affairs of Pakistan, ripples of which were not far away from its immediate neighbour, considering the economic fragility of Pakistan with regard to its ability to repay loans. Ironically, the chicken came home to roost; as per a study by AidData, a US-based research institute, Pakistan owes a cumulative amount of $67.2 billion to China (surpassing the World Bank estimate of $46 billion). Therefore, it will not be an understatement to say that India's stance against the BRI, rooted in its contempt for the CPEC, was far-sighted. India foresaw the potential dangers of the Chinese strategies of 'debt-trap diplomacy' and 'string of pearls' unfolding right at its doorstep, with the Hambantota Port situation serving as a stark example.

Granted, India's approach towards the BRI has been atomistic, guided by its own strategic and economic interests. Mala Sharma divides the Indian semantics on the BRI into three categories—the optimistic, the cautionary, and the sceptical. While the first overstates the economic gains and argues for integration into the project to gain bargaining power vis-à-vis China on issues of its concern, the sceptical side warns India against China's strategic attempts to encircle its territory, involving military and diplomatic implications. The cautionary, however, calls for a more nuanced and multilateral participation fused with the strategy of leveraging its other partnerships, as a hedge against the Chinese rise. One must note that India has adopted a cautionary yet multifaceted approach.

Its non-participation in the two BRI forums held in 2017 and 2019 is representative of its repudiation of the Chinese edifice, while its promotion of sub-regional organizations, like the Quadrilateral Security forum, Bangladesh-Bhutan-India-Nepal (BBIN) initiative, and the Asia-Africa Growth Corridor (AAGC), is a product of its strategic urgency to offset the influence of the 'dragon' in South Asia. Furthermore, alongside strengthening the Act East Policy, these forums serve as a 'benevolent alternative' to the BRI. Thus, India has so far remained consistent with its policy, but it refuses to acknowledge or endorse the BRI through platforms like the Shanghai Cooperation Organization (SCO).

India's refusal to join the BRI sowed the initial seeds of its intent to 'decouple' from China, a decision that later materialized in its foreign policy. The Chinese connectivity plan fuelled the ever-present scepticism in New Delhi's heart and soul, about the former's intentions. This marked a shift in India's bilateral policy that is now extra-cautious regarding China's meddling in the strategic landscape of South Asia, Southeast Asia, the Pacific Rim region and Oceania, from the earlier policy that was defined by merely economic considerations. This wariness is said to be a reason for India's withdrawal from the world's largest free trade agreement, the Regional Comprehensive Economic Partnership (RCEP), in 2019.

Alongside this, New Delhi's pivot towards exploring multilateralism prioritizing transparency, democratic values and a rules-based order has compelled it to seek closer partnerships with other like-minded powers that denounce Chinese expansionism in the Indian Ocean Region (IOR). Simultaneously, India is promoting its own vision of regional connectivity, in the form of the India-Middle East-Europe Economic Corridor (IMEC) as announced during the G20 Summit, offering an alternative to the Chinese model, thereby actively shaping the global developmental and strategic landscape, and not just responding to it.

2016

67. INDIA JOINS THE MISSILE TECHNOLOGY CONTROL REGIME

Traditionally, India has been hesitant to partake in global nuclear groupings due to concerns about constant scrutiny over its indigenous nuclear programmes, coupled with its commitment to challenging their perceived discriminatory stance towards developing nations. Significantly, the 2008 NSG waiver redefined India's geopolitical outlook in being able to contribute to the global non-proliferation climate, earning it recognition as a 'responsible nuclear power'. Following this, India's strategic priorities have shifted. The appetite to validate its nuclear power status, and foster a deep trust with the rest of the world, has taken precedence over its historical apprehensions. In the last few decades, India has been actively lobbying to join the Nuclear Suppliers Group (NSG) as a full member.

After a failed bid at the NSG in June 2016, India earned its spot in the Missile Technology Control Regime (MTCR) as a full member, making it the 35th member of the group. MTCR is a voluntary group aiming to control the horizontal proliferation of missiles and missile technology with the potential of delivering weapons of mass destruction (WMDs). It regulates missiles and other unmanned aerial systems (UAV) capable of carrying a payload of 500 kilograms to a range of 300 kilometres and beyond. In 1992, the regime expanded its domain by including technology related to biological and chemical weapons.

The MTCR membership is an important element of the India-US strategic partnership. India initially applied for membership in 2015. However, a consensus was thwarted by Italy's objection. While India has always remained committed to the non-proliferation objectives of MTCR, it updated its domestic laws and its Special Chemicals, Organisms, Materials, Equipment and Technologies (SCOMET) List, fully aligning it with the MTCR guidelines. This move was met with approval from the US and other like-minded partners. In 2016, the joint statement released by President Barack Obama and PM Narendra Modi called for India's 'imminent entry' into the NSG and MTCR, reaffirming the American policy to validate India's position. This unconditional support bolstered India's case, creating a positive perception of its candidacy and shedding the concerns of the past.

While the ministry of external affairs, in its statement, reassured that India's membership in MTCR would help strengthen its global non-proliferation objectives, critics argued that India's ambitions weren't as altruistic as they seemed. They alleged that the MTCR membership would allow India to advance its missile programme since all the constraints over its possession of ballistic missiles would now be lifted.

However, India already enjoys concessions with respect to retaining its nuclear arsenal from the US. Moreover, it cannot be denied that the membership will open newer avenues for enhanced trade in aerial weapons, military hardware and missile technology, given that India will now be treated as a nuclear-weapon state in practical terms. The fear of sanctions will not be a major factor in future trade arrangements. Besides, India has attempted to acquire armed drones from the US in the past, but the latter has shown reluctance. However, in a major development with India's MTCR inclusion, in June 2023 the Pentagon announced a mega drone sale worth $4 billion to India, to meet the maritime security needs of its 'major defence partner'. Commentators have discouraged such deals, owing to the sensitivity of India's geopolitical location, claiming that it will give an unnecessary boost to India's offensive capabilities in cross-border operations, implicitly hinting towards Pakistan.

One must note that the US still exercises enough reservations on the export of critical technology to India. India has been willing to acquire anti-ballistic capabilities since the Kargil War. Despite Israel's continued interest to sell its Arrow II interceptor missile system to India, the US has been a major roadblock, as it vetoed such a bid in 2002. Even though the newly forged membership was seen as a gateway to materializing this deal, it remains in limbo.

Nonetheless, the Indian Space Research Organisation (ISRO) has benefited considerably as a result of the MTCR membership. It suffered a major blow in an attempt to prep up its indigenous satellite launch capability in the early 1990s, when the decision to import cryogenic technology from Glavkosmos (the Soviet space agency) was framed as a violation of the MTCR guidelines. The deal was cancelled on the pretext of the US's scepticism over the evolution of India's Intercontinental Ballistic Missile (ICBM) Programme using Russian cryogenic engines or French 'Victor' rockets, having the potential to threaten mainland America. Now, with the MTCR inclusion, India can gain access to the very high-end technology that it was previously denied, facilitating an uninterrupted expansion of its space programme.

The membership also opens the doors for collaboration with foreign vendors. It allows India to tap into foreign expertise, to give an impetus to indigenous programmes like 'Make in India'. India also stands at the crossroads of augmenting its defence exports—for example, the Indo-Russian joint venture, the BrahMos supersonic cruise missile, is highly sought after among Southeast Asian nations. The same can be construed from India's present position in the list of the top twenty-five arms-exporting nations in the world.

As India stands closer to joining the NSG, its foreign policy vision has adapted itself to growing regional security dynamics. The MTCR membership has significantly added to India's regional power projection. It has advanced India's position as a 'net security provider', capable of deterring Chinese assertiveness. This event reflects the enhanced role of 'pragmatic realism' in India's foreign policy, marking a shift from its hard-line 'soft power' diplomacy.

2017

68. QUAD 2.0

The Indo-Pacific region, which stretches from the Indian Ocean to the Pacific Ocean, has become a major geopolitical flashpoint in recent decades. Managing new-age security threats necessitated a relatively robust collaboration across many domains, such as defence, resource sharing, democracy promotion, counterterrorism, health security, and climate change. Against this dynamic backdrop, Quad 2.0—a reimagined impression of the Quadrilateral Security Dialogue established in 2007, encompassing the US, Japan, India and Australia—has become a focal point of strategic cooperation in the Indo-Pacific. Unlike the older version, the new plurilateral alliance takes a definitive stance on the rising hegemony of China in the region, pushing the concerned regional powers to re-invest and scale up the extent of their engagement. The revival of Quad, hence, is an inevitable consequence of the same realization.

Conceived alongside the 2017 East Asia Summit, Quad 2.0 aims to maintain the status quo in the Indo-Pacific region by furthering a Free and Open Indo-Pacific strategy (FOIP) rooted in a rules-based international order. Building on the former US Secretary of State Hillary Clinton's call to redefine the 'Asia-Pacific' as 'Indo-Pacific' by assuming an enhanced leadership role in the region, Quad 2.0 embodies the liberal vision of a 'positive sum game' promoting mutual gain and common good.

More aptly, Xi Jinping's ascent to office in 2013 supercharged China's quest to reclaim the ancient Sino-centric rhetoric of the 'Chinese Dream', projecting China as the centre of the world order. The growing assertiveness and expansionism characterizing Beijing's foreign policy, as a result, signalled an increase in its territorial claims and military presence. The continual Chinese claims of its perceived sovereignty over the South China Sea, represented by the 'nine-dash line' and 'grey zone diplomacy', coupled with its refusal to accept the UNCLOS verdict in a maritime dispute with the Philippines in 2016, generated a justified sense of uneasiness in the littoral states. Japan's Prime Minister Shinzo Abe, thus, described the Quad reincarnation as a 'democratic security diamond', implicitly providing a counter to the Chinese 'string of pearls' strategy. Even the Australian leader Kevin Rudd, who initially opposed Quad, acknowledged the Dragon's wrath in his second innings. He conceded, 'The extent to which political and strategic circumstances may have changed a decade later is another matter entirely.'[14]

Despite all this, the grouping remained dormant even after its revitalization. It failed to take any collective action or issue any joint statement until 2021. The only event that remained constant in the otherwise fractured Quad was the Malabar exercise, the joint naval endeavour that continued even after the Australian withdrawal in 2008 (excluding disruptions during the Covid-19 pandemic), first bilaterally and then multilaterally.

Given the incremental nature of military confrontation and the deliberate obstruction to its multilateral ambitions (the NSG and the UNSC), China has been a major source of India's pivot to revive Quad. In 2015, India launched the Security and Growth for All in the Region (SAGAR) policy that explicitly mentioned a breakaway from the 'disproportionate dependence' on one country, advocating that all stakeholders' prosperity, sovereignty and connectivity are an article of faith for India. Soon, the strategy was extended in the form of the Indo-Pacific Oceans Initiative (IPOI), which sought to strengthen maritime boundaries in the Indo-Pacific region, particularly with regard to sustainability and security. Captain Gurpreet S. Khurana, executive director of the National Maritime Foundation, New Delhi, argues that though Quad is a 'flexible arrangement', with limited military content for India at present, its strategic potential to deter and contain China cannot be overlooked.[15]

Notably, 'The Spirit of Quad' joint statement released after the joint meeting in 2021 emphasized other non-traditional security aspects to strengthen a free and inclusive Indo-Pacific, defying the military character of Quad. This included a vaccine partnership to circulate one billion vaccines in the region, which gave a boost to India's 'Vaccine Maitri' initiative and countered Beijing's vaccine diplomacy. Significantly, India hosted a CT-TTX (counter-terrorism tabletop exercise), the first of its kind, and regularly steered the Quad Plus format. Similarly, there have been modular configurations under the Quad banner, the Indo-Australia collaboration in the disaster relief domain during cyclones Fani and Seroja, the India-US Clean Energy Agenda 2023, and the US-Japan-India trilateral initiative in quantum technology, all of which helped India deepen its ties, interoperability, and capacity-building vis-à-vis like-minded powers.

Quad countries officially refute any talk of it being a military alliance. However, sceptics claim that this narrative is an act of disservice to countless smaller Asian states that rely on the group's collective strength for protection against China. Quad's careful dance to avoid angering China undermines the very thing these smaller nations seek: a security architecture that deters Chinese aggression. However, one cannot deny that the ambiguity maintained by the grouping acts as a double-edged sword for India, for it is the only country out of the four that shares its border with China; therefore, any form of tiptoeing will be preferred, so that it does not provoke the Dragon.

Notwithstanding the criticism, Quad offers immense potential for India's Neighbourhood First and Act East policies. Similarly, India's fervour within the organization cannot be understated. Quad has galvanized Indian foreign policy towards leveraging its maritime capacity in the Indian Ocean, marking a significant departure from its continental outlook. India's forthrightness within this new security architecture has added to its power projection, instituting it as a key node of influence.

69. THE DOKLAM STANDOFF

Before the Himalayan winter set in over the Doklam Plateau in 2017, India and China engaged in a military standoff, an unprecedented event in their confrontational history since 1962. The clashes arose from Chinese intrusion, involving sabotage of the stone bunkers used sporadically by the Bhutanese armies, in an attempt to construct a road in Doklam. Also known in Chinese as Donglang or Donglang Caochang (meaning 'pasture' or 'grazing field'), Doklam has endured disputed territorial claims from both China and Bhutan, India's close ally, in the past because of its strategic location at a tri-junction border area, touching India, China and Bhutan alike.

Soon, India responded by sending a contingent of around 270 armed soldiers via Sikkim, as a part of Operation Juniper, to counter the Chinese incursion. After a short-lived scrummage, on 28 August, both India and China announced the withdrawal of their troops from the site of the standoff, which the former termed as an 'expeditious disengagement'. The decision came in the run-up to the BRICS Summit, where PM Modi and President Xi Jinping met to decide the future course of their bilateral and multilateral relationships. Xinhua, the state-run Chinese news agency, quoted President Xi verbatim, as he said the following to PM Modi during the summit, 'China and India should see each other as development opportunities, not threats,' and 'peaceful coexistence, win-win cooperation is the only correct choice for China and India.'[16] Many reports highlighted that the Doklam standoff, more than being counter-productive, was a huge blunder on China's part. The PLA's decision to stick to their patrolling rights, even after the de-escalation, was nothing short of a face-saver after the impasse.

On a closer inspection, China's actions in Doklam transcended a mere territorial dispute. The release of a map depicting Doklam as Chinese territory, supposedly supported by Article 1 of the

1890 Convention of Calcutta signed between Britain and China, raised concerns. The Chinese presence in Doklam, apart from being a normative predicament, acted as a major security threat for India with respect to the Siliguri Corridor, the narrow strip of land connecting the Indian mainland to the northeastern states. This posed a significant strategic disadvantage, with the potential to disrupt the movement of security forces in case of a conflict. Recognizing this, the ministry of external affairs asserted that the Chinese attempt to unilaterally subvert the status quo violated the 2012 agreement requiring the determination of tri-junction boundary points between India, China and a third country through consultation among the said countries. The Indian government also posited its intention to resolve the conflict peacefully.

Simultaneously, Beijing officially accused India of disrupting its border talks with Bhutan, and framed it for trespassing and impinging on the territorial sovereignty and independence of both nations. China also claimed that it had notified India of its plan to construct the road 'in advance in full reflection of China's goodwill'.[17] However, the MEA did not provide any definitive confirmation of the same, and maintained its position by questioning the undiplomatic nature of the Chinese construction.

The Doklam crisis served as a crucible for India's foreign policy outlook, exposing a critical cognitive dilemma. It showcased India's measured response, prioritizing diplomatic channels to de-escalate tensions, in the face of the assertive rhetoric from the Chinese defence ministry. The deployment of forces in response also carried the risk of escalation, yet New Delhi's calibrated approach to maintain back-channel diplomacy was reflective of its adroit balancing act.

However, Chinese belligerence prompted India to scale up its security game, lifting the veil from the vulnerabilities of its security apparatus. It further tasked New Delhi to strengthen its eastern frontier by augmenting the border infrastructure and military capability, focusing on deterrence. The security dilemma posed by the event saw increased reconnaissance and deployment of security forces along the LAC from both sides. This was exacerbated by the Galwan clashes in 2020, urging New Delhi to restructure one of its three strike corps facing Pakistan to face China instead, to handle the eastern theatre. Doklam reiterated India's ability to stand its ground vis-à-vis Chinese aggression, resonating with the other regional powers and boosting its regional standing. However, it also advanced the realist case of 'self-help', where India was left to navigate the evolving dynamics of the complex world order without any support from the big or surrounding powers, including Bhutan.

Significantly, the event has underscored its need to develop permanent consultative mechanisms to resolve border disputes with China in a phased manner, a need that has become more apparent than ever. Considering the non-cooperative history of China, India shall be ready to step in to initiate and assert its strategic interests in such a reality.

2018

70. INDIA'S VISION OF THE INDO-PACIFIC

The Indo-Pacific is a geopolitical construct brought into the international relations lexicon due to the rising power competition in the Indian and Pacific Oceans. Due to the assertiveness of China in the Pacific Ocean and the West's strategy of using countries like Japan, Australia and India as balancing powers, it became prudent to treat the two vast oceans as one geopolitical entity. This was concretized during the Trump administration, when the United States Pacific Command (USPACOM) was renamed the US Indo-Pacific Command in 2018. For India, the Indo-Pacific is a broader geographical and strategic expanse, stretching from Africa's eastern coast to the islands of the South Pacific.

In his keynote address at the Shangri La Dialogue in 2018, PM Modi articulated how the Indian Ocean and the Pacific Ocean are connected not only by the geography of the Malacca Strait and the South China Sea, but also by India's multidimensional partnerships with the countries in the region. He listed the key elements of how India envisions this region.[18] First, the region should be free, open and inclusive, welcoming of countries not exclusive to this geography, to contribute to common progress and prosperity. Second, Southeast Asia and ASEAN would be central in establishing a peace and security architecture in the region. Third, a common rules-based order established through dialogue needs to evolve in the region. Fourth, all nations should have access to the use of common spaces in the sea as well as the air, under international law characterized by the freedom of navigation, trade and commerce and the peaceful settlement of disputes. Finally, connectivity, not only of infrastructure but also of trust, is vital to ensure that competition does not turn into conflict.

PM Modi also highlighted how India's Indo-Pacific vision was guided by the 2015 SAGAR policy and India's well-known commitment to ensuring that global transit routes remained secure, peaceful and open for all, especially through forums like the Indian Ocean Naval Symposium, IORA, and Forum for India-Pacific Islands Cooperation (FIPIC). India's Act East Policy bears a special place in India's Indo-Pacific strategy as it remains the key link joining India, especially its northeast region, with the economies of ASEAN, East Asia, Australia and New Zealand. Given the importance of the region, which accounts for half of global trade and commerce moves (including 90 per cent of India's trade), and its vulnerability to numerous challenges such as piracy, cyber security and natural disasters, India does not wish to lag behind in shaping the regional trade and security architecture.

At the time of the formulation of India's Indo-Pacific strategy, India was beset with the task of balancing its relations with the West, which wanted India's support for its China containment strategy, and with China, with which India wanted to resolve the border situation peacefully. Even Russian Foreign Minister Sergey Lavrov called the focus on the Indo-Pacific a ploy of Western countries to draw New Delhi into 'anti-China games'. However, India clarified that it had never deemed the Indo-Pacific a place with limited members, to be seeking to dominate one particular country. Moreover, questions were raised about India's willingness to expand beyond diplomatic and commercial engagements in the region, given that its contemporary focus was on the Western Indian Ocean and South Asia. Nevertheless, analysts such as T.V. Paul pointed out that India did seek to balance China's rise in the region by playing a leading role in shaping the regional architecture.

The coming together of the ASEAN nations, and their demand for a dialogue-based resolution to the competing claims in the South China Sea, created the narrative for the evolution of a new rules-based order in the region. This gave India the foundation to build its balancing strategy towards China. India began to consistently voice its support for the rule of international law, the adherence to The Hague's 2016 arbitration ruling against China, and the peaceful resolution of disputes. The revival of the Quadrilateral Security Dialogue, with India as its member, gave it a ground to stand upon and the opportunity to shape the regional architecture. It is also argued that India's shift of focus to the Pacific, particularly the South China Sea, was due to China making deep inroads into India's neighbourhood and sowing discontent against India. Hence, India decided to do the same in China's sphere of influence. For example, during Minister of External Affairs S. Jaishankar's visit to the Philippines in March 2024, India reiterated its support for the Philippines's territorial claims in the South China Sea.

Thus, India's Indo-Pacific strategy includes strengthening partnerships with regional countries and forming issue-based groupings or coalitions with like-minded partners to address the strategic challenges in the region. This is reflected in India's deepening relations with Southeast and East Asian countries, like Vietnam and the Philippines, particularly in terms of defence cooperation. India is also engaging with countries like the US, France, Japan and Australia in their respective Indo-Pacific strategies. An important aspect of these relations is India's engagement at Quad and the launch of the Indo-Pacific Economic Framework to support Quad's strategic initiatives. While there is no overt attribution of Quad to China's aggression in the region and on India's border, India is also using its relations with countries in the Indo-Pacific to voice its disapproval of China's actions.

2019

71. THE DILUTION OF ARTICLE 370

On 5–6 August 2019, the President of India issued two orders—Constitution (Application to Jammu and Kashmir) Order 272 and 273—effectively rendering Article 370 of the Indian Constitution inoperative. Article 370 provided a special status to the state of Jammu and Kashmir (J&K) in the federal structure of India, in terms of a separate Constitution, the rights of residents, and the autonomy of its internal administration. The newly promulgated Presidential Orders took this special status away from Jammu and Kashmir, and provided that the Constitution of India in its entirety would be made applicable in the state of Jammu and Kashmir. Further, on 9 August, the parliament passed the Jammu and Kashmir Reorganisation Act, 2019, bifurcating the state into two union territories. The Presidential Orders were judicially contested, but on 11 December 2023, a five-judge Constitution Bench of the Supreme Court unanimously upheld those orders, putting to rest all the debates regarding their constitutionality.

Article 370 of the Indian Constitution evolved from the Instrument of Accession through which the erstwhile princely state of Jammu and Kashmir acceded to India post-Independence, in return for protection from invading Pakistani tribes. The invasion from Pakistan started a war with India which ended with a UN-mediated ceasefire. The ceasefire established a status quo, with Pakistan occupying territories in Kashmir which legally belong to India. Pakistan never recognized the Instrument of Accession to India, and harped on a plebiscite to decide the future of Jammu and Kashmir. Since then, Pakistan has fought three more wars in 1965, 1971 and 1998. In 1962, India's war with China in the Aksai Chin region of Ladakh resulted in them occupying the region. China's friendship with Pakistan also makes them a supporter of Pakistan's claim on Kashmir.

During the parliamentary debates, several questions were raised about the action of the government. The Congress Party opposed the unilateral manner in which Article 370 was removed. It argued that Kashmir was a bilateral issue between India and Pakistan, and that the issue was pending at the United Nations. However, the BJP-led government accused the former of toeing the line in favour of Pakistan by calling it a bilateral issue. The home minister clearly stated that all of Kashmir belonged to India, even Pakistan-occupied Kashmir and Aksai Chin (under the illegal occupation of China), and that the PoK seats were still a part of the Jammu and Kashmir legislature. He also added that the abrogation of Article 370 was necessary to further curb terrorism and separatism, and to advance the goals of development in the state.

On the issue of the applicability of the UN Charter on Jammu and Kashmir, the home minister responded that it was Pakistan which violated the provisions of the charter by attacking India in 1965. This continued illegal occupation of a part of Kashmir also voided any question of a referendum. Hence, the breach of faith by Pakistan allowed the Government of India, through the parliament, to exercise full rights to decide matters within its territory. On the question of the duration for which Jammu and Kashmir would continue to be governed as union territories, the home minister assured the parliament members that once the situation in the region normalized, and it was free of terror threats, its statehood would be restored. With respect to this, the Supreme Court had also ordered the Election Commission of India to hold assembly elections there before 30 September 2024.

Pakistan expressed outrage at the Indian government's actions with regard to Article 370. It expelled India's high commissioner and recalled its top diplomat from New Delhi. Bilateral trade was suspended. Its foreign ministry called India's actions a violation of UN resolutions. General Bajwa of the Pakistan Army said, 'Pakistan army firmly stands by the Kashmiris in their just struggle to the very end… We are prepared and shall go to any extent to fulfil our obligations in this regard.'[19] Pakistan's former PM Imran Khan said, '…incidents like Pulwama are bound to happen again… I can already predict this will happen.'[20] Through their resentful statements, both General Bajwa and Imran Khan showed to the world that Pakistan's army and state supported separatist activities and terrorism in Kashmir.

China also came out in support of Pakistan's stance and voiced its opposition to making Ladakh a union territory. At the same time, one change was noted in the stance of Western governments—for example, the US, unlike before, called India's move an 'internal matter' and did not seek to mediate between India and Pakistan, urging both parties to resolve the dispute peacefully. Perhaps this was because of growing strategic relations between India and the West, specifically the US. Nevertheless, there were elements in these countries that feared another conflict between the nuclear-power states India and Pakistan. In this regard, the UN Secretary-General called for 'restraint'.

India stated in clear terms that the entire state of Jammu and Kashmir was an inalienable part of India, and included PoK and

Aksai Chin. On many occasions since, the minister of external affairs has stated that Kashmir is not a bilateral issue, and the only issue to be discussed at the talks with Pakistan is the question of when Pakistan plans to give up its illegal occupation of PoK.[21] However, India recognizes the differences in the perception of the boundary question in the Aksai Chin region. But China's unilateral moves and its aggression on the boundary forced India to push back. With the rising strategic importance of India in order to rebalance China, the West has also come out in support of India, and distanced itself from Pakistan.

2020

72. THE GALWAN VALLEY CLASH

In June 2020, the Chinese and Indian armies clashed along the LAC in eastern Ladakh's Galwan Valley, resulting in the death of twenty Indian soldiers and at least five Chinese soldiers. The clash was the worst of its kind since 1975, when Chinese troops ambushed India's Assam Rifles at Tulung La in Arunachal Pradesh. The Galwan clash led to a military standoff with both sides deploying over 50,000 troops in the area. Despite several rounds of diplomatic, political and military-level talks to defuse the crisis, the two sides remained engaged at the Depsang Plains and Demchok. The Army Chief General Manoj Pande said that the situation was 'stable but sensitive', as operational preparedness remained very high and the deployment of the armed forces was robust and balanced.

According to Hu Shisheng, a senior analyst affiliated with the Chinese Communist Party (CCP) and a director of the South Asia Institute of the China Institutes of Contemporary International Relations (CICIR), there are three reasons why China acted this way. First, it was India's revocation of Article 370 and the change in the political status of Jammu and Kashmir. Second, Hu accused the Indian Army of becoming unduly aggressive, continuously extending the patrol route and building bridges and roads, such as the Darbuk-Shyok-Daulet Beg Oldie (DSDBO) Road, for better connectivity. Third, Hu alleged that PM Modi made the border issue a central aspect of bilateral relations, thus violating the 1988 agreement to put the border dispute aside while developing other aspects of the relationship.

Even before Galwan, China had attempted to unilaterally change the status quo at the LAC. This could be seen from the clashes that erupted at Pangong Tso in Ladakh and Naku La in Sikkim in May 2020. In April 2020, the Chinese had amassed thousands of soldiers, tanks and armoured carriers along the LAC in Ladakh. According to General M.M. Naravane, at Patrolling Point 14 (PP-14) in Galwan, the Chinese PLA reacted violently when the Indian Army asked them to remove their illegally set-up camps. Despite the ongoing crisis in eastern Ladakh, on 9 December 2022, Chinese troops tried to transgress the LAC in the Yangtse area of the Tawang sector. This shows how China's PLA repeatedly provoked the Indian Army.

International reaction to the Galwan clash has largely been in support of India. This is because China has antagonized many regional powers with its aggressive territorial claims in the South China Sea and financial debt traps. In an unprecedented move, the US publicly criticized China's aggressive actions at the LAC and expressed solidarity with the families of the Indian soldiers who died during the clash. The White House, for the first time, said that it would stand with India if a military conflict arose between India and China. The US also helped India with critical intelligence information, cold-weather clothing, and other equipment during the border crisis. Japan, France and Italy also publicly supported India. The European Union and the UN called for restraint on both sides, and urged for de-escalation and dialogue to resolve the situation. Russia also welcomed the de-escalation efforts made by both sides.

At present, both sides are building up infrastructure, including land and air connectivity, not just in Ladakh but along the entire LAC in order to remain vigilant about each other's actions. In accordance with its 2021 land borders law, China built significant civilian and military infrastructure near the border. To counter these Chinese actions, India has also boosted its infrastructure projects, and plans to build seventy-three strategic roads along the LAC, including some in Arunachal Pradesh, and several tunnels to cut transportation time in border regions. The Indian government has also launched its Vibrant Village Programme to build important socio-economic infrastructure in villages on the Indian side of the LAC. This significant build-up of infrastructure at the border points to the existence of longer plans on both sides to maintain their presence in the region, which would constitute a hurdle in resolving the border dispute.

Currently, both China and India are pushing different narratives in their effort to resolve the border crisis. Beijing is pushing the narrative that the situation at the LAC is normalizing and is generally stable. However, India argues that China's normalizing narrative is an attempt to concretize the latter's new gains at the LAC. India's Minister of External Affairs S. Jaishankar has described the situation at LAC as 'very fragile' and 'quite dangerous'. Moreover, China wants to keep the border issue on the back burner and focus on other aspects of bilateral relations. However, India has called for restoring the April 2020 status quo in Ladakh, with Jaishankar stating that 'peace and tranquillity in the border areas is a sine qua non' for the normalization of bilateral relations. Because of China's continuous provocations, India has joined the West as well as Indo-Pacific countries like the Philippines in openly criticizing China's aggressive actions. Countries with an anti-China stance are also supporting India's rise, both to balance China and as a voice of the Global South.

2021

73. THE VACCINE MAITRI INITIATIVE

At the 75th session of the UNGA on 26 September 2020, PM Modi assured the global community that India would use its vaccine production and delivery capacity to help other countries fight the coronavirus pandemic. On 20 January 2021, India began its Vaccine Maitri (Vaccine Friendship) initiative by sending 150,000 and 100,000 vaccines to Bhutan and the Maldives, respectively. Underscoring the importance of its Neighbourhood First policy, India sent vaccines to Bangladesh, Nepal, Myanmar, Seychelles, Mauritius, Afghanistan and Sri Lanka. The next priority was its extended neighbourhood, especially the Gulf, and the smaller and more vulnerable nations in various regions, from Africa to the Caribbean Community (CARICOM). Overall, India sent vaccines to more than 100 countries including the US.

India's Vaccine Maitri initiative was in keeping with the traditions of 'Vasudhaiva Kutumbakam', its 2015 Security and Growth for All in the Region (SAGAR) policy, and its ambition to serve as the region's 'net security provider' through HADR measures. India employed its capabilities as the 'pharmacy of the world' not only to vaccinate its domestic population, but also to manage the needs of its external partners. Besides vaccines, India provided essential medicines, testing kits, personal protection equipment, respirators, and telemedicine services to several countries. India also sent teams of military doctors to Nepal, Maldives and Kuwait to help them manage the pandemic.

Because of these generous donations to foreign countries, the government was criticized for prioritizing its foreign relations at the expense of critical domestic vaccination needs. However, the government made it clear in the parliament that the supply of vaccines to foreign nations was done only after ensuring adequate availability at home. For this reason, India temporarily curtailed its supplies during the second wave of the pandemic in April 2021, and resumed it as soon as supplies normalized. External Affairs Minister S. Jaishankar also informed that India had been using raw materials sourced from other countries to make these vaccines, and hence, it had a moral responsibility to supply the vaccines back to those countries.

The vaccine diplomacy served as an effective instrument of India's soft-power influence, and deepened its ties in the neighbourhood and beyond. Bhutan's prime minister thanked PM Modi for the Indian people's compassion and generosity, and their concern for the well-being of humanity. Bangladesh's health minister likened India's actions to how it stood by their country during the 1971 Liberation War. The Brazilian president thanked PM Modi with a picture of Lord Hanuman carrying the holy herb 'sanjeevani'. India also received praise from the seventy-nine-member African, Caribbean, Pacific (ACP) group and the fifteen-member CARICOM. Praising India's actions, WHO Director-General Dr Tedros Adhanom Ghebreyesus said that India displayed humanitarian responsibility at a time when 'the developed countries monopolised the Pfizer and Moderna vaccines for their populations'.[22] UN Secretary-General António Guterres called India's vaccine production capacity the 'best asset' in the world's fight against the pandemic.

India's Vaccine Maitri initiative also helped the country mend its lately strained relations with its neighbouring countries to counter the rising Chinese influence in the region, especially in Sri Lanka. With Bangladesh, India's ties had nosedived over its 2019 Citizenship Amendment Act. With Nepal, its relations had taken a downturn due to disagreements on some territories at the border. Through Vaccine Maitri, New Delhi showcased its ability to deploy its capabilities for diplomatic purposes and build trust with its neighbours. Seeing India's increasing goodwill in the region, China's *Global Times* began questioning the safety and efficacy of India's vaccines.[23] This was in response to countries like Cambodia, Nepal and Bangladesh refusing to take China's vaccines because of their huge cost, quality concerns, and the conditions of supply. However, India continued its humanitarian efforts and even partnered with the Quad countries in 2021 to accelerate the production of vaccines and extend development finance to countries in the Indo-Pacific to manage the pandemic.

India's strong capabilities in manufacturing and delivering vaccines domestically as well as internationally bolstered its status as a rising power. Its vaccine diplomacy pointed at the success of not only its Neighbourhood First policy, but also its ability to position itself as a leader of the Global South. India had already begun shouldering global responsibilities by providing HADR support and partnering with countries in tackling climate change through initiatives like the International Solar Alliance. Now, with its Vaccine Maitri initiative, India also showcased its ability to provide critical support to countries in managing global health crises. Through its actions, India also intends to demonstrate that in the changing world order, constructive, human-centric actions that benefit all countries must be prioritized, instead of self-serving power-centric ones, so as to build a better world order.

2022

74. INDIA REFUSES TO JOIN THE WEST'S SANCTIONS AGAINST RUSSIA

After Russia invaded Ukraine on 24 February 2022, a number of countries, led by the West, announced sanctions against Russia in order to condemn its actions and push it to end the war. The massive list of sanctions included economic and financial sanctions such as asset freezes and bans on financial transactions, travel, trade and commerce. Sanctions were also imposed on Russian individuals linked with the government. While several nations joined the West-led sanctions regime against Russia, India refused to join the bandwagon. India's stance, based on its core national interests, disappointed the West, and many questions were raised about its implicit support for Russia during the war.

India's response to the Russian war on Ukraine has been to remain neutral, but also to voice its concerns. It has consistently declined to call Russia out as an aggressor, and has abstained from voting against it at the UNSC, General Assembly and Human Rights Council. However, PM Modi had told President Putin in Samarkand in September 2022 that 'today's era is not of war'. In October 2022, S. Jaishankar said, 'We have been very clearly against the conflict in Ukraine. We believe that this conflict does not serve the interests of anybody.'[24] He also highlighted how the war is a humanitarian catastrophe, not just in terms of the lives lost, but also in the way the Global South's low-income countries are facing a shortage of resources such as fuel, food and fertilizers. On the issue of supporting the West-led sanctions against Russia, India reiterated its policy of supporting only UN-backed sanctions, and not supporting any unilateral measures against a particular country.

At the same time as India refused to condemn Russia, it voiced its support for respecting the territorial integrity of both Ukraine and Russia. On the issue of the killings of civilians in Bucha in Ukraine, India condemned it unequivocally and supported the calls for an independent investigation into the matter. Moreover, till February 2024, India had sent fifteen consignments of humanitarian aid to Ukraine. India has also extended financial assistance for the reconstruction of schools and community development projects. While no Indian minister has visited Kiev, PM Modi met the Ukrainian President Volodymyr Zelenskyy in Japan, on the sidelines of the G7 meeting in March 2023, and assured him that India would do everything in its capacity to resolve the situation.

The West, especially the US, was disappointed by India's stance because it reflected a divergence between their value commitments on the rules-based world order—that force must not be used to occupy another country's territory. However, India justified its stance based on the following factors: firstly, the immediate evacuation of thousands of India's citizens, especially students, based in Ukraine; secondly, India wanted to preserve its historically tested friendship with Russia; and thirdly, India still heavily depended on Russia for its military equipment and defence technology. According to the Stockholm International Peace Research Institute (SIPRI), India imported 66.5 per cent of its arms from Russia between 2000 and 2020.

Against the backdrop of the war and the shortage of oil, India began importing huge quantities of oil from Russia. Thus, from less than $2.5 billion in 2021–22, India's imports of Russian crude oil increased to over $31 billion in 2022–23. This decision taken by India drew widespread criticism, especially from the Western media, which accused India of funding the Russian war. India's Minister of External Affairs S. Jaishankar stated that India's stance was based on a balance of its interests and values. He retorted that the West could not morally question India when they themselves were importing large amounts of Russian oil and gas.[25] He justified India's purchases of Russian oil citing India's need for energy security and the availability of Russian oil at a time when Western sanctions had kept Iranian and Venezuelan oil off the market.

India's stand on the war in Ukraine is variously described as 'strategic neutrality' or 'strategic ambivalence'. However, India has clearly put forward its stance taking into account its national interests and values. In the wake of the West's disapproval of India's reticence to join the sanctions regime against Russia, India successfully convinced the West of its own strategic interests. Moreover, India's position of openly talking to the leaders in the US, Russia and Ukraine led to it being invited to the Ukraine Peace Summit in Switzerland in June 2024.[26] This shows India's importance not only in terms of its strong diplomatic credentials, but also in its ability to leverage its strategic weight to gain a leading power status in the emerging international order.

2023

75. INDIA'S G20 PRESIDENCY

India assumed G20 presidency on 1 December 2022, prioritizing a 'reformed' and 'reinvigorated' multilateralism to address various global challenges such as recovery from the Covid-19 pandemic, debt issues in developing nations, and climate change. At the G20 Summit of September 2023, organized according to the theme of Vasudhaiva Kutumbakam, India sought to offer the world an alternative to the crisis-ridden status quo, a shift in the global conversation from 'GDP centrism' to 'human centrism'. India aimed to bridge the divide among countries, amplify the voice of the Global South, and focus on development. India's G20 presidency also displayed its soft-power potential, as more than 200 official events were organized in different parts of the country highlighting its diverse cuisine, ancient traditions and modern innovations.

During its presidency, India hosted the 'Voice of the Global South Summit', bringing together 125 developing nations and setting the tone for a G20 where the concerns and priorities of the Global South were brought to the forefront of international discourse. A significant strategic win for India in mainstreaming the voice of the Global South lay in it securing a permanent membership for the African Union at G20, which had hitherto been accused of 'elite multilateralism'. This move did not just strengthen the G20's reach and inclusivity, but also ensured that the G20 prioritized the development efforts of the least developed countries.

The New Delhi Leaders' Declaration (NDLD), adopted at the end of the summit, aimed to triple the global renewable energy capacity by 2030 and proposed the Green Development Pact to balance environmental protection with food security. India also generated consensus on implementing the 2023 Action Plan to Accelerate Progress on SDGs, by setting up a New Collective Quantified Goal on climate finance from a floor of $100 billion a year. In this context, India co-launched the Global Biofuel Alliance to expedite the global uptake of biofuels. The Declaration also committed to embracing 'Lifestyles for Sustainable Environment' (LiFE) principles, which promoted sustainable production and consumption to reduce carbon emissions. India showcased its achievements in digital welfare infrastructure (Aadhar and United Payments Interface) to secure the commitment of leaders to establish a global digital public infrastructure (DPI), to reduce the digital divide and enable service delivery and innovation.

Russia's absence at the summit made addressing the Ukraine conflict difficult in the New Delhi Leaders' Declaration. For India, it was a test of its long-standing commitment to 'strategic autonomy' or 'omni-alignment', evading the connotations of being 'anti-West' from its criticism of the war. By doing so, India also risked isolation from anti-Western groups like SCO and BRICS, whose presidency it was about to assume. However, in a seasoned display of its diplomatic manoeuvre, India emerged as a 'Vishwamitra' in building consensus on both sides. While Russia found satisfaction in the fact that its direct mention was avoided, with the statement referring to 'the war in Ukraine' instead, the Western nations had the assurance of the statement echoing UN Charter principles urging all states to refrain from using force for territorial gain or violating another state's sovereignty. This also served as a subtle message to India's neighbour China, which chose to opt out of the summit owing to contemporary border tensions. Moreover, the omission of Ukrainian President Zelenskyy from the summit's guest list underscored New Delhi's renewed push for a return to the G20's core focus on economic concerns. The unanimous adoption of the NDLD by all G20 members stands as a testament to India's multilateral prowess, marking the success of its presidency.

In addition to its global impact, India's G20 presidency has left a lasting legacy, as highlighted by Italy's emphasis on including the African Union and the Global South in the upcoming G7 summit. Thus, India's G20 presidency was not merely a successful international summit, but also a transformative moment on the world stage. The 'People's G20' moniker aptly captures the essence of this leadership, as it emerges as an eminent voice of the Global South. This global recognition from leaders like President Biden, who in his UN address commended the India-led G20 for delivering solutions and achieving ground-breaking feats, solidified India's position as a leading power, with a vision for a more inclusive and sustainable future. As India steps down from the G20 presidency, the world undoubtedly sees it in a new light: a responsible and influential player shaping the narrative of the emerging global order.

Prime Minister Narendra Modi delivering the opening remarks to mark the commencement of the G20 Summit 2023, hosted in New Delhi, India.

Source: PIB

Epilogue

It has become a cliché to suggest that the global order today is in a state of flux. The disarray in the world continues unabated as multiple conflicts shape the global environment, fault lines have sharpened further among major powers, and international institutions have continued on their declining streak. The fragmentation of the global economic order has accelerated as emerging technologies have become the most important determinant of the international balance of power. Exacerbating these complex changes has been a leadership void at the global level, which has also contributed to the inability of the extant international system to effectively make provisions for global public goods.

From Russia-Ukraine to Israel-Hamas, it is becoming clear that war is back as the central feature of interstate relations. The instrumentality of force is now not only visible as a key part of the contemporary global order, but its potency is also a reminder that the anarchic nature of international politics continues to exert its pressure on the behaviour of states. Institutions, markets and norms offer no respite, as the strong continue to do as they wish, while the weak continue to suffer as they must. The new normal in today's world is the age-old normal that the international system seems to have forgotten at its own peril.

These conflicts are happening at a time when the great power contestation between the US and China is also beginning to broaden. In more ways than one, the cockpit of this struggle is the Indo-Pacific, where tensions continue to be at an all-time high. This global disorder demands a collective leadership that is conspicuous in its absence. And this means that the world could be entering a phase where the assumptions of the past may no longer be enough to ascertain the trends of the future.

The brooding shadow of violence has always defined the parameters for interstate interactions. But the ferocity with which hard power is making its presence felt is also a reflection of the complacency with which certain actors were engaging with global affairs. As China was accumulating its hard power, Europe was busy dismantling its military structures. The struggle of the EU to emerge as a relevant actor in global geopolitics today is a reflection of its desire to give up on its hard power. And as American adversaries are joining hands, the formidable US fiscal-military machine is also finding it hard to balance them out in multiple theatres.

Not surprisingly, most nations today are trying to fend for their own security by relying on their own capabilities, and the Indo-Pacific is the critical theatre, where the centre of gravity of global politics and economics has shifted. It is here that military expenditures are booming and defence forces are trying to adapt to new strategic realities. It is in the Indo-Pacific where the EU has been forced to come to terms with its own inadequacies in shaping the regional and global balance of power. Even Germany and Japan have started reassessing their strategic choices with a single-minded focus on their hard-power capabilities, which stands as a testament to our changing times.

It is at this crisis-ridden time that India had to showcase its G20 presidency. This allowed India to be at the helm of a troubled global order, and advocate for New Delhi's brand of multilateralism. India's aim was to steer the diverging great powers back to the negotiating table at the G20, and in doing so, to bolster its credentials as a leading power on the global stage.

India's G20 presidency was aimed at steering the world away from polarization, and, instead, moving it towards a greater sense of solidarity. Its own reality of being a multicultural democracy prepared it well, in bringing together highly diverse stakeholders to cogitate, and act, on global challenges. The theme of G20 India 2023—Vasudhaiva Kutumbakam, 'One Earth, One Family, One Future'—encapsulated India's conceptualization of the global order and its own role in it. And New Delhi has demonstrated well that it does not dwell merely on rhetoric. In 2020, as Covid-19 began to surge, it insisted on the need for the international community to work together and help those struggling with the least resources, even as developed nations increasingly focused inwards, with some of them hoarding enough vaccines to inoculate each adult five times over.

At a time of grave worldwide crisis, New Delhi has effectively used all the instruments and platforms available to India to make a case that instead of nations becoming more and more inward-looking, global engagement should be the norm. This is also an attempt to fill the leadership vacuum in the global order, when both China and the US have exposed their vulnerabilities. India has shown that a nation with limited capabilities can also emerge as a leader, by outlining the concerns of like-minded countries and working with them to build capacities in smaller states. The contrast between a world struggling to generate a sense of order and an India ready to shape global outcomes in a positive manner, couldn't have been starker in recent years.

It is in this complex geopolitical environment, and its catalytic effect on Indian foreign policy, that the purpose of this volume was located. The analysis provided insight on the roots of contemporary Indian foreign policy, highlighting, in chronological order, the most significant events of the first three quarters of post-Partition India's first century as an independent nation. To this end, while the volume maintained Leopold von Ranke's objectivist rigour in examining each event, it ultimately fell prey to the inherent challenge of achieving complete objectivity—one of the key critiques Ranke faced. Despite striving for neutrality, the unavoidable influence of presentism shaped the decisions on which events to include or exclude. However, it is this very bias of presentism that enabled the volume to achieve its second-order purpose for the benefit of its audience of future foreign policy analysts, for whom this work will provide a window into how Indian foreign policy and its roots were perceived, as independent India entered the fourth quarter of its first century. Building from the structure of this volume, several realities are highlighted for New Delhi as it enters its Amrit Kaal.

While structural changes have propelled India to the forefront of global politics, leadership within India has also played an important role in re-defining the nation's global priorities. The last decade, however, has witnessed a phenomenal change in both the scale and the scope of global politics. At the same time, politics in India has undergone a tectonic shift. Inevitably, India's foreign policy was bound to be affected as well. But it's not just that. Beyond global shifts, it is also the current Prime Minister Narendra Modi's personal involvement in the realm of external relations that has allowed India to thrive in this complex environment, and has accorded India a unique place in contemporary international affairs today.

Proving the Critics Wrong

It is easy to forget that when Prime Minister Modi came to power in 2014, his critics had painted him as a provincial politician who didn't have adequate experience of engagement with foreign policy. His 'Hindu nationalist' credentials were deemed to be a liability that would constrain India's outreach to the Islamic world in particular. But Prime Minister Modi has managed to keep his detractors as well as supporters on tenterhooks by following a pragmatic foreign policy, keeping the 'India first' mantra at its core. Right from the time he surprised everyone by inviting all South Asian nations to his swearing-in ceremony in 2014, to the current day when a visit to Bhutan is in the works in the midst of a gruelling election campaign, Indian foreign policy has been

'Modi-fied' in ways that were not expected when he took the reins a decade ago.

Of course, India's emergence as the centrepiece of contemporary global political discourse has a lot to do with the structural changes shaping the international order. The shifting balance of power, and growing disillusionment with China in the West, has focused the world's attention on India, which has emerged as the fastest growing major economy in the world. India's favourable demographics, its position as an attractive alternative to China, and its centrality in the key strategic geography of the Indo-Pacific, have together contributed to making this India's century.

Towards Being a 'Rule-Shaper'

What has also changed is New Delhi's growing willingness to be more proactive on the global stage, which is in line with its aim of taking on the role of a 'rule-shaper'. Prime Minister Modi's diplomacy on the global stage has managed to give wings to India's aspirations to play a larger international role. Consequently, Indian foreign policy has made the most of this inflection point in world affairs. In the last decade, India's image of being a perpetual naysayer in global politics has changed to that of a nation that is more than willing to contribute to global governance. The rescue by the Indian Navy, in March 2024, of a commercial ship that had been hijacked by pirates off Somalia's coast, for example, underscored the point that Indian policymakers today are ready and willing to assume operational burden in order to ensure the safety of commercial shipping as well as the freedom of navigation in strategically vital waterways.

The artificial divide between the domestic and the foreign also seems to have faded under Prime Minister Modi. India's key priority remains its domestic developmental transformation, and for that, an all-hands-on-deck approach is crucial. Indian diplomacy, too, is geared towards harnessing the country's developmental aspirations. This has brought about an inherent pragmatism in New Delhi's external outreach, wherein, though partnerships have become key, India's needs, and not its ideologies, determine the contours of its engagements. From building robust ties with the West to sustaining an important partnership with Russia through the tricky landscape of the Ukraine crisis, India has managed to insulate its global engagement from the growing turbulence around it.

'Neighbourhood First'

The Modi government's regional outlook, under the 'Neighbourhood First' approach, has sought to promote regional stability and prosperity, recognizing the importance of a secure and cooperative neighbourhood for India's overall development and security. The focus of New Delhi's South Asia policy has shifted from its fixation on Pakistan to the more productive Bay of Bengal maritime geography, which lends itself to a more organic connection between South and Southeast Asia. This permanent de-hyphenation of India and Pakistan is perhaps the single most important achievement of the last decade, allowing New Delhi to focus on the real strategic challenge: China.

Prime Minister Modi had initially started off by reaching out to China in an effort to manage its rise through diplomatic engagement. Beijing, however, had other plans. India's stance, after the Galwan Valley crisis of 2020, that Sino-Indian relations cannot be normal unless the border situation is resolved, is audacious, and there has been no going back on that. India's growing footprint in East and Southeast Asia, and its inclination to shape the strategic contours of the wider Indo-Pacific region, underscore a new reality: New Delhi will not be diffident as it seeks a greater regional and global role for itself.

Dropping the Ideological Baggage

Over the last few years, New Delhi has not been averse to challenging adversaries and courting friends, and it has done these things without the ideological baggage of the past. From being the only global power to challenge Xi Jinping's Belt and Road Initiative as far back as 2014, responding to Chinese military aggression with a strong military pushback, trying to work with the US without entering into the full embrace of an alliance, to engaging the West for building domestic capacities, India has been pragmatic to the core, and willing to use the extant balance of power to its advantage. India's focus today is on enhancing its capabilities in every possible sector, and that allows for a more clear-eyed engagement with its partners.

A Responsible Stakeholder

Today the world, which has been more used to a pontificating India in the past, hears an Indian voice on the global stage that is capable of articulating the narrative of a responsible stakeholder which, despite being firmly steeped in its own ethos, is not willing to shirk global commitments. New Delhi led the way in shaping the regional response to the Covid-19 pandemic in South Asia, which then became global in scope. India's decision to support its neighbours with critical supplies of medicines, and later vaccines, as part of the Vaccine Maitri initiative was a reflection of a new confidence that it could offer solutions to global problems. India's G20 presidency is just a recent example of how the nation's leadership on the international front has made a mark.

This is a challenging time in global politics, but New Delhi seems to have found a unique and special voice over the last decade. More than any other major power today, Indians view their future in aspirational terms, and that is shaping their domestic as well as foreign engagements. Prime Minister Modi has been successful not only in tapping into that sentiment effectively, but also, in a sense, shaping that aspiration into his own image.

This is an inflection point for the global order, and for India as well. India is on the cusp of achieving something dramatic: it is not only a top-tier economic power that is also a multicultural democracy, but is also a top-tier geopolitical player that can lead, and not simply balance. The choices that New Delhi will make over the next few years will define the contours of that rise.

Notes

Rediscovering Indian Foreign Policy: An Introduction

1 This is roughly transliterated to 'Vasudhaiva Kutumbakam'.
2 World Bank, 'This chart shows the growth of India's economy', 2024, World Economic Forum, 2022. https://tinyurl.com/pt3hpsvd. Accessed on 22 October 2024.
3 West Asia, from an Indian perspective.
4 India's GDP grew by 8.2 per cent in 2023–24, as estimated by the National Statistics Office. Ministry of Statistics and Programme Implementation (MoSPI), Government of India, *PRESS NOTE ON PROVISIONAL ESTIMATES OF ANNUAL GDP FOR 2023-24 AND QUARTERLY ESTIMATES OF GDP FOR Q4 OF 2023-24*, https://tinyurl.com/3spt55b3. Accessed on 18 October 2024.
5 Growth is represented by the annual percentage change of real GDP.
6 IMF, *World Economic Outlook Update*, 2023, https://tinyurl.com/4aa7d2f9. Accessed on 18 October 2024.
7 UNDESA, *India overtakes China as the world's most populous country*, 2023, https://tinyurl.com/yc4bt5bs. Accessed on 18 October 2024.
8 Prime Minister Modi stated in August 2022 that India 'completed 75 years of its independence on August 15 [2022] and [has now] entered the "Amrit Kaal" of independence.' PIB, 'English Rendering of Prime Minister's address from the ramparts of Red Fort on 76th Independence Day', 2022, https://tinyurl.com/3anmr6et. Accessed on 18 October 2024.
9 Pant, Harsh V., 'A quiet but decisive shift in India's foreign policy', Observer Research Foundation, 30 January 2019, https://tinyurl.com/3zrh63y6. Accessed on 18 October 2024.
10 Ministry of External Affairs, GOI, 'IISS Fullerton Lecture by Dr. S. Jaishankar, Foreign Secretary in Singapore', 2015, https://tinyurl.com/262t8f4m. Accessed on 18 October 2024.
11 Ministry of External Affairs, GOI, 'External Affairs Minister's speech at the 4th Ramnath Goenka Lecture', 2019, https://tinyurl.com/mr3ywa9s. Accessed on 18 October 2024.

12 Katju, Vivek, 'In India's balancing act, echoes from the past', *The Indian Express*, 10 April 2022, https://tinyurl.com/5n6mdnrw. Accessed on 18 October 2024.

13 Ministry of External Affairs, GOI, 'External Affairs Minister's remarks on the topic "Preparing for a Different Era" at Center for Strategic and International Studies, Washington D.C. (October 01, 2019)', 2019, https://tinyurl.com/3b5cpcwx. Accessed on 18 October 2024.

Wave 1: 1947–64: State-building and the Nehruvian Outlook

1 The pact opens with both nations 'solemnly agree[ing] that each shall ensure, to minorities throughout its territory, complete equality of citizenship, irrespective of religion, a full sense of security in respect of life, culture, property and personal honour, freedom of movement within each country and freedom of occupation, speech, and worship, subject to law and morality'.

2 'New Evidence On North Korean War Losses', Wilson Centre, 1 August 2001, https://tinyurl.com/yc2z9wtm. Accessed on 18 October 2024.

3 Roy, Nabarun. 'India's Forgotten Links to the Korean War', *The Diplomat*, 27 October 2018, https://tinyurl.com/zfvpjdaj. Accessed on 18 October 2024.

4 Ministry of External Affairs, GOI, 'Treaty of Peace and Friendship, 31 July 1950', https://tinyurl.com/2btb7sme. Accessed on 18 October 2024.

5 Nehru, Jawaharlal, 'Jawaharlal Nehru, "Note on Visit to China and Indo-China"', Wilson Centre, https://tinyurl.com/y4sukj9s. Accessed on 18 October 2024.

6 Rao, Nirupama, 'The Politics of History: India and China, 1949-1962', The Watson Institute for International Studies at Brown University, Working Paper No. 2014-18, https://tinyurl.com/3388cdjs. Accessed on 18 October 2024.

7 Hyer, Eric, 'China's Policy of Conciliation and Reduction and its Impact on Boundary Negotiations and Settlements in the Early 1960s', 2017, Wilson Centre, CWIHP Paper Series, https://tinyurl.com/y4rrbytr. Accessed on 18 October 2024.

8 An excerpt from Nehru's speech at the Moscow Dynamo Stadium on June 23, 1955: 'More particularly we have long felt that the non-recognition by the U.N. of the great People's Republic of China is not only an anomaly and not in keeping with the spirit of the Charter,

but is a danger to the promotion of peace and solution of the world's problems. One of the most vital problems today is that of the Far East and this cannot be settled without the goodwill and co-operation of the People's Republic of China. I trust that we shall soon see the People's Republic of China taking its rightful place in the U.N. and that attempts being made to find a solution to the problems of the Far East will meet with increasing success.'

9 For further reading to India's offer for a seat on the UNSC, please see Harder, Anton, 'Not at the Cost of China: New Evidence Regarding US Proposals to Nehru for Joining the United Nations Security Council', 2015, Woodrow Wilson International Center for Scholars, Working Paper 76, https://tinyurl.com/4uvv9byh. Accessed on 18 October 2024.

10 'Minutes of Chairman Mao Zedong's Third Meeting with Nehru', Wilson Centre Digital Archive, https://tinyurl.com/mrnn9n6n. Accessed on 18 October 2024.

11 Ministry of Foreign Affairs, People's Republic of China, 'Partners May Have Differences, But They Seek Common Ground', 2022, https://tinyurl.com/4h8nck4v. Accessed on 18 October 2024.

12 Paranjpe, V.V., 'Jawaharlal Nehru & Zhou Enlai: Contrasting Personalities', *World Affairs: The Journal of International Issues*, Vol. 2, No. 2, 1998, pp. 51–55, https://tinyurl.com/8ch5269k. Accessed on 18 October 2024.

13 'Note by the Prime Minister on the Visit of Soviet Leaders to India, November-December, 1955', Nehru Memorial Museum & Library, Subimal Dutt Collection, Subject File No. 17, New Delhi. A summary was published in Nehru, Jawaharlal, *Selected Works of Jawaharlal Nehru*, Second Series, Vol. 31 (1 February-30 April 1956), Jawaharlal Nehru Memorial Fund, New Delhi, 2003, pp. 303–306.

14 Nayudu, Swapna Kona, 'Nehru's India & the Suez Canal Crisis of 1956', *India in Transition*, CASI, 7 November 2016, https://tinyurl.com/34d7vanh. Accessed on 18 October 2024.

15 Dates reported by Bhabha Atomic Research Centre (BARC), 2006.

16 Quoted in Sethna, H.N., 'India's Atomic Energy Programme Past and Future', *IAEA Bulletin*, Vol 21, No. 5, October, 1979, pp. 2–11, https://tinyurl.com/ycsfrut5. Accessed on 19 December 2024.

17 Description of Apsara by the Director of the Reactor Group of the Bhabha Atomic Research Centre in 2006.

18 Dhanda, Suresh, 'India's Nuclear Weapons Programme: Retrospect and Prospects', *Indian Foreign Affairs Journal*, Vo. 4, No. 1, January-

March 2009, pp. 82–102, https://tinyurl.com/w7e4fe3b. Accessed on 19 December 2024.

19 The Dooars had been ceded to the British in the Treaty of Sinchula in 1865, in return for an annual subsidy of ₹50,000.

20 Tobgye, Justice Sonam, 'The Development of Bhutan's Relations with India', *Kuensel*, 9 February 2019, https://tinyurl.com/2envw73r. Accessed on 18 October 2024.

21 'Discussion between N.S. Khrushchev and Mao Zedong', Wilson Centre Digital Archive, https://tinyurl.com/398696k5. Accessed on 18 October 2024.

22 Salman, Salman M.A., and Kishor Uprety, *Conflict and Cooperation on South Asia's International Rivers*, World Bank Publications, 2002, p. 42; Baxter, R.R., 'The Indus Basin', *The Law of International Drainage Basins*, Garretson, et al. (eds.), Oceana Publications, New York, 1967, pp. 449–457, https://tinyurl.com/sw3t6kcr. Accessed on 18 October 2024.

23 The delivery of water had been discontinued from the Ferozpur headworks to the Dipalpur Canal, and to the main branches of the Upper Bari Doab Canal.

24 Ministry of External Affairs, GOI, 'Notes, Memoranda and Letters Exchanged and Agreements signed between The Governments of India and China: Correspondence Nehru-Zhou', WHITE PAPER III, November 1959–March 1960, https://tinyurl.com/yhjfrf3b. Accessed on 18 October 2024.

25 'Premier Chou En-Lai's Written Statement; the text of the written statement issued by Premier Chou En-Lai at the press conference in New Delhi on April 25', *Peking Review*, 3 May 1960, pp. 18–19; 'Joint Communiqué of Chinese and Indian Premiers,' *Peking Review*, 3 May 1960, p. 17, https://tinyurl.com/2s2b423m. Accessed on 19 October 2024.

26 'Report from the Chinese Foreign Ministry, "The Soviet Union's Stance on the Sino-Indian Boundary Question and Soviet-Indian Relations"', Wilson Centre Digital Archives, https://tinyurl.com/bpasz8kh. Accessed on 19 October 2024.

27 Chari, P. R., 'Indo-Soviet Military Cooperation: A Review', *Asian Survey*, Vol. 19, No. 3, 1979, p. 234, https://tinyurl.com/38cj4n4c. Accessed on 19 October 2024.

28 Government of India, *Annual Report 1976-77: Ministry of Defense*, p. 28.

29 Nonviolent activists.

30 Similar incidents of firing on Satyagrahis were recorded in Daman and Diu. For further insights into the brutal suppression, please see Pathak, G. S., 'Treatment of Indian Nationals by Portugal and The Law Of Nations', *India Quarterly*, Vol. 12, No. 1, 1956, pp. 22–31, https://tinyurl.com/3km4wnuf. Accessed on 19 October 2024.

31 'International Reactions to Indian Attack on Goa. - Soviet Veto of Western Cease-fire Resolution in security Council', *Keesing's Record of World Events*, Volume 8, 1962, p. 18659, https://tinyurl.com/4e6wbnxj. Accessed on 19 October 2024

32 Singhal, D.P., 'Goa—End of an Epoch', *The Australian Quarterly*, Vol. 34, No. 1, 1962, pp. 77–89, https://tinyurl.com/ms9mzdtr. Accessed on 19 October 2024.

33 Please see previous note regarding Zhou Enlai's visit to India in 1960.

34 Kissinger, Henry, *On China*, Penguin, New York, 2012.

35 Lamb, Alastair, 'The Sino-Pakistani boundary agreement of 2 March 1963', *Australian Outlook*, Vol. 18, No. 3, 1964, pp. 299–312, https://tinyurl.com/mx2amm5y. Accessed on 19 October 2024.

36 Cheema, P.I., 'Significance of Pakistan-China Border Agreement of 1963', *Pakistan Horizon*, Vol. 39, No. 4, 1986, pp. 41–52, https://tinyurl.com/32d84fmx. Accessed on 19 October 2024.

Wave 2: 1964–85: Regional Consolidation and Antagonisms

1 Central Intelligence Agency, 'OUTCOME OF INDIA-PAKISTAN WARFARE', https://tinyurl.com/3anbwvk4. Accessed on 19 October 2024.

2 Menon, Vandana, Raghav Bikhchandani, and Laeeq, Humra. 'Hungry India, a nawabi US President, "Mexican blood"—The real story of Green Revolution', *The Print*, 19 February 2022, https://tinyurl.com/mr4r6vc8. Accessed on 19 October 2024.

3 Subramaniam, Arjun, 'Book Extract: Full Spectrum: India's Wars 1972-2020 by Arjun Subramaniam'. *The Indian Express*, 13 September 2020, https://tinyurl.com/u3ueaepm. Accessed on 19 October 2024.

4 The resolution called upon the Conference of the Eighteen-Nation Committee on Disarmament 'to give urgent consideration to the question of non-proliferation of nuclear weapons and, to that end, to reconvene as early as possible with a view to negotiating an international treaty to prevent the proliferation of nuclear weapons,

based on the following main principles: (a) The treaty should be void of any loopholes which might permit nuclear or non-nuclear Powers to proliferate, directly or indirectly, nuclear weapons in any form; (b) The treaty should embody an acceptable balance of mutual responsibilities and obligations of the nuclear and non-nuclear Powers; (c) The treaty should be a step towards the achievement of general and complete disarmament and, more particularly, nuclear disarmament; (d) There should be acceptable and workable provisions to ensure the effectiveness of the treaty; (e) Nothing in the treaty should adversely affect the right of any group of States to conclude regional treaties in order to ensure the total absence of nuclear weapons in their respective territories.'

5 Indira Gandhi Abhinandan Samiti, *The Spirit of India, Vol. 1*, Asia Publishing House, Bombay, 1975, https://tinyurl.com/vk4ynp9u. Accessed on 22 October 2024.

6 Article IV states that the Treaty 'respects India's policy of non-alignment and reaffirms that this policy constitutes an important factor in the maintenance of universal peace and international security and in the lessening of tensions in the world'.

7 Foreign Minister Swaran Singh, in his address to the Lok Sabha, declared: 'This Treaty is, in its true sense, a treaty of peace. It strengthens our policy of non-alignment, respect for which is expressly mentioned in the Treaty. We sincerely hope that the policy of non-alignment will be further strengthened and will become an effective instrument for the safeguarding of our national interests as well as an important factor in the maintenance of universal peace and international security and in the lessening of tensions in the world.'

8 Noted by Michael Gerson (2010) in a report (ASCO, 2010, 027) titled 'The Sino-Soviet Border Conflict: Deterrence, Escalation, and the Threat of Nuclear War in 1969', at the Centre for Naval Analyses (CAN) Strategic Studies, under the Defence Threat Reduction Agency of the US Department of Defence, p. iv, https://tinyurl.com/ms7eye8w. Accessed on 19 October 2024.

9 Unnikrishnan, Nandan, '1971: When Delhi and Moscow came together', Observer Research Foundation, 16 August 2021, https://tinyurl.com/2dtxhmnk. Accessed on 19 October 2024.

10 See *Organiser*, Vol. 25, No. 2, 21 August 1971, pp. 1–2, cited in Singh, S.P., 'Indo-Soviet Treaty – A Critique', *Proceedings of the Indian History Congress*, Vol. 40, 1979, p. 1058, https://tinyurl.com/mv2anynz. Accessed on 19 October 2024.

11 Ibid.

12 Mascarenhas, Anthony, 'Genocide', *The Sunday Times (UK)*, 13 June 1971, https://tinyurl.com/yfwfn953. Accessed on 19 October 2024.
13 Rummel, R.J., *Statistics of Genocide*, L LIT Verlag, Germany, 1998. Also, Rahman, Arif, *Three Million Deaths: Excess or Reality?*, Nandanik, Dhaka, 2015, cited in Ahmed, Imtiaz, *Recognising the 1971 Bangladesh Genocide: An Appeal for Rendering Justice*, Ministry of Foreign Affairs, Government of the People's Republic of Bangladesh, 2022, p. 4, https://tinyurl.com/49y5bmhv. Accessed on 19 October 2024.
14 Walter, Michael, 'The U.S. Naval Demonstration in the Bay of Bengal during the 1971 India-Pakistan War', *World Affairs*, Vol. 141, No. 4, 1979, pp. 293–306, https://tinyurl.com/mw2y2fj2. Accessed on 19 October 2024.
15 See literature on game theory.
16 MEA, 'Agreement Between the Government of India and the Government of the Islamic Republic of Pakistan on Bilateral Relations (Simla Agreement)', 1972, https://tinyurl.com/2k547d29. Accessed on 19 October 2024.
17 'DOCUMENTS', *Pakistan Horizon*, Vol. 27, No. 4, 1974, pp. 159–200, https://tinyurl.com/49ekzzrc. Accessed on 19 October 2024.
18 Bakshi, K.N., 'Simla Agreement (1972): From Military Victory to A Diplomatic Defeat?' *Indian Foreign Affairs Journal*, Vol. 2, No. 3, 2007, pp. 105–19, https://tinyurl.com/ymjmkzru. Accessed on 19 October 2024.
19 Bhargava, G.S., 'THE SIMLA AGREEMENT—An Overview', *India Quarterly*, Vol. 29, No. 1, 1973, pp. 26–31, https://tinyurl.com/4epwpu36. Accessed on 19 October 2024.
20 The multilateral export control regime was established and initially consisted of seven members, West Germany, Canada, France, Japan, USSR, UK and US.
21 Kennedy, Andrew, 'India's Nuclear Odyssey: Implicit Umbrellas, Diplomatic Disappointments, and the Bomb', *International Security*, Vol. 36, No. 2, 2011, pp. 120–153, https://tinyurl.com/2nkkf3cu. Accessed on 19 October 2024.
22 The Group of 77 (G-77) was established in 1964 by the developing nations, and rapidly grew to become, as is stated in its aims, 'the largest intergovernmental organization of developing countries in the United Nations, which provides the means for the countries of the South to articulate and promote their collective economic interests and enhance their joint negotiating capacity on all major international economic issues within the United Nations system, and promote South-South cooperation for development'.

23 The GATT was the precursor to the World Trade Organization (WTO), which it replaced in 1995 under the Marrakesh Agreement.

24 The theory of the drain of wealth broadly proposes that India's increasing poverty could be attributed to the British colonial system, which was designed to cater to a net outflow of capital and assets from India to the United Kingdom. Dadabhai Naoroji's ideation manifested in the foundation of the Indian National Congress in 1886, with Naoroji serving several terms as its president. Interestingly, these ideas are also present in several Maharashtrian intellectuals in the 1840s, see Naik, J.V., 'Forerunners of Dadabhai Naoroji's Drain Theory', *Economic and Political Weekly*, Vol. 36, No. 46/47, 2001, pp. 4428–4432, https://tinyurl.com/3m5yyb3f. Accessed on 19 October 2024.

25 The dependency theory proposes that a world system of dependency is perpetuated by the rich nations, situated at the core of the world system, and it is characterized by the outflow of resources from poor nations, situated at the periphery of the world system.

26 For related works, please see *The Prison Notebooks* by Antonio Gramsci; and Immanuel Wallerstein, Andre Gunder Frank, Ha-Joon Chan, Amartya Sen, and Susan Strange, among others.

27 For further details, see the authors of critical theories of development mentioned in the previous footnote.

28 Quotation taken from Franczak, Michael, 'Losing the Battle, Winning the War: Neoconservatives versus the New International Economic Order, 1974–82', *Diplomatic History*, Vol. 43, No. 5, November 2019, pp. 867–889, https://tinyurl.com/y8y2mcwf. Accessed on 19 October 2024.

29 'Telegram 10183 From the Consulate General in Hong Kong to the Department of State', *Foreign Relations Of The United States, 1969–1976, Volume E–8, Documents On South Asia, 1973–1976*, Department of State, United States of America.

30 Doc. 2267, 'Telegram from Indian Embassy, Peking to the Ministry of External Affairs, 01 May, 1970', *India-China Relations 1947-2000: A Documentary Study,* Vol 5, A.S. Bhasin (ed), Geetika Publishers, New Delhi, 2018, p. 4810.

31 As described by a former foreign minister, in Jiaxuan,Tang, *Heavy Storm and Gentle Breeze: A Memoir of China's Diplomacy*, HarperCollins Publishers, New York, 2011, p. 171.

32 Lin, Biao, and Zedong Mao, 'Mao Zedong's Talk at a Meeting of the Central Cultural Revolution Group (Excerpt)', March 15, 1969, *Zhonghua renmin gongheguo shilu* [A Factual History of the People's Republic of China], Vol. 3, Part 1, Jilin renmin chubanshe, Changchun,

1994, pp. 467–469, History and Public Policy Program Digital Archive, https://tinyurl.com/b5z2d9hd. Accessed on 19 October 2024.

33 'January 28, 1976, Forty Years Ago: Indo-China Relations', *Express News Service*, https://tinyurl.com/yjb2bkzu. Accessed on 19 June 2024.

34 The Minister of External Affairs. quoted in *The New York Times*. Borders, William, 'India to Send Ambassador to China, First in 15 Years', *The New York Times*, 16 April 1976, https://tinyurl.com/4wdv9c8e. Accessed on 19 October 2024.

35 Notably, while the two 'package deals' in 1980 and 1982 were mentioned by Deng Xiaoping during Prime Minister Indira Gandhi's tenure, a similar 'package deal' was unsuccessfully offered in April 1960 by the Chinese premier Zhou Enlai to Prime Minister Jawaharlal Nehru.

36 The former was a result of the Anglo-Nepalese War of 1814–16, and the latter was a consequence of the support provided to the British during the events of 1857.

37 'Toasts of the President and Prime Minister Indira Gandhi of India at the State Dinner', Reagan Library, https://tinyurl.com/54xh9j9x. Accessed on 19 October 2024.

38 Many of the details and the accounts of Operation Lal Dora was brought to light in 2013 by an Australian scholar, David Brewster, and a former Indian Director of Naval Intelligence, Ranjit Rai, in their research article 'Operation Lal Dora: India's Aborted Military Intervention in Mauritius', *Asian Security*, Vol. 9, No. 1, 2013, pp. 62–74, https://tinyurl.com/pxysx4dm. Accessed on 19 October 2024.

39 The island of Diego Garcia is a British Indian Ocean Territory which is claimed by Mauritius and has a major US Indian Ocean naval base stationed in it. The prospect of a US intervention seemed likely, with the memory of its gunboat diplomacy, and the intrusion by USS *Enterprise* into the Bay of Bengal, towards the close of the 1971 War with Pakistan.

40 Estimates by the *Hindustan Times* indicate that just a fifth of the deaths at the Siachen Glacier were caused by enemy combat, the majority being victims of the altitude and the terrain. 'Of 1,000 soldiers lost in Siachen, only 220 fell to enemy bullets', *The Hindustan Times*, 14 February 2016, https://tinyurl.com/4rw233h6. Accessed on 19 October 2024.

41 Nair, P., 'The Siachen War: Twenty-Five Years On', *Economic and Political Weekly*, Vol. 44, No. 11, 2009, p. 37, https://tinyurl.com/yzxwhkdb. Accessed on 19 October 2024.

42 Zain, O. F., 'Siachen Glacier Conflict: Discordant in Pakistan-India Reconciliation', *Pakistan Horizon*, Vol. 59, No. 2, 2006, p. 78, https://tinyurl.com/mvb96p37. Accessed on 19 October 2024.

Wave 3: 1985-2004: Opening up to the World

1 Bohlen, Celestine, 'Gandhi, Gorbachev Sign Pacts For Soviet Loans, Trade With India', *The Washington Post*, 23 May 1985, https://tinyurl.com/y5e6nw5e. Accessed on 19 October 2024.

2 Markham, James M., 'Rajiv Gandhi, in Speech to Nation, Pledges a Continuity of Policies', *The New York Times*, 13 November 1984, https://tinyurl.com/ms5bbwnx. Accessed on 20 December 2024.

3 Mydans, Seth, 'GANDHI STRESSES INDIA-SOVIET LINK', *The New York Times*, 23 May 1985, https://tinyurl.com/2fs6utvu Accessed on 19 October 2024.

4 This data has been gathered from the Stockholm International Peace Research Institute (SIPRI), Military Expenditure Database.

5 Central Intelligence Agency, *India-USSR: Strains in Relations*, https://tinyurl.com/2kdcvhef. Accessed on 19 October 2024.

6 Thakur, Ramesh, 'India and the Soviet Union: Conjunctions and Disjunctions of Interests', *Asian Survey*, Vol. 31, No. 9, 1991, pp. 826–46, https://tinyurl.com/5n8zu7fb. Accessed 19 October 2024.

7 Estimates calculated by the World Bank, 2022, https://tinyurl.com/5fvvauv8. Accessed on 19 October 2024.

8 Burr, William, 'China, Pakistan, and the Bomb: The Declassified File on U.S. Policy, 1977-1997', NSA Archive, https://tinyurl.com/jf2m3sjz. Accessed on 19 October 2024.

9 Battle, Joyce, 'India and Pakistan – On the Nuclear Threshold', NSA Archives, https://tinyurl.com/mr2aarrk. Accessed on 19 October 2024.

10 The Symington Amendment of the Foreign Assistance Act of 1961 barred US economic and military assistance to any country that imported or exported spent nuclear fuel for reprocessing, or uranium enrichment equipment, materials, or technology, but failed to comply with the International Atomic Energy Agency (IAEA)'s full-scope safeguards.

11 In January 1972, the union territory of Arunachal Pradesh was created, previously known as the North-East Fronter Agency (NEFA).

12 Maxwell, Neville, 'Sino-Indian Border Dispute Reconsidered', *Economic and Political Weekly*, Vol. 34, No. 15, 1999, pp. 905–18, https://tinyurl.com/45zu7ds9. Accessed 21 October 2024.

13 The Reorganised Army Plains Infantry Division (RAPIDS) was the introduction of compact, integrated formations that afforded greater flexibility, mechanization, firepower, mobility, and air-to-land battle capabilities.

14 'Brass Tacks and Kashmir: India-Pakistan Military Crises in the 1980s', ADST, https://tinyurl.com/5fhx7jd3. Accessed on 21 October 2024.

15 Badhwar, Inderjit, 'General Sundarji leaves behind a legacy most fiercely disputed in the history of the army', *India Today*, 15 May 1988, https://tinyurl.com/4782wp7k. Accessed on 19 October 2024.

16 'Estimates of GDP Growth (annual percentage) – Nepal', World Bank data, https://tinyurl.com/5deavvaj. Accessed on 21 October 2024.

17 In December 1960, King Mahendra led a coup d'état and wrested control of the Nepalese government from the democratically elected cabinet of Prime Minister B.P. Koirala, and set up the Panchayat system.

18 Later, between 1996 and 2006, Nepal faced a civil war between the Nepalese state and the Maoist Communist Party of Nepal.

19 Crossette, Barbara, 'Nepal's Economy Is Gasping as India, a Huge Neighbor, Squeezes It Hard', *The New York Times*, 11 April 1989, https://tinyurl.com/2p9um5wv. Accessed on 21 October 2024.

20 The minority communities include the Madhesi, Janjati, and Tharu communities, among others.

21 Bobb, Dilip, 'Prime Minister Rajiv Gandhi's visit to China marks a new beginning in bilateral relations', *India Today*, 15 January 1989, https://tinyurl.com/ypacs3v8. Accessed on 20 December 2024.

22 Ministry of Information and Broadcasting, GOI, 'Rajiv Gandhi Selected Speeches and Writings', Vol. 4, https://tinyurl.com/53rybnhy. Accessed on 22 October 2024.

23 The NWS, as recognized by the NPT, are the US, Soviet Union, UK, France, and China.

24 See Note 38.

25 PTI, 'Rajiv Gandhi's ideas on nuclear-free world will show the way: Mani Shankar Aiyar', *The Economic Times*, 21 May 2012, https://tinyurl.com/yc8tmwa9. Accessed on 20 December 2024.

26 This arms-control treaty marked the first instance in which the two superpowers agreed to reduce their nuclear arsenals, eliminate an entire category of weapons, and employ extensive on-site inspection for verification. Unfortunately, in 2019, the Trump administration withdrew from this pact, alleging Russian non-compliance, which was soon followed by Russia's withdrawal from the same.

27 This was largely an outcome of the mismanaged military build-up on both sides of the border, caused by India's Operation Brasstacks (see Note 41).

28 Bhagwati, Jagdish, and Padma Desai, *India: Planning for Industrialization*, Oxford University Press, London, 1970. See also, Panagariya, Arvind,

'India in the 1980s and 1990s: A Triumph of Reforms', IMF Working Paper, March 2004, https://tinyurl.com/dx57xvef. Accessed on 20 December 2024.

29 Canalized imports refer to the monopoly rights of the state to import selected items.

30 The difference between globalization and neoliberal globalization is worth noting, and can be understood further in the works of Henry Wai-Chung Yeung, Ben Fine, Kyung-Sup Chang, Linda Weiss, and Ha-Joon Chang.

31 Among others, reasons for this have been located in the nation's labour laws. For further reading, please see Panagariya, Arvind, 'India in the 1980s and 1990s: A Triumph of Reforms', IMF Working Paper, WP/04/43, 2004, https://tinyurl.com/2bwtm2jt. Accessed on 21 October 2024.

32 For further reading, please see Utsa Patnaik, Vicente Navarro, Kathy Le Mons Walker, Kalim Siddiqui and John Rapley, among others.

33 ASEAN currently includes Indonesia, Malaysia, the Philippines, Singapore, Thailand, Vietnam, Brunei, Laos, Myanmar and Cambodia.

34 'India's Look East policy', *The Economic Times*, 12 February 2007, https://tinyurl.com/4k23cvvx. Accessed on 22 October 2024.

35 Singh, B.P., 'INDIA'S LOOK EAST POLICY: AN ASSESSMENT', *The Indian Journal of Political Science*, Vol. 76, No. 1, 2015, pp. 101–16, https://tinyurl.com/2meaxhft. Accessed 21 October 2024.

36 Haokip, T., 'India's Look East Policy: Prospects and Challenges for Northeast India', *Studies in Indian Politics*, Vol. 3, No. 2, 2015, pp. 198–211, https://tinyurl.com/37vynf4x. Accessed on 21 October 2024.

37 A simultaneous increase in inflation and unemployment.

38 For further readings on the evolution of the global economic system, read Nitsan Chorev, Richard Peet, Elaine Hartwick, Ha Joon-Chang, Jostein Hauge, John Ruggie, among others.

39 General Agreement on Trade in Services (GATS).

40 Agreement on Trade-Related Investment Measures (TRIMS).

41 Agreement on Trade-Related Aspects of Intellectual Property Rights (TRIPS).

42 Chorev, N., 'Fixing Globalization Institutionally: US Domestic Politics of International Trade', *International Sociology*, Vol. 25, No. 1, 2010, pp. 54–74, https://tinyurl.com/yc5d43zd. Accessed on 21 October 2024.

43 Special Secretary, Ministry of Commerce, and Chief Negotiator for India at the Uruguay Round of multilateral trade negotiations.

44 The Gulf Cooperation Council (GCC) includes the states of Saudi Arabia, United Arab Emirates, Kuwait, Qatar, Oman and Bahrain.

45 As stated in Article I of the Treaty.
46 The PTBT had prohibited nuclear weapons tests in the atmosphere, outer space, and underwater, but did not include those conducted underground. This exclusion was partly due to the inability of detection and supervision of underground testing.
47 The treaty describes that states included in Annex 2 are those that were 'members of the Conference on Disarmament as at 18 June 1996 which formally participated in the work of the 1996 session of the Conference and which appear in Table 1 of the International Atomic Energy Agency's April 1996 edition of "Nuclear Power Reactors in the World", and of States members of the Conference on Disarmament as at 18 June 1996 which formally participated in the work of the 1996 session of the Conference and which appear in Table 1 of the International Atomic Energy Agency's December 1995 edition of "Nuclear Research Reactors in the World"'.
48 Information gathered from the Comprehensive Nuclear-Test-Ban Treaty Organization (CTBTO), 2024.
49 The CD was set up initially in 1978, as a thirty-eight-member body replacing the Eighteen Nation Disarmament Committee set up in 1961.
50 India's Ambassador and Permanent Representative to the UN in Geneva.
51 'India's Official Stand on the CTBT', statement by Arundhati Ghose, India's Ambassador and Permanent Representative to the UN in Geneva, at the Plenary Session of the Conference on Disarmament, Geneva, 20 August 1996 (Ministry of External Affairs, Government of India).
52 Terms like 'qualitative improvement of nuclear weapons', 'advanced new types of nuclear weapons', 'nuclear weapon test explosions', 'other nuclear weapons', among others, have not been defined in technical terms.
53 Article Analysis of the Comprehensive Nuclear Test Ban Treaty, Arms Control and Disarmament Agency, USA, in Jayaprakash, N.D., 'Nuclear Disarmament and India', *Economic and Political Weekly*, Vol. 25, No. 7, 2000, p. 528.
54 Chellaney, Brahma, 'The Military Nuclear Option Poses a Grave Dilemma for India', *International Herald Tribune*, 26 January 1996, p. 8.
55 With the inclusion of Nepal and Bhutan in 2004, the group was renamed the Bay of Bengal Initiative for Multi-Sectoral Technical and Economic Cooperation, retaining the BIMSTEC acronym.
56 Association of Southeast Asian Nations.

57 South Asian Association for Regional Cooperation.

58 For a detailed insight into the Gujral Doctrine, see Sen Gupta, Bhabani, 'India in the Twenty-First Century', *International Affairs*, Vol. 73, No. 2, 1997, pp. 297–314, https://tinyurl.com/2wnsrfsk. Accessed on 21 October 2024.

59 'The Gujral Doctrine: Text of "Aspects of India's Foreign Policy", A Speech by I.K. Gujral at the Bandaranaike Center For International Studies in Colombo, Sri Lanka On January 20, 1997', *Stimson*, 21 January 1997, https://tinyurl.com/3dsxrstb. Accessed on 21 October 2024.

60 Gujral, I.K., *Matters of Discretion*, Hay House, Carlsbad, 2011.

61 Mehta, Rupal N., 'India: Erstwhile Ally and Nuclear Reversal', *Delaying Doomsday: The Politics of Nuclear Reversal,* Oxford Academic, New York, 2020, https://tinyurl.com/yc3zkfzk. Accessed on 21 October 2024.

62 For further insight into the economic impacts of these sanctions, see Morrow, Daniel, and Michael Carriere, 'The Economic Impacts of the 1998 Sanctions on India and Pakistan', *The Nonproliferation Review*, 1999.

63 For further insight, see Gupta, Vipin, and Frank Pabian, 'Investigating the Allegations of Indian Nuclear Test Preparations in the Rajasthan Desert', *Science and Global Society*, 1996, pp. 101–189. Interestingly, speculations also exist about India considering another nuclear explosion in early 1982. See Bhattacharya, Shubhabrata, 'Another Nuclear Blast at Pokhran?', *Sunday*, 12 May 1982, pp. 12–14.

64 See Subrahmanyam, K, 'Nuclear India in Global Politics', *World Affairs: The Journal of International Issues*, Vol. 2, No. 3, 1998, pp. 12–40; Ganguly, Sumit, 'India's Pathway to Pokhran II: The Prospects and Sources of New Delhi's Nuclear Weapons Program', *International Security*, Vol. 23, No. 4, 1999, pp. 148–177, https://tinyurl.com/534mh8s7. Accessed on 21 October 2024.

65 Burns, John F., 'India's New Defense Chief Sees Chinese Military Threat', *The New York Times*, 5 May 1998, https://tinyurl.com/vfw8hesp. Accessed on 21 October 2024.

66 'Indian's Letter to Clinton on the Nuclear Testing', *The New York Times*, 13 May 1998, https://tinyurl.com/4fcfcx4a. Accessed on 21 October 2024.

67 Described by Samuel Huntington during a trip to India in the 1990s.

68 The Brown Amendment overturned the Pressler Agreement, under which Pakistan was barred from receiving US economic aid and military sales, due to concerns of its continued nuclear proliferation. Under the new amendment, Pakistan would receive $368 million worth of military aircraft, missiles, and other equipment. See Lippman, Thomas,

'Conferees Loosen Ban on Arms to Pakistan, Soften Senate Language on Russia', *Washington Post*, 24 October 1995, https://tinyurl.com/e84up3t5. Accessed on 21 October 2024.

69 This was a great concern for India, given its position that the NPT sought to create a discriminatory regime, which only controlled horizontal proliferation. See Note 23.

70 New Delhi had previously, in 1965, attempted to secure a nuclear guarantee, with its foreign minister, Swaran Singh, visiting the Soviet Union, UK, and US. Unfortunately, this was to no avail, with the nuclear weapons states ultimately failing to provide any nuclear guarantees. See Ganguly, 'India's Pathway to Pokhran II', 1999, p. 155.

71 Minister of External Affairs, GOI, 'Media Centre: Press Releases: The Cabinet Committee on Security Reviews Operationalization of India's Nuclear Doctrine', 4 January 2003.

72 These documents can be easily accessed here: 'The Lahore Declaration: February 21, 1999', *World Affairs: The Journal of International Issues*, Vol. 3, No. 1, January–March 1999, pp. 151–156, https://tinyurl.com/mve6ksxj. Accessed on 21 October 2024.

73 As defined by the Carnegie Council for Ethics in International Affairs, nuclear deterrence refers to a principle in international relations where the retaliatory potential and destructive force of nuclear weapons prevents nations from launching a nuclear attack.

74 For further insight into the conciliatory stance taken by both sides, see Noorani, A.G., 'The truth about the Lahore Summit', *Frontline*, Vol. 19, No. 4, 2002.

75 Baruah, Amit, *Dateline Islamabad*, Penguin, UK, 2007.

76 Khalil, Umair, 'The Role of Confidence-Building Measures in the Pakistan-India Relationship', *Pakistan Horizon*, Vol. 67, No. 1, 2014, pp. 81–88, https://tinyurl.com/bdhpe6rc. Accessed on 21 October 2024.

77 These forward posts were vacated seasonally, with Indian troops occupying them only during the summer months.

78 Cheema, Mussarat Javaid, 'International Community on Kargil Conflict', *A Research Journal of South Asian Studies*, Vol. 28, No. 1, 2013, pp. 85–96, https://tinyurl.com/3af4ku5z. Accessed on 21 October 2024.

79 'I learnt about Kargil from Vajpayee, says Nawaz', *Dawn*, 26 May 2006, https://tinyurl.com/tvf98ywp. Accessed on 21 October 2024.

80 'Kargil planned before Vajpayee's visit: Musharraf', *The Indian Express,* 13 July 2006.

81 'Musharraf advised against Kargil, says Benazir', *Daily Times*, 2 July 2003.

82 See Ganguly, Sumit, and Devin Hagerty, *Fearful Symmetry: India Pakistan Crisis in the Shadow of Nuclear Weapons*, Oxford University Press, New Delhi, 2005, p. 9.

83 Kapur, S. Paul, 'Ten Years of Instability in a Nuclear South Asia', *International Security*, Vol. 33, No. 2, 2008, p. 72, https://tinyurl.com/ycywu3fx. Accessed on 21 October 2024.

84 Riedal, Bruce, 'How the 1999 Kargil conflict redefined US-India ties', *Brookings*, 24 July 2019, https://tinyurl.com/5edfxfpn. Accessed on 21 October 2024.

85 It is common knowledge that the ties between these terrorist organizations and Pakistan's intelligence services facilitate a covert instrument of Pakistan's national security policy. See Bajoria, Jayshree, and Eben Kaplan, 'The ISI and Terrorism: Behind the Accusations,' *Council on Foreign Relations*, 4 May 2011, https://tinyurl.com/bdevrtyd. Accessed on 21 October 2024. Steve Coll further argues: 'Pakistan's support for jihadi groups that launched attacks in India had a rational premise: the groups offered a potent, cost-effective way for Pakistan's generals to tie down India's large force in Kashmir. But they also had a religious aspect, because some officers in Pakistan's Army had come to identify with the global ambitions of the jihadi cause.' In Coll, Steve, 'The Stand Off', *The New Yorker*, 5 February 2006, https://tinyurl.com/5n957e7k. Accessed on 21 October 2024.

86 Both groups, soon after the attacks, were designated as terrorist groups by the US.

87 'Musharraf declares war on extremism', *BBC*, https://tinyurl.com/5bwxjn87. Accessed on 21 October 2024.

88 See Gordon, Michael, 'India Presses Its Conditions for Pullback from Border', *The New York Times*, 18 January 2002, https://tinyurl.com/y4jbrbz5. Accessed on 22 October 2024.

89 Talbot, Ian, 'Pakistan in 2002: Democracy, Terrorism, and Brinkmanship', *Asian Survey*, Vol. 43, No. 1, 2003, p. 200, https://tinyurl.com/ybrkm2cv. Accessed on 21 October 2024.

90 LaFraniere, Sharon, and Rajiv Chandrasekaran, 'Musharraf Pledges to Rein In Militants', *The Washington Post*, 27 May 2002, https://tinyurl.com/crdrvx7j. Accessed on 21 October 2024.

91 The US State Department Spokesperson Richard Boucher stated that 'Deputy Secretary Armitage was given assurances by President Musharraf on 6 June that ending of infiltration across the Line of Control would be permanent'; See 'Musharraf firm on Kashmir infiltration', *BBC*, 25 June 2002, https://tinyurl.com/54tcz74a. Accessed on 21 October 2024.

92 Ladwig, Walter C., 'A Cold Start for Hot Wars? The Indian Army's New Limited War Doctrine', *International Security*, Vol. 32, No. 3, 2007, pp. 158–90, https://tinyurl.com/ymt9yn6m. Accessed on 21 October 2024. See also, Gady, Franz-Stefan, 'Is the Indian Military Capable of Executing the Cold Start Doctrine?', *The Diplomat*, 29 January 2019, https://tinyurl.com/58r9j4m4. Accessed on 21 October 2024.

93 This war would continue to be waged for nearly two decades, ending with the US's withdrawal in 2021, and the recapture of Afghanistan by the Taliban.

94 The US's Afghanistan policy had similarly dictated the importance of US-Pakistani relations after the Soviet invasion of Afghanistan in 1979–89.

95 This estimate is provided by the Institute for Conflict Management.

96 Coll, 'The Stand Off'.

97 Between 1993 and 2003, several visits had taken place, with the Chinese President Jiang Zemin's visit to India in 1996, the Indian Minister of External Affairs Jaswant Singh's visit in 1999 (this visit took place after the 1998 nuclear tests to reiterate that neither side was a threat to the other), the Indian President K.R. Narayanan's visit in 2000, and the Chinese Premier Zhu Rongji's visit in 2002.

98 For the Sino-Indian Joint statement released, please see 'Declaration on Principles for Relations and Comprehensive Cooperation between the Republic of India and the People's Republic of China', Prime Minister's Office, Press Information Bureau, GOI, 24 June 2003.

99 Notably, this was the first Sino-Indian comprehensive document on the development of bilateral relations signed at the highest level. See Ministry of External Affairs, GOI, 'India-China Bilateral Relations', January 2012.

100 See Mathou. Thierry, 'Tibet and Its Neighbors: Moving toward a New Chinese Strategy in the Himalayan Region', *Asian Survey*, Vol. 45, No. 4, 2005, pp. 503–21, https://tinyurl.com/j94cn8f6. Accessed on 21 October 2024.

101 China's decision to go to war in 1962 was partly based out of the feeling of being cornered, with increasing hostilities between China and the US and Soviet Union. See Whiting, Allen, *The Chinese Calculus of Deterrence: India and Indochina*, University of Michigan press, Ann Arbor, 1975.

102 See Mansingh, Surjit, *India-China Relations in the Context of Vajpayee's 2003 Visit*, Sigur Center for Asian Studies, Elliott School of International Affairs: The George Washington University, 2005.

103 Mathou, Thierry, 'Tibet and Its Neighbors', *Asian Survey*, Vol. 45, No. 4, 2005, https://tinyurl.com/j94cn8f6. Accessed on 21 October 2024.

104 'Indo: China Relations: A Historic Reopening', *Economic and Political Weekly*, Vol. 41, No. 29, 2006, pp. 3132–3132, https://tinyurl.com/4m4prztk. Accessed on 21 October 2024.

105 Estimates were made by the Asian Development Bank (ADB). See 'A Historic Reopening', *Economic and Political Weekly*, Vol. 41, No.29, 2006, pp. 3132–3132, https://tinyurl.com/4m4prztk. Accessed on 22 October 2024.

Wave 4: 2004—Present: On the Path to Global Leadership

1 Grossman, Marc, 'The Tsunami Core Group: A Step toward a Transformed Diplomacy in Asia and Beyond', *Security Challenges*, Vol. 1, No. 1, 2005, pp. 11–14, https://tinyurl.com/4rj827ud. Accessed on 21 October 2024.

2 'U.S.-INDIA ATOMIC ENERGY COOPERATION: STRATEGIC AND NONPROLIFERATION IMPLICATIONS', https://tinyurl.com/bdffpt9x. Accessed on 21 October 2024.

3 Pant, Harsh V., *Indian Foreign Policy*, Manchester, Manchester University Press, 2016.

4 Chaudhury, Nilova Roy, 'China lays claim to Arunachal', *The Hindustan Times*, 19 November 2006, https://tinyurl.com/3u4k2fsu. Accessed on 21 October 2024.

5 'Background Briefing by Administration Officials on U.S.-South Asia Relations', US Department of State Archive, https://tinyurl.com/yc7scbtf. Accessed on 22 October 2024.

6 'Senate debates US-India nuclear deal', *The Economic Times*, 1 October 2008, https://tinyurl.com/36txdsr3. Accessed on 22 October 2024.

7 Tellis, Ashley J., 'Atoms for War: U.S.-Indian Civilian Nuclear Cooperation and India's Nuclear Arsenal', Carnegie Endowment for International Peace, https://tinyurl.com/8yd5ayhj. Accessed on 22 October 2024.

8 'NSG should address "aspirations" of others too: China', *The Economic Times*, 6 September 2008, https://tinyurl.com/4crhaptn. Accessed on 21 October 2024.

9 'NSG waiver has attendant risks, govt. tells Lok Sabha', *The Hindu*, 17 November 2021, https://tinyurl.com/ybt6vbvf. Accessed on 21 December 2024.

10 Sareen, Sushant, 'Deconstructing the Joint Statement', IDSA, https://tinyurl.com/5n8jpcps. Accessed on 21 October 2024.

11 IANS, 'Seven seas will not wash shame at Sharm el-Sheikh: BJP', *The Hindustan Times*, 29 July 2009, https://tinyurl.com/2p9jj32n. Accessed on 21 October 2024.

12 Ministry of External Affairs, GOI, *Fourth BRICS Summit - Delhi Declaration*, 29 March 2012, https://tinyurl.com/23pvyx4y. Accessed on 21 December 2024.

13 Hillary Rodham Clinton, 'Remarks on India and the United States: A Vision for the 21st Century', *U.S Department of State*, 20 July 2011, https://tinyurl.com/y97rdrw2. Accessed on 21 December 2024.

14 Lee Lavina, Lee John, 'Japan-India cooperation and Abe's democratic security diamond: Possibilities, limitations and the view from Southeast Asia', *Contemporary Southeast Asia*, Vol. 38, No. 2, 2016, pp. 284–308. https://tinyurl.com/4dnruhw7. Accessed on 21 October 2024.

15 Rej, Abhinjan, 'Reclaiming the Indo-Pacific A Political Military Strategy For QUAD 2.0', *ORF*, 27 March 2018, https://tinyurl.com/23rk3aka. Accessed on 21 October 2024.

16 MFA, The People's Republic of China, 'Xi Jinping Meets with Prime Minister Narendra Modi of India', 2017, https://tinyurl.com/yeytsv34. Accessed on 21 October 2024.

17 PTI, 'China claims India reduces troops from 400 to 40 at Doklam', *The Economic Times*, 13 July 2018, https://tinyurl.com/4s8jzphf. Accessed on 21 December 2024.

18 MEA, GOI, 'Prime Minister's Keynote Address at Shangri La Dialogue, June 01, 2018', 2018, https://tinyurl.com/4s2fhszd. Accessed on 21 October 2024.

19 'Pakistan army: Prepared to "go to any extent" to help Kashmiris', *The Indian Express*, 6 August 2019, https://tinyurl.com/4wchn88d. Accessed on 21 December 2024.

20 Mishra, Vivek Kumar, 'THE ABROGATION OF ARTICLE 370 INTERNATIONAL REACTIONS', *Indian Journal of Asian Affairs*, Vol. 33, No. 1/2, 2020, pp. 120–29, https://tinyurl.com/329rze8h. Accessed on 21 October 2024.

21 'India's stand clear on Kashmir, won't accept third party mediation: Jaishankar', *India Today*, 1 October 2019, https://tinyurl.com/46zjcr2d. Accessed on 21 October 2024.

22 United Nations General Assembly Human Rights Council, 'Joint written statement* submitted by Association PANAFRICA, Al-Hakim Foundation, Centre du Commerce International pour le Développement., Organisation pour la Communication en Afrique et de Promotion de la Cooperation Economique Internationale- OCAPROCE

Internationale, non-overnmental organizations in special consultative status', 2 June 2022, https://tinyurl.com/rm9uprr6. Accessed on 21 December 2024.

23 'GT Voice: Transparency, caution key to vaccine drive in India', *Global Times,* 17 January 2021, https://tinyurl.com/y8vsac84. Accessed on 21 October 2024.

24 AP, 'Ukraine war serves no one's interests: S Jaishankar', *The Times of India,* 10 October 2022, https://tinyurl.com/2p87j66u. Accessed on 21 October 2024.

25 'India stands firm on buying Russian oil amidst sanctions; EAM Jaishankar says Moscow has never hurt New Delhi', *The Economic Times*, 20 February 2024, https://tinyurl.com/3c578zkp. Accessed on 21 October 2024.

26 Later in August 2024, the Indian Prime Minister made an important visit to Kyiv, marking the first prime ministerial visit from India since Ukraine's independence in 1991.

Acknowledgements

As the landscape of Indian foreign policy evolves, and approaches the final quarter of its first century, it presents an important moment for reflection and assessment of its journey thus far. This book not only aims to take stock of the progress heretofore, as it navigates this crucial period, but it also endeavours to make Indian foreign policy more accessible to the general reader, inviting engagement from those eager to explore this critical field with growing anticipation.

This work represents a collective aspiration to foster a deeper understanding of India's role in the global arena. We hope this book serves as a catalyst for dialogue and curiosity among readers, encouraging them to delve into the intricacies of Indian foreign policy, and its implications for our future. We would like to extend our appreciation to Rupa Publications, and particularly Yamini Chowdhury, Richa Tewari and M.D. Mahasweta, for their editorial support and in bringing this book to publication. Their collective efforts have been instrumental in bringing this project to fruition. We would also like to express our gratitude to Satyam Singh, Vaishali Jaipal and Shiva Menon, who helped us with various aspects of this project.

As we navigate this dynamic landscape, we are reminded of the importance of informed discourse, and the role each of us plays in shaping the narrative. Thank you to all who have supported this journey, and to the readers who will engage with these ideas.

Index